urban political geographies

A GLOBAL PERSPECTIVE

SAGE has been part of the global academic community since 1965, supporting high quality research and learning that transforms society and our understanding of individuals, groups, and cultures. SAGE is the independent, innovative, natural home for authors, editors and societies who share our commitment and passion for the social sciences.

Find out more at: **www.sagepublications.com**

urban political
geographies

A GLOBAL PERSPECTIVE

ugo rossi & alberto vanolo

Los Angeles | London | New Delhi
Singapore | Washington DC

First published 2012

SAGE Publications Ltd
1 Oliver's Yard
55 City Road
London EC1Y 1SP

SAGE Publications Inc.
2455 Teller Road
Thousand Oaks, California 91320

SAGE Publications India Pvt Ltd
B 1/I 1 Mohan Cooperative Industrial Area
Mathura Road, Post Bag 7
New Delhi 110 044

SAGE Publications Asia-Pacific Pte Ltd
33 Pekin Street #02-01
Far East Square
Singapore 048763

Library of Congress Control Number: 2011936975

British Library Cataloguing in Publication data

A catalogue record for this book is available from the British Library

ISBN 978-0-85702-883-9
ISBN 978-0-85702-884-6 (pbk)

Typeset by C&M Digitals (P) Ltd, Chennai, India
Printed and bound by CPI Group (UK) Ltd, Croydon, CRO 4YY
Printed on paper from sustainable resources

Contents

Contents

Figures

About the Authors

Ugo Rossi gained his PhD in Human Geography at the University of Naples 'L'Orientale' (Italy) and obtained a Master's Degree from the University of Durham (UK). He held post-doctoral appointments at the University of Amsterdam, the Johns Hopkins University and over the last four years at the University of Cagliari in Italy, where he is currently also a temporary lecturer. He has published in academic journals both in Italian and in English. He co-edits the book review forum section of Dialogues in Human Geography. His research interests variously relate to the politics of urban and regional development.

Alberto Vanolo gained his PhD in Geography and Spatial Planning at the University of Turin. In the last five years he has held a permanent research and lecturer position in the Faculty of Economics of the same university. He has also held post-doctoral and visiting fellowships at the universities of Helsinki and Paris I. His work has been published in national and international journals of geography and urban studies; he is also author of key textbooks of economic geography and globalization studies, which are widely used in Italian universities. His research interests have touched on a variety of issues falling within the fields of urban studies and economic geography, including the deconstruction of the geographies of globalization and the contested image of the creative city.

Foreword: the Athenian Symptom

Ola Söderström, Institute de Géographie, Université de Neuchâtel (Switzerland)

On 20 June 2009, the museum hosting the archaeological treasures of the Acropolis and the Parthenon, designed by Swiss architect Bernard Tschumi, was inaugurated in Athens. The Greek government estimated that the museum, in which some 80 million euros were invested, would attract two million visitors a year, contributing to renewing the image of the city capital as well as to increasing the inflow of tourists in Athens. The project and its implementation sparked lively debates in Greece. The fact that a non-Greek architect was commissioned for a project touching the heart of the nation aroused strong criticism among the wider public, considering also that demolitions of Art Deco and neoclassical buildings were necessary in order to make way for the 25,000 square metre building.

The establishment of the new Acropolis Museum is evocative of at least three dimensions of contemporary city life: the urban-marketing campaigns, the growth-led strategies of urban development and their contestation. *Urban Political Geographies* is centred on the analysis of these interrelated but also conflicting dimensions. The book is conceived as an advanced textbook for students and urban practitioners (policymakers, planners, urban activists), but it is also aimed at a specialist audience, by offering a theoretically situated account of the politics of urban development in times of globalization and neoliberalism.

In recent years, Athens and Greece have been hit by an unprecedented financial and political turmoil. As a consequence of the sovereign debt crisis, but also of related financial speculations, Greece finds itself, as a member of the European Union, in an uncomfortable position similar to that experienced in previous decades by developing countries that had to deal with the structural adjustment programmes demanded by the International Monetary Fund and the World Bank as the conditionality for granting loans at reasonably low interest rates. In response to this situation, Greece has had to self-impose severe restrictions on government expenditure in order to receive the financial support it needs to achieve macroeconomic stability and restore market confidence. Over the medium run, economic prospects for Greece and the city of Athens look dire. After having enjoyed a period of spectacular growth, driven by the huge investments linked to the 2004 Olympic

Games – a veritable 'holy grail' of urban entrepreneurialism – Athens has to reconsider and limit its ambitions.

The Greek crisis is to be viewed against the backdrop of the broader crisis of the world economy, which was triggered from 2008 onward by the collapse of the hyper-speculative subprime mortgage market and the subsequent financial crash, eventually leading to the global economic recession that has not yet come to an end three years later. The expansionary fiscal policy which encouraged property ownership (but led to a shrinkage in state budgets), the deregulation of the financial sector and the rise of cities and regions as relatively autonomous politico-economic agents are distinctive features of the neoliberal era analysed in the book. Athens' story, therefore, raises important questions about whether we are witnessing the coming of a post-neoliberal era of urban development; an era in which urban policies could be less centred on the imperative of representation through the mobilization of culture and creativity, while being more oriented towards – let's be optimistic! – the redistribution of wealth and public revenue.

The future is by definition unpredictable, but the crumbling of the certainties on which cities relied until a very recent past is evident. The recent and still ongoing economic crisis has had the effect of making the hegemonic economic-political pattern even more decipherable, once its underlying mechanisms have shown their weaknesses. Ugo Rossi and Alberto Vanolo take us on a journey around the ascent and crisis of urban liberalism, providing a clear and highly readable analysis of key issues and debates in the field of urban political geography at a time in which the neoliberal era seems to be unravelling.

Representation/government/contestation

The book fundamentally builds on a political economy approach to the study of urban development issues. According to the authors, the rise of urban neoliberalism, with its relentless transformations, contradictions and dynamics of diffusion across the globe, is key to the understanding of the contemporary geographies of urban politics. The authors, therefore, draw on what has become a sort of new 'grand narrative' within English-language urban scholarship over the last two or three decades. However, their account of urban neoliberalism is not conventional, but it is problematized by using theoretical and conceptual sources that depart from the conventional political economy literature. In doing so, the book identifies the pillars of what is called the 'triad of urban politics': representation, government and contestation, each being understood by making reference to one key thinker.

In the first instance, the geographies of urban politics are presented by looking at the performative power of representations, referring to the images associated with strategies of urban branding, as well as to those arising from the realm of everyday life, both acting as frameworks (in the sense of Goffman's 'framing') for the rationalization of urban issues.[1] Edward Said's *Orientalism*, which shows that the social and the political are constructed through cognitive processes, is an essential reference on the 'politics of representation'. The second pillar supporting the triad is about 'politics as government', which is analysed in the book as a study of the practices of government, drawing on the Foucauldian notion of governmentality, rather than as a study of the models of governance.[2] This approach allows an understanding of the long-term process of 'governmentalization' of urban life, which has evolved – as the authors point out using the work of Nikolas Rose – by making citizens and local communities increasingly responsible entities as regards the improvement of societal well-being. Last but not least, the third dimension of urban politics relates to acts of resistance and citizenship and is conceptually based on Jacques Rancière's distinction between 'politics' and 'police'. The former takes the form of the techniques of 'partition of the sensible' by which the preservation of the extant political-economic order is pursued, while the latter is associated with the contentious processes and acts challenging the established order and its reproduction. By scrutinizing the potential of a wide range of contestation movements, Rossi and Vanolo succeed in highlighting different modes of insurgent action coexisting in contemporary urban environments.

Along with the clarity of its structure and the fluidity in the writing, the strength of the book lies therefore in the theoretical grounding of each chapter. Non-specialist readers of the book, such as students and urban practitioners, will have at their disposal a useful learning tool, dealing with issues that are central to contemporary urban scholarship, such as the entrepreneurialization of governance, the militarization of urban life, the cultural turn in urban planning and policy processes. In many parts of the book, the authors approach these important themes from unconventional perspectives. The globalization of gated communities, for instance, is dealt with against the backdrop of Zygmunt Bauman's reflections on the various forms of insecurity in postmodern societies (Chapter 4). This allows the authors to identify the selectivity of the public discourse on 'security', which is understood merely as the preservation of physical integrity, rather than as the pursuit of social wellness. The chapter focusing on urban struggles begins with a detailed and nuanced reconstruction of the philosophical debate on social justice. This discussion, which critically reviews John Rawls's foundational theory of distributive justice, Harvey's neo-materialist critique as well as Iris Marion Young's neo-feminist insights, helps the reader conceptualize different types of social movements, such as those committed to identity-based claims and those transcending specific positionalities.

The representation/government/contestation triad is not intended to be inclusive of all dimensions of the contemporary geographies of urban politics. For instance, the book admittedly does not take account of the 'more than human' geographies exploring the implicitly political significance of the complex relations between humans, technologies, objects and non-human organisms. Equally, in the introduction to the book the authors admit that they have not drawn on the 'more-than-representational' geographies looking at the political implications of the feelings, emotions and body gestures inherent in the urban experience, while admiring this lively strand of research. Therefore, rather than a conventional text-book providing a comprehensive overview of the main strands of thinking and investigation currently available in the academic market, *Urban Political Geographies* offers an intentionally partial point of view on urban affairs. Paradoxically, thanks to this intentional incompleteness the authors find themselves in a convenient position to provide a clear view of the current state of urban affairs, being able to zoom in on specific regions of the urban political universe in unconventional ways. Time will tell us whether its publication coincides, as one might expect in view of recent upheavals and economic turbulences across the globe, with a turning-point in geographical research and urban studies.

Notes

1 For example, consider the different ways in which poverty can be 'framed' either as a social justice issue or as a security issue.
2 According to Foucault, governmentality concerns 'the conduct of conduct', which includes a variety of practices ranging from techniques of 'government at a distance' to the self-regulation of individual behaviour. The study of governance, on the other hand, more conventionally consists of analysing different modes of coordination or conflict between private, public and civil-society actors.

Foreword: the Nine Lives of Neoliberalism

Jamie Peck, Department of Geography, University of British Columbia (Canada)

In February 2011, a report from the Independent Evaluation Office of the International Monetary Fund (IMF) was issued in Washington, DC, barely causing a ripple. The brief of this arm's-length watchdog agency had been to review the performance of its parent organization, the IMF, in the run-up to the financial crisis of 2008 and the global recession that followed. Couched in characteristically restrained tones, the report's findings were nevertheless damning. It revealed how the IMF had maintained a dangerously sanguine outlook in the months preceding the crash, failing to warn of systemic risks in the global financial system, or to voice concerns about the reckless regulatory posture of the US and UK authorities, where the crisis was being fomented. (Unlike the Asian financial crisis of the late 1990s, this one could not so easily be blamed on 'crony capitalism'.) For years, risks of contagion had been radically underestimated by the IMF, along with the possibility that those 'advanced' economies that were not only following *but writing* the neoliberal playbook might be vulnerable to self-inflicted financial failure. Instead, the IMF's 'banner message was one of continued optimism', right up to the moment that Wall Street tipped the world economy into a spiralling economic collapse, for which solutions would have to be improvised in a fog of political uncertainty, bordering on outright panic. The lemming economists at the IMF had jumped off the proverbial cliff, along with the financial elites of New York and London:

> The IMF's ability to correctly identify the mounting risks was hindered by a high degree of groupthink, intellectual capture, a general mindset that a major financial crisis in large advanced economies was unlikely, and inadequate analytical approaches. Weak internal governance, lack of incentives to work across units [or] raise contrarian views ... also played an important role, while political constraints may have also had some impact ... Looking forward, the IMF needs to ... create an environment that encourages candor and considers dissenting views; [to strengthen] incentives to "speak truth to power;" to overcome [its] silo mentality and insular culture; [while delivering] a clear, consistent message on the global outlook and risks.[1]

Just a few days later, tens of thousands started taking to the streets in Madison, Wisconsin in an escalating series of protests against newly elected Republican Governor Scott Walker's draconian 'budget' plan. Having rushed through an emergency package of corporate tax cuts, Walker had proposed a budget that not only rolled back social benefits for most of the state's public-sector workers (with the notable exception of those police-service unions that had supported his campaign), but which sought unilaterally to remove collective-bargaining rights. Once a pioneer of public-sector unionization, back in the 1950s, Wisconsin had now become a test-case for what was already threatening to become a rolling, state-by-state programme of legislative deunionization. Walker evasively argued that his uncompromising budget package was a fiscal necessity. Yet even after unions accepted the need for wage and benefit clawbacks – as long as their bargaining rights were maintained – the Governor flatly refused to negotiate. His union-busting charter was eventually passed, using a procedural ruse, having been detached from those budget measures that had supposedly been its rationale. It was, apparently, a matter of principle.

These two episodes – the dramatic events in Wisconsin and the non-event in Washington, DC – call attention to some sobering political realities of these nominally post-crisis times in the United States, and indeed beyond. Certainly, the brief period of post-neoliberal optimism, during the early stages of the crisis, now seems little more than a distant memory, if not a dream. At the time, prominent figures from across the broad left – from Naomi Klein to Eric Hobsbawm and Joseph Stiglitz – had been quick to declare the death of neoliberalism, quite rightly pointing to the damning indictment of 'the system' manifest in the devastating convergence of predatory financialization, negligent regulation, and craven mismanagement. There were even a few *mea culpas* from the architects of the crisis, and plenty of earnest political promises that lessons had been learned and mistakes would never be repeated. This was promptly followed by a disorienting period in which both the world, and neoliberal principle, seemed to be turned upside down: the United States, the home of 'free-market' capitalism, would witness massive bank bailouts, corporate rescues on an industrial scale and an historic surge in pseudo-Keynesian 'stimulus' spending.

But almost in reflex, the summer of 2009 saw the birth of a kind of grassroots neoliberal uprising in local communities across the country, in the form of the stridently neoliberal tea-party movement. On the surface, this was fuelled by inchoate, and spontaneous, populist rage against the Obama administration's 'socialist' excesses, but less visibly, it was enabled by the same corporate bankrollers that for decades had been constructing an extra-governmental apparatus of conservative think tanks, lobby groups, and political-action committees. Among the more prominent financiers of this free-market counter-revolution are the billionaire Koch brothers, who had pumped significant sums into conservative and libertarian causes like the Heritage Foundation and Cato Institute, before establishing the front organization, Americans for Prosperity, in 2011 to channel funding to an ideologically approved slate of Republican candidates – including Governor Scott Walker of Wisconsin.[2]

The Koch brothers would later open a lobbying office in Madison, as the protest movement reached its peak, while running anti-union ads on Wisconsin TV.

As crisis conditions have been normalized across the United States, effectively (re) defining Obama's domestic programme, they provide an object lesson in the unforgiving politics of market rule. Despite its practical inadequacy, as a source of workable policy measures, new pages are continually being added to the neoliberal playbook. Analytically, this reveals some recurring truths about the nature of neoliberalization, as it is practised at scales from the global to the local.

First, the extra-local 'rules of the game' continue to be structured according to selectively competitive principles, with most of the multilateral agencies still working actively to extend free-trade agreements, to restrain public expenditure, to further liberalize private investment flows and to deregulate the operating environments for corporations and banks. Save for that brief moment of bastard-Keynesianism, when the crisis was in its free-fall phase, there has been no sign of meaningful change in the pattern of free-market 'groupthink' in the finance ministries and international agencies. (It remains to be seen if and how those absent 'dissenting views' might be sought or accommodated in the halls of the IMF.) Deep in the neoliberal silos, the entrenched ideological preference for rolling deregulation has evidently become such that default setting politics involve riding successive waves of speculative expansion, never to seek to manage them. As Keynes once said of Hayek, the neoliberal prophet's fundamental problem was that he never knew 'where to draw the line' in terms of the containment of market forces and the regulatory roles of the state.[3] Little seems to have changed. Today, the bonus culture is brazenly resurgent on Wall Street and in the City of London; regulatory reform has been timid at best; and political elites on both sides of the Atlantic have argued that the public should pay to refloat the system, by way of long-run fiscal austerity and social-state retrenchment. As if this were not bad enough, it is probably only a matter of time before the free-market lemmings are leaping blindly off the cliffs again.

Second, it follows that the neoliberal predisposition to crisis is not accidental, but immanent. Crisis conditions, however, tend to further animate and energize the neoliberalization process. Indeed, the pattern so far is that they have tended to spur reinventions of neoliberal governance, not its reversal. One of the many tragic ironies of the Wall Street crash of 2008, widely acknowledged to have been brought on by negligent regulatory surveillance and craven profiteering, is that its downstream political consequences have included a Republican revival on a scale sufficient to take back not only Congress, but to secure the control of 21 of the 50 states. Having chronically short-changed the states in the initial round of stimulus spending, the Obama administration must now bear witness to an orgy of righteous budget-slashing, entitlement rollbacks and union-busting across Republican-controlled statehouses (and, in muted form, in more than a few Democratic ones, too). Wisconsin, all sides acknowledge, represents a sign of things to come.

Malign devolution is, by now, a tried-and-tested neoliberal tactic. Yet again, the costs of financial overreach and corporate failure are being downloaded onto cities and states, and onto the most socially vulnerable, in the form of new and apparently long-term programmes of public austerity. These dynamics are playing out all over the place, not only across the United States, but in Britain too, where David Cameron's coalition government has initiated cavalier public-spending cuts on a scale sufficient to threaten a rapid return to negative growth, while offering local governments the sparse consolation of budgetary flexibility in the administration of this unprecedented fiscal retrenchment. The equivalent of presenting local authorities with the knife, while inviting them to decide which fingers to amputate ('in accordance with local priorities'), this is being sold in the euphemistic language of Cameron's 'Big Society' (conveniently enabled by yet-smaller government, of course).

It is through such means – of downloaded responsibilities and unfunded mandates; of deregulatory hand-offs to private enterprises, to community and third-sector organizations, and ultimately to households and individuals – that the bait-and-switch scale politics of neoliberalization are being prosecuted. And it is in this context that what we have come to understand as 'neoliberal urbanism' has been shaped, as a distinctive geohistorical form.[4] Evolving through time, and variable over space, neoliberal urbanism nevertheless exhibits a series of recurrent features and enduring contradictions. Neoliberalized cities have come to fulfil fundamentally paradoxical roles. On the one hand, they are among the preeminent sites of experimentation in (and relay stations for) neoliberal reforms. On the other hand, cities have been the epicentres of struggles against these self-same incursions. The results of this dialectical process have been anything but uniform and singular, as Rossi and Vanolo powerfully demonstrate in the pages that follow, but they have nonetheless been far-reaching.

This geographically variegated face of neoliberalism represents, at the same time, a deeply consolidated and a crisis-driven form of market rule. Maybe it is still being guided, in some way or another, by Hayek's rusty old compass, trained on the unattainable (and stark) utopia of a free-market society, but the vanguard momentum of the 'revolution from above', such as the Reagan/Thatcher moment of unapologetic confrontation and 'conviction politics', has long since given way to alternating currents of opportunist attacks on the social state and social collectivities; to decentralized, trial-and-error experimentation and regulatory races to the bottom; and to increasingly networked forms of local resistance politics. The geographies of this process may be complex but they are far from chaotic. They involve a metastasizing fiscal crisis of the local state, not only in the US and the UK – the dubious 'dividend', presumably, of three decades of relentless neoliberalization – but much more broadly. They are triggering new forms of local resistance, the downstream consequences of which cannot be predicted.

It was clearly too soon, however, to read the last rites for neoliberalism as the global crisis took hold. Perhaps the tawdry ideology of neoliberal 'market rule' has lost another of its nine lives, but in adapted form it remains very much with us. Crises themselves need not be fatal for this mutable, mongrel model of governance, for neoliberalism has always been a creature of crisis. As such, it has become increasingly mired in the unending challenge of managing its own contradictions, together with the socioeconomic fallout from previous deregulations and malinterventions – for all its reproductive tenacity. In these late-neoliberal times, however, one thing that has become clear is that the spatial and scalar transmission belts for crises are becoming ever more deeply interwoven and integrated. Globalizing rules of the interurban game are repeatedly redrawing the ideological and fiscal parameters of 'local' politics, while the reverberations of urban-scale experiments and social struggles continue to spiral unpredictably, both upward and outward. It is in the city trenches that the crises, contradictions, and counterpolitics of neoliberalization are finding some of their most vivid and consequential expressions, where new worlds are being imagined, made, and unmade. These real-time dynamics can be difficult to map. But in *Urban Political Geographies*, we have a timely and astute field guide to this unfolding process.

Notes

1   Independent Evaluation Office of the International Monetary Fund (2011) *IMF Performance in the Run-Up to the Financial and Economic Crisis*. Washington, DC: Independent Evaluation Office of the International Monetary Fund.
2   E. Lipton (2011) Billionaire brothers' money plays role in Wisconsin dispute. *New York Times*, 22 February: A16.
3   See J. Peck (2010) *Constructions of Neoliberal Reason*. Oxford: Oxford University Press, Chapter 2.
4   N. Theodore, J. Peck and N. Brenner (2011) Neoliberal urbanism: cities and the rule of markets. In G. Bridge and S. Watson (eds) *The New Blackwell Companion to the City*. Oxford: Wiley-Blackwell, 15–25.

Foreword: Politics Between the Lines

AbdouMaliq Simone, Department of Sociology, Goldsmiths College, University of London (UK)

This is an incisive and lucid account of contemporary urban politics, and envisions the terms through which it is possible to nurture a politics beyond neoliberal melancholia. As such, it is important to reaffirm the ways in which the solidarities, reciprocities and collaborations that are generated from the quotidian density of relationships and potentialities across city districts continue to exceed the frameworks through which residents are either accounted for or included in prevailing narratives of citizenship and economic efficacy. Take a young man logging transactional data for American Express credit cardholders in a Mumbai BPO (business process outsourcing) firm every night. He lives in a time zone 12 hours behind that of Mumbai but simultaneously engages in an intricate, everyday urban politics of redevelopment and neighbourhood upgrading to bring better services to his settlement. The efforts of ordinary citizens are closely tied to opportunities that are simultaneously enabled and foreclosed by the aggrandizement of urban space. While it is possible to discern clear trajectories of 'development' – as settlements like where the young man lives are replaced by 'spatial products' like the technopark where he works, there are also continuous oscillations of ascendancy and decline. Populations pushed to the periphery stretch urban 'cores' and develop new logics of dwelling and economy, while standardized development zones sometimes rapidly acquire new functions and designs, or even eventually fade from existence. The topologies of urban transformations are simultaneously clearly charted and opaque – a constant reworking of colonization and decolonization, innovation and exhaustion, recuperation and ruin.

Conventional strategies of urban development simultaneously promote an uneasy bundling together of heterogeneous spatial forms, forms of economic action and settlement histories with particular political nominations such as the 'urban poor'. This results in puzzling patterns of political struggle, which engage collective economies and energies but require adjustments that always escape the rationalities of planned urban growth and the resulting calculations of the costs of displacement and resettlement. What, then, can serve as a basis for the conditions in which any consideration of rights to the city can be imagined and concretized outside of this mirroring framework in which rights are framed in reaction to a landscape of mega-projects and compensatory developments? In cities across the 'majority world', residues of colonial planning, post-colonial practices of 'regularization' and landed investments into maintaining economic heterogeneity are rapidly being erased and replaced by such landscapes of mega-development – a process this book thoroughly documents.

This continuous aggrandizement of urban space by large-scale property developments crowds out existing central city districts that intersect diverse income groups, settlement histories, built environments and local economies. Yet, caught within an analytic logic of poverty and residency rights, these districts simultaneously become invisible as incubators of potentialities that cannot be pinned down within normative logics of efficacy. As bounded spaces, these districts occupy a distinctive position vis-à-vis contemporary mega-development. In particular they proffer location advantages and bring with them the colonial residues of proximity to off-the-grid and exploited populations. In the efforts to dominate the narrative of urban change, as well as what can be seen and talked about across the urban landscape, such mega-developments ironically run interference for a plurality of other urban domains that pose neither a clearly discernible threat – environmental or political – but yet continue to provide dwelling and livelihood for large numbers of urban residents.

Urban Political Geographies stretches questions of how to address cities beyond the conventional formulations concerning agency, civil society, governance, polarization, dispossession and accumulation, which have largely dictated the terms of how cities in the urban South are talked about. It raises the possibility that there are interstices – analytical, empirical – in which residents work out ways of putting together modalities of collective life that, even if compelled by accommodations to the agendas of powerful elites, still harbour materialized propositions of how urban space can be transformed. As such the book is not interested in appropriating particular kinds of urban residents – rich, poor, middle class – to exemplify theoretical imaginations about the city.

Of course politics – and its concomitant instruments of policy, mobilization and re-imagination – must address unequal access to resources, growing uncertainty in how everyday livelihood is attained, and the growing access to a larger world of information and experiences folded in to the most desperate of urban conditions. But there is also a need to recognize more provisional ensembles and associations that come together momentarily at the cusp of transformations and in the interstices of shifting spatial alignments, using specific instantiations of the strategic possibilities of urban life that change shape, durability and viability all of the time. Such collectivities are not consolidated into political vanguards. Nevertheless, they register an effect and gradually articulate different facets of the city, and different ways of life. In the past several decades, urban governance has emphasized decentralization, individual entrepreneurialism and enforced mobility, as if they are self-contained tools of change. But these interventions have also called attention to the extent to which unplanned intersections of highly discrepant walks of life actually manage to bring out new capacities amongst the proliferating fragments that make up a city and enable them to have something concrete to do with each other.

In part, issues concerning the social composition of cities and their impact on urban life in general have become challenges in relation to the political strategies and technical instruments that have predominated in the efforts to organize the urban poor since 1976 after the first international gathering to consider urban settlement issues (Habitat I, Vancouver). As such, policies geared towards accommodating swelling populations of the cities gravitated toward sites and services schemes where basic demarcations of plots and skeletal services were to be provided that would be 'filled in' over time through the initiatives and resources of the poor themselves.

The idea was to establish a basic, identifiable platform on which residents could establish a secure foothold in the city. This infrastructure also provided a basic political address for the urban poor, calling them into being as it were. By applying their own logics of spatial development, it was expected that the poor would also 'domesticate' the city in ways that would enable them to 'recognize themselves' within it. While such policies have been markedly contested all along, their implicit traction has been to defer difficult challenges about rights, inclusion and responsibilities to a future time. Everyone could then argue that development was under way, that a trajectory of progressive inclusion in urban life had been charted. Furthermore, these projects were framed as a response to the supposed failure of low-income populations to bring their practices of habitation into synch with the expectations materialized in state sponsored public housing projects. These lacks were to be addressed with various capacity building programmes centred on teaching the poor how to save and govern themselves.

Demands for citizenship rights were therefore coupled with discourses that valorized the capacities of the poor to manage their own lives and settlements. In order not to internalize the violence directed toward them – as manifested through forced removals and the harassment around livelihood activities – urban social movements emphasized the unyielding capacities of low-income residents to make the city their own regardless of efforts to exclude them. Thus when residents were to look upon dense, underserviced and insalubrious urban environments, they would also recognize specific abilities to be part of urban life, to have concretized their rights to the city. These efforts by local associations, made visible to a larger international audience through the efforts of organizations such as Habitat International, Shack/Slumdwellers International, the Asian Coalition on Housing Rights – to name a few, helped generate a broader interest by researchers, architects, and artists in various city-making practices 'from below'.

As such, urban literature in recent years has been replete with examples of the efficacies of slums or the productivity of urban frisson. This proliferation in turn raises the question about representation and the politics of a subaltern urbanism. Here, a wide range of claims, from more modest ethnographic examinations of the toiling of the poor just managing to keep their heads above water to claims that the subaltern shows us what all cities 'really are' – a field of constant improvisation – turn the city into essentially destabilized, fluid assemblages of bodies, materials and affect.

Whereas cities embody a critical inability to hold together stable relationships amongst such elements, it is another thing to insist that this notion of the city is 'proved' by its most vulnerable inhabitants – thus equating vulnerability and the exigencies of constant compensation and adjustment with some 'essence' of urbanity. The actions of the poor can certainly point to how the city is not all that it is 'cracked up' to be. Still, these fissures in the normative – i.e. the constituent gaps that enable urban governance and urban norms to consolidate themselves – do not become visible and useable by unveiling a prior and more 'real' version of the city. Rather, as *Urban Political Geographies* emphasizes, they become instrumental through the active disruption of municipal power and capitalist relations. It is in the fight of the poor to overcome the very conditions that supposedly embody the fractal character of urban life that concretizes its potentialities – not just in the game of 'show and tell'.

The challenges posed by the exclusion or encampment of the urban poor are in part discursive problems that end up obscuring the question of the fundamental political and empirical challenges of describing an 'urban majority' and attributing to a population the status of a majority. In the practice of urban democracy, what then is to be made of a so-called 'urban majority'? For in many cities, reference to a majority would entail talking about different ways of doing things, calculating chances and opportunities and using resources on the part of those who statistically might be grouped as similar in terms of length of urban residence, household income, educational background and so forth. If a critical advantage is to be accrued through engaging a majority as heterogeneously composed, what is to be gained by sustaining the notion of a 'majority'? Is it simply to exclude them from the 'pool' of residents from which conclusions about urban dynamics are commonly made, and in this way maintain the majority as some kind of constituent exception? If so, is there a way to bring such a majority back in to analysis? And for what purpose would we do so?

Given these questions and challenges, *Urban Political Geographies* attempts to make sense of the heterogeneity of contemporary cities – their heterogeneity of housing situations, livelihoods, resource dispositions, settlement histories and social identities. As such it attempts to explore scales of city-making that go beyond the conventional identities, such as the poor, the slum, the gated community, or the mega-development. The question becomes how growing urban populations are employed, housed and fed in cities that 'hitch' themselves to imaginaries of urban vitality and economic growth which would seem to make irrelevant the backgrounds and capacities of the majority of the city's population. In such circumstances, discourses on efficient, democratic urban governance, sustainability and security seem to displace the political and economic practices that make urban life at least minimally viable for that majority. In light of the substantial growth of urban middle classes across the majority world or the so-called South – for which the discourses of civil society, accountability, transparency and good governance seem consonant – there is a need to reconsider the economic heterogeneity of cities as the very conditions in which any consideration of rights to the city can be imagined, let alone concretized.

The seemingly wide divergences between contemporary economic spaces – between traditional wet markets and hypermarkets, shopping malls and streets full of small shops and stalls – pose many challenges to how lines of articulation and mutual implication can be drawn. Big projects cast long and ominous shadows over vast numbers of small enterprises and labour markets even as they promise to accelerate new job creation. Different temporalities are involved, and so the cost savings and efficiencies anticipated by expanded scale also tend to flatten the intricate gradations once available to residents in terms of how they balanced their management of shelter, education, mobility, proximity to work and social support, opportunistic chances and household consumption. They change how residents 'paced' themselves over time and calculated what kind of time that had to work with.

These gradations did not so much stand alone as class positions or characteristics of neighbourhoods, but were more provisional markers that provided clues for how households, associations and networks might collaborate, and how they would use available resources of all kinds. So the challenge is how to redraw the lines of connection. Here the day-to-day struggles of municipal politics and the attempts to remake 'messy environments' remain critical.

Such observations do not obviate the fact that conventional mobilizations and organizational politics are necessary. The fact remains that in many districts, claims to space, resources and life are made by those who have no right, or where claims to rights are simply based on a game that only involves seizing or being seized. In many districts today, eligibility, preparation, status and waiting – all elements that have conventionally been associated with the ability to attain certain positions or opportunities – are frequently pushed aside. This is being demonstrated by the often highly speculative acts of residents to collaborate with each other in ways that cut across formal attributions of identity and discernible organizations and movements.

Even when acts of speculation are undertaken as individual initiatives, they become a way to configure possibilities for residents of a district to be in a larger world together – in ways that do not assume a past solidity of affiliations, a specific destination nor an ultimate collective formation to come. It is a way of being together without recourse to being able to see, coordinate or command each other. If in each individual initiative, back and forth, here and there, is a proposition for how spaces across a city could be articulated, the question is how are these propositions amassed? Or, more importantly, how do they have traction with and imply each other? What kinds of openings – spatial and temporal – and what kinds of stories and practices of engagement are important for such 'gatherings' to take place, to find and seep through the interstices of urban promises and their ruins, of seamless and probabilistic control and the rampant uncertainties they also unfold?

Introduction

Key Issues and Themes

The introductory chapter begins by presenting two exemplar stories of urban economic development in recent times (Beijing and Bilbao), illustrating the complex relationship between globalization and the urban experience. Globalization is understood as an inherently conflictual process and as an assemblage of narratives and representations.

The field of urban politics is outlined and reinterpreted as a 'triad' (reflected in the structure of the book): politics as representation, as government and as contestation.

Part One 'Politics as Representation' is concerned with the ways in which politico-economic elites produce and circulate images and discourses sustaining strategies of urban development and capital accumulation.

Part Two 'Politics as Government' explores the ways in which cities are being governed in a neoliberal and global era, through the mobilization of a variety of technical, intellectual and policy tools.

Part Three 'Politics as Contestation' takes into account the role of resistance movements forming around issues of social justice and urban citizenship.

I.1 Globalization and the urban experience

This book analyses the ways in which the intimately interconnected processes and forces of globalization, post-Fordism, postmodernity and neoliberalism have given rise to path-breaking changes in our urban experience. In this context, an 'urban change story' helps the reader – perhaps more convincingly than any theoretical framework – to understand what this book aims to offer: namely, a critical exploration of the variety of trajectories and strategies of urban development coexisting today within an increasingly globalized world economy. The two stories of urban change which will be presented in the following pages, despite their obvious differences, powerfully highlight the strong relationships linking the so-called 'new urban politics' to globalization, in the first instance, but also to other key phenomena of our times.

I.1.1 The new Beijing

The city of Beijing grows and evolves at a rapid pace, radically transforming its economic, social and institutional foundations. The general features of the process of widespread change currently under way in the Chinese capital, like in the whole country, are now widely known. However, in order to understand the relationship between globalization and contemporary urban issues in China and in many respects also in the larger East Asian context, it is worth analysing in greater detail the ways in which the process of change in this city is leading its urban community to experiment with radically different lifestyles and modes of societal organization. The multitude of physical changes, the new high-rise buildings and shopping malls (such as the spectacular Oriental Plaza), the demolition of vast portions of the historical built environment (including the traditional alleys called Hutong), the reconversion of old, Soviet-style factories into exhibition sites for local and international artists: these are only some examples illustrating the wide array of socio-spatial changes presently being observed in Beijing.

Over the three decades of Mao Zedong's leadership (from the late 1940s to the mid-1970s), Chinese governing elites largely neglected urban development and regeneration issues. In fact, during those decades government policies embraced an explicitly anti-urban stance towards economic and regional planning issues: migration flows from the countryside to the urban regions were severely regulated; urban dissidents and minorities were persecuted in the name of the 'cultural revolution'; civil society suffered from a lack of autonomy from the established authorities; private consumption was strongly limited. In this context, Beijing appeared as a city with an austere life and an inward-looking identity, with the economy being limited to the industrial sector, and its inhabitants forced to wear the Maoist uniform. Automobiles were almost unknown, as were places for leisure and nightlife. On the whole, the city was far from experiencing the vibrancy of urban life and the cosmopolitan imaginary which were already common in the major cities of the advanced capitalist countries. In the 1970s, only a quarter of the existing hotels were open to foreigners: at that time, a conventional belief held that there were more visitors in London over a week than in Beijing over a year. It was only in 1978 that, at the dawn of the epochal economic reforms undertaken in the subsequent years, the Central Committee of the Communist Party proclaimed that cities should play a role as drivers of 'socialist modernization' and as places where material and immaterial resources had to be concentrated and processes of industrial growth and economic internationalization had to be based on. During the 1980s, the changing approach to economic and spatial planning led to the establishment of four 'special economic zones' and fourteen 'coastal towns', in order to attract foreign direct investment, including capital inflows originating from the then British overseas territory of Hong Kong (Cook, 2006).

In the subsequent years, cities across the country experienced high growth rates, testifying to the success of the new strategy of economic and spatial development.

In light of these achievements, national elites became increasingly aware of the importance of urban development in strengthening China's economic competitiveness. As a consequence, China's major urban agglomerations (such as Beijing, Shanghai, Canton and Tianjin) started internationalizing their economies. Within the space of few years, the internationalization of urban development would become a key factor in China's rapid ascent in the global economy. In particular, political elites believed that large cities and metropolitan regions needed to be endowed with adequate infrastructures and producer services in order to enhance economic and cultural relationships and exchanges with existing 'global cities' across the world, and prospectively even to challenge their hegemony. As the country's political capital, Beijing was expected to play a crucial role in this strategy, attracting large amounts of public and private (foreign) capitals for investments in transport infrastructures, urban renewal projects, research and development laboratories, and the like. Today, just after Hong Kong, Beijing boasts the highest concentration of multinational firms in China. In this process, political motivations have been inextricably intertwined with economic interests: the lack of transparency in the public sector induces private firms to locate their headquarters in the capital, so as to take advantage of the spatial proximity to the sites of political power (Zhao, 2003). The 2008 Olympic Games, with their slogan 'New Beijing, Great Olympics', were the event in which this strategy of urban competitiveness reached its peak, celebrating worldwide the destiny of Beijing as a global city.

The changing approach to economic and spatial governance and planning has been accompanied by a process of political and administrative devolution (for example, on matters of fiscal responsibility) from the national level to the local level. The liberalization of domestic markets along with the attraction of foreign investors has enabled local governments and private actors to be less dependent on state revenues. On the whole, these changes have weakened the primacy of the state within the politico-economic realm (Logan, 2002). When Mao was President of the People's Republic, urban-renewal initiatives were promoted and directly managed by the central government. Today, municipal authorities play a growing role in the regulation of land use, in cooperation with other administrative entities operating at the sub-urban level. The private ownership of urban land is now allowed, even though each city and metropolitan area has its own regulations in this field. However, despite the process of economic liberalization and politico-administrative devolution, ordinary citizens find it hard to act as collectively organized actors and to actively contribute to the formulation of economic and regional policies through transparent mechanisms of negotiated decision-making, because of the persistent lack of institutions representing civil-society interests. Urban policies and planning processes are, therefore, no longer an exclusive domain of the national government, but are managed and supported also by local and regional elites. The latter, however, are reluctant to allow emerging actors and social groups to become involved in the decision-making processes.

The most marginalized social group is undoubtedly that of rural migrants residing in urban areas. Regular immigrant flows from the countryside overlap with irregular movements directed towards cities where the economic boom has vitalized the job market, even though the majority of available jobs are unregistered, poorly paid and offered on a casual basis. Migrants associate on the basis of regional origin and they support each other within informal neighbourhood communities, mostly located in poor and geographically peripheral urban areas, giving rise to networks of social cooperation and mutual help. In such 'urban villages', migrant communities reproduce and reinvent their collective identities through the sharing of local dialects, the socialization of cooking spaces and the pursuit of community-based survival strategies. Informal networks take the form also of spontaneous protest movements contesting the repressive regime in China. These movements act in unusual ways according to Western standards: under the rule of a persistently authoritarian regime, those in the forefront of grassroots movements are committed to building not only horizontal ties of solidarity and mutual help, but also 'vertical' connections with members of the local power structures (Shi and Cai, 2006).

The event of the Olympic Games has provided an exceptional opportunity for a variety of urban actors: the politico-economic elites have enthusiastically celebrated the country's modernization project as well as its hegemonic ambitions at the international level; urban social movements have striven to acquire visibility and legitimacy in the attempt to renegotiate on more democratic bases the relationship between the state and civil society. The Olympic Games, therefore, have set the scene for the assertion of a wide range of claims and protests: for religious freedom and against the repression of pro-Tibet movements; for human and social rights; and against the expropriation of private properties for the building of Olympic facilities and shopping areas. In conclusion, the evolution of contemporary Beijing shows that globalization has not only vigorously fostered economic growth and created opportunities for processes of urban and regional development, but has also prepared the ground for the rise of a lively urban community claiming a variegated set of political, social and human rights.

I.1.2 Bilbao after the Guggenheim

Until the 1990s, Bilbao was far from being an example of socio-spatial innovation and change. Fifth biggest agglomeration in Spain (today it has about 350,000 inhabitants), the city's image was commonly associated with its heavy industries, especially the iron and steel factories located in the industrial belt of Greater Bilbao. Like most European cities and regions specialized in the industrial and manufacturing sector, in the 1980s Bilbao witnessed a process of deindustrialization and structural decline. In 1986, the unemployment rate rose to an unprecedented 26 per cent of the workforce.

The situation of economic crisis and restructuring was concomitant with the transition occurring at the political and administrative levels. Until the mid-1970s, the Franco dictatorship prevented civil society from undertaking any independent

Figure I.1   Urban transformations in Beijing's Olympic Village (2007)

Source: photo © Alberto Vanolo

initiative, but the process of devolution started in 1978 when the recognition of the Basque Autonomous Community in the Spanish Constitution created new opportunities for urban and regional regeneration. In 1989, after the adoption of Bilbao's first strategic planning scheme, a series of ambitious urban projects were launched: the cleaning of the highly polluted river Nervión (known as the 'estuary of Bilbao'), the relocation of the harbour area outside of the city centre, the building of a new metro system. These initiatives were managed by newly established governing bodies, such as 'Bilbao metropolis 30', a public–private partnership committed to promoting the image of the city, and 'Bilbao Ría 2000', which was responsible for projects of physical renewal and redevelopment of the built environment.

During the 1990s, these initiatives of physical renewal were conducted within the framework of an emerging vision laying emphasis on the opportunities offered by a stronger connection to the global economy. Local elites became increasingly concerned with the generation of a cultural economy capable of positioning Bilbao within the cross-national flows of people, commodities and ideas. The shaping of this context preceded the ground-breaking event in Bilbao's recent history: the

Figure I.2   The Guggenheim in Bilbao: an urban icon (2007)

Source: photo © Alberto Vanolo

opening of the Guggenheim Museum in 1997. The related mega-project financed the construction not only of the spectacular museum building, but also of skyscrapers (such as the towers designed by the Japanese architect Isozaki), of a new airport and a pedestrian bridge designed by the famous Spanish architect Santiago Calatrava. The Guggenheim Museum, designed by the Canadian archistar Frank Gehry, has rapidly become a major cultural attraction: millions of tourists coming from all over the world have enjoyed the spectacle of a building which has rapidly become a landmark of the new Bilbao. It is estimated that 82 per cent of tourists visiting the city have chosen the Basque capital only for the Guggenheim (Landry, 2006). The museum has been so successful that it has been imitated worldwide: a phenomenon known as McGuggenheimization, which has been narrated even in the popular TV series *The Simpsons* as the imaginary town of Springfield (see Chapter 2). To put it briefly, one building has proved capable of shedding a new light on a declining city as was post-industrial Bilbao in the 1980s.

The pathway leading to the reinvention of the image and the economy itself of Bilbao, with the prominent role played by the tourist sector, has been based on material and discursive strategies of urban development which are typical of the times in which we live. As Sara Gonzalez (2006) has argued, the strategy devised by the Basque political-economic elites has dynamically re-positioned the city within the globalising world. This process of re-scaling has shifted the city's prevailing identity from being a regional capital, peripheral even at a national level, to an emerging positionality as an internationalizing city striving to re-connect itself in innovative ways to the material and immaterial flows of globalization. As said above, this process has to be regarded as an achievement of the local government as well as of other regional and local authorities, including the public-private coalition 'Bilbao Metropolis 30'. These actors have shared the goal of turning Bilbao into an internationally competitive, service-oriented city. The responsibilities that have been devolved to international private actors such as the Guggenheim Foundation, along with the cooptation of globally renowned architects, have been central to the strategy of economic regeneration and symbolic change (cf. Sklair, 2005).

Without denying the important changes that have been just shortly described, Bilbao's urban-change story can be told from a different perspective. In Guggenheim's opening day, a museum employee was injured when a bomb exploded nearby. The urban vision conveyed by the politico-economic elites collided with the reaction of ETA, the armed Basque nationalists, an organization with socialist background actively participating in the anti-Franco resistance whose reputation has been subsequently ruined by countless terrorist attacks and horrendous crimes against politicians, civil servants and civilians alike. Not only the Basque terrorists, however, have been opposing the new Bilbao strategy. The image of the Basque capital as a 'city of culture' appears to be detached from the social values of large portions of the population, accustomed to the hardness of factory work and the working class culture. It is no surprise then that, in light of Bilbao's example, the announced opening of other branches of the Guggenheim Museum aroused protests and dissident voices in New York City and São Paolo. In conclusion, Bilbao's path of urban change has drawn the attention of both those willing to exploit the regeneration potential of the global economy (the politico-economic elites) and those from an oppositional side (the grassroots movements) protesting over the effects of cultural homologation and societal annihilation.

What do these urban change stories have in common? Despite their obvious differences, they tell us about the transformations linked to the advent of globalization and the geographical diffusion of the so-called 'new urban politics' (centred around issues of inter-urban competition and internationalization) beyond the original boundaries of Anglo-American and even Western capitalism. In particular, the described urban pathways point to the ways in which globalization takes shape in different and at the same time similar forms across the globe, producing changes within the urban governance strategies and regulations which do not arise from the abstract realm of urban-management theories and normatively defined 'best practices', but from the tremendously wide array of social, cultural and institutional realities of cities and regions across the world. Urban success strategies, on the one hand, and resistance movements claiming 'rights to the city', on the other hand, mobilize varying and in many respects contrasting networks of actors, coalitions and partnerships. The city is, therefore, a crucial field in which globalization gives rise to dynamics of economic development that are concrete and visible but also based on conflicts and constantly evolving power relationships between spatialities and social groups.

I.1.3 The contested terrain of globalization

The distinguishing features of globalization – namely, the re-scaling of societal and spatial governance, the expansion of social and economic relationships at a potentially global scale, the widespread belief that our lives depend on events originating somewhere distant and rapidly migrating elsewhere – have urged scholars to revise the commonly held stance towards cities and urban issues. For instance, classic theorizations of the urban process and the city morphology in terms of living 'organism' are clearly no longer adequate. Cities, alongside the socio-spatially uneven fragments within them (the 'quartered cities': Marcuse, 2000), are to be viewed as nodes of a multitude of urban networks and as sites partaking in wider spaces of flows, producing multi-scalar and qualitatively variegated spatialities. Observing the process of globalization from the vantage point of urban-development trajectories throws light on the materiality of social phenomena and the interplay of local and global issues, as defined by dynamics of connectivity, cooperation and antagonism mobilizing a wide range of spatialiaties and temporalities. In the following pages of this book, these themes and issues will be addressed from a specific standpoint: one focusing on the relationship between the political and the urban in its multifarious variants. Until recently, spatial planning and the management of urban issues were either of national competence or were devolved to the local and regional levels of government. Recent transformations that are conventionally ascribed to the advent of globalization – such as the shift towards nationally and regionally differentiated varieties of neoliberalism, the establishment of influential international bodies of regulation, the belief that economic actors and processes are 'out of control' for the nation-states – have radically changed the meaning and the practical experience of urban politics (opening the way for the 'new urban politics', as was defined almost twenty years ago by geographer Kevin Cox, 1993): the 'global city', the 'entrepreneurial city', the 'creative city' and most recently the 'resilient city', along with other powerful representations of the contemporary city, paradigmatically testify to the radical changes that have occurred within the urban realm.

The social sciences and the broader public debate are informed, therefore, by the commonly held view that globalization has given rise to groundbreaking transformations all over the world: in the 'global North' and in the 'global South', as the conventional lexicon puts it. Without entering the rich and complex debate about globalization, two ways of approaching this theme can be identified: globalization as a social process and as a discursive practice.

First, globalization should be understood as a 'social process', which is characterized by an increasing interdependence between actors being conscious that, while operating 'at a distance', their lives are being increasingly socialized on a planetary scale (Elliott and Urry, 2010). The general social-science literature widely accepts the idea that globalization is not a 'final stage' in the development of human civilization, but should be viewed as a dynamic process exerting influence on the evolution of a multitude of simultaneously separate and interrelated dimensions of social life: economic, political, cultural, social and environmental. The process of globalization is typically marked by features of unevenness and imbalance: regions across the world unevenly take advantage of, or conversely are threatened by, globalization. As regards urban-development trajectories, evidence shows that the experience of globalization in São Paolo, for example, has a number of converging as well as diverging aspects with that of New York City. In particular, by looking at the societal formations of contemporary cities one cannot fail to notice the multitude of differences and similarities and the ways these are reflected in the collective senses of belonging variously based on gender, ethnicity, age as well as on urban citizenship. A Catholic woman of the Philippine diaspora, employed as a cleaner in Rome in Italy, is likely to cope with social integration issues that are similar to, and at the same time different from, those experienced by a Muslim man of Turkish origin employed in a German manufacturing industry, or by a self-made entrepreneur of Chinese nationality setting up a commercial business in San Francisco.

Cities across the world witness, therefore, the shaping of a contradictorily globalizing human condition: the duality of globalization is typically epitomized by the situation of hopeless exclusion and inequality affecting the so-called 'underclass' in capitalist cities (Mingione, 1996) and by the disproportionate affluence enjoyed by the new global elites (Sklair, 2002). On the other hand, rigidly dualistic representations of globalized societies are inadequate to describe the present situation, as social boundaries are increasingly blurred, and collective identities constantly change, evolving towards hybrid configurations. An individual or a territorial entity (a city, a region, etc.) is likely to develop multiple allegiances, partaking in a number of economic, social and cultural networks under conditions of relational proximity as well as time-space 'distanciation' (Amin, 2002). Likewise, while some urban areas and neighbourhoods find themselves to be highly connected to the process of globalization, other areas in the same city are relegated to a condition of marginality and physical decay. Underlining the contradictory and indeterminate character of globalization entails embracing an explicitly politically orientated perspective: the globalizing world is constitutively unstable, and the present and the future of cities are subject to largely unpredictable trajectories of evolution and change. The globalizing world can take the form either of an arena characterized by unchallenged individualism, ruthless competition and unregulated capitalism, or of a space imbued with values and practices of egalitarianism, democracy and exchange between equals. It is the political connotation of inherently conflictual processes, many of which take place at the urban scale, that makes the difference in the evolution of constitutively contingent and unpredictable socio-spatial realities like those of contemporary cities.

A second way of approaching globalization looks at this term as an assemblage of narratives and representations shedding light on different and even contrasting meanings of the present politico-economic context. Of course, there is no agreement on whether globalization is a positive or a negative phenomenon. On the one hand, there are those conveying an optimistic view of the globalizing world, such as those commentators that since the early 1990s have portrayed globalization as a promising horizon for humankind, opening spaces for a 'borderless world' (Ohmae, 1990) and for a pattern of social development providing novel opportunities to the poor (Baghwati, 2004). On the other hand, there are the critical views of those stressing the weaknesses of mainstream approaches to economic development and the related policy recommendations adopted by established institutions and international organisations (Stiglitz, 2002) and envisaging an incipient process of 'de-globalization' in the world economy (Bello, 2004). The ongoing global recession, which started in 2008 in the mortgage and financial sectors and then quickly spread to the wider economies, particularly supports the sceptical views, questioning the neoliberal orthodoxy that has driven the early stages of globalization. In any case, it is evident that each vision of globalization reflects the role of specific cultural, political and economic actors, intervening in the scholarly debate and the public sphere in order to exert an influence on the evolution of social and economic processes and on the way in which globalization is concretely managed: from the neoliberal elites leading the most influential international organisations to NGOs activists and representatives as well as the intellectuals and advocates of new social movements. Globalization is not to be regarded, therefore, as a process whose qualities are generally accepted by political, social and economic commentators. On the contrary, it is a discursive category which is created and sustained by 'experts' and opinion-makers voicing the interests of the emerging global elites and, on the other hand, is contested and deconstructed by those advocating alternative strategies of development and post-development.

Such a variety of subjective positions takes form along ideological lines, but has also strong economic motivations. Discussions over urban-regeneration processes and strategies provide evidence of the diversity of positions and related policy 'recipes': for instance, the discourse and the related academic theory stressing the economic potential of the urban creative class have been enthusiastically welcomed and in many cases translated in the policy realm by urban elites and city managers across the world, but critical scholars and social movements have warned about the gentrification effects and the commodification of the arts and culture associated with creative class policies and initiatives (see Chapter 2). The future of cities is, therefore, a highly controversial issue, especially when it comes to defining the way in which the process of decision-making is actually pursued: identifying an urban-development strategy is alternatively (or jointly) the outcome of a decision taken 'from above' by one legitimate authority or of a consultation process involving a plurality of policy options and actors. In conclusion, globalization is not an objectively definable historical-geographical scenario, but is a meta-narrative having multiple meanings and capable of directing individual and collective agency towards pre-fixed objectives. Globalization is also mobilized as a discursive device by economic and social actors on the basis of their positionality in terms of power and political role: local and global elites make use of globalization as a rhetorical justification of their development and wealth accumulation strategies (Jessop, 1997); justice movements, on the other side, refer to globalization as a convergence space for protest actions as well as for experimental practices of solidarity and grassroots cooperation (Routledge, 2003).

BOX 1	**KEY WORDS**

What do we mean by 'politics'?

o Recent decades have seen a resurgence of political theorizing in academic research, which has exerted an important influence also on the interdisciplinary field of urban studies. North American universities have been at the forefront in what has been defined 'the return to political philosophy' (Rancière, 2001). This process has occurred in at least three stages. First, in the 1980s the academic departments of humanities and philosophy in the US (particularly those in the progressive Western coast) made a decisive contribution to the academic popularization of the ideas of contemporary thinkers and critics from Continental Europe (most notably France) such as Jacques Derrida, Michel Foucault, Roland Barthes, Gilles Deleuze. According to some commentators, this import of philosophical ideas from the old continent has significantly transformed an originally loose and diversified intellectual movement into a sort of academic commodity commonly labelled as 'French theory' (Cusset, 2003). Even so, there is no doubt that this strand of thinking has been central to the 'poststructuralist' turn that has occurred within the human and social sciences, with an increasing emphasis being laid on discourse, representation and deconstruction (see Part One, 'Politics as Representation').

o A second stage in the resurgence of political theory can be associated with the debates on the changing forms of societal government, most notably those conducted within the framework of discussions on 'dialogic democracy', on 'governance' and lately on 'governmentality'. These debates, which have been

(Continued)

(Continued)

particularly lively since the mid-1980s onwards, were originally inspired by the following strands of thinking: the work of social and political theorists, led by Hannah Arendt and Jürgen Habermas, dealing with the dynamics of pluralistic democracy and the communicative turn in late-modern societies; the theoretical perspective elaborated by institutional economists and political scientists such as Oliver Williamson and Paul DiMaggio investigating the fragmentation of governmental processes within socio-economic organizations (the governance paradigm); the neo-Foucauldian rethinking of government as a complex assemblage of procedures, intellectual techniques and strategic agency (see Part Two, 'Politics as Government').

o   Finally, a third stage in the resurgence of political theory has occurred in more recent times in the form of a radicalized stance towards politics. In the late 1990s, this 'radical turn' has found fertile ground in the rise of the so-called anti-globalization movement across the world, which has posed demands for a new progressive and democratic politics transgressing conventional North–South geographical dichotomies and cultural boundaries (see Part Three, 'Politics as Contestation'). The main streams of this radical political movement have been the following: first, the feminists and the ethno-racial scholars that since the mid-1980s have placed notions of difference, subaltern subjectivity and positionality at the centre of critical political theory (from Donna Haraway to Judith Butler to Cornel West); second, a heterogeneous neo- and post-Marxist movement, including Italian Marxist 'autonomists' theorizing the potential politics in post-Fordist capitalism (Antonio Negri, Paolo Virno), the French theorists of absolute and libertarian democracy such as Jacques Rancière, and finally the advocates of a renewed idea of revolution tracing its origins back to the ideals of the twentieth century, such as Alain Badiou and Slavoj Žižek.

I.2 The triad of urban politics

The origins of the field of enquiry which can be conventionally defined 'the politics of urban development' trace back to the pioneering studies of the 1960s and 1970s dealing with issues of spatial organization and planning in the urban agglomerations of the United States and Western Europe. Those in the forefront of these foundational studies dealing with the politics of urban development were prominent human geographers and urban planners such as Jean Gottmann (1961) in France and subsequently in the US, Peter Hall (1966) in Britain, Allan Pred

(1977) in the US and Francesco Compagna (1967) in Italy. From the mid-1980s onwards, these studies have been revived by the advent of globalization as a discourse and social process and by the related greater emphasis being placed on the role of cities and regions as relatively autonomous agents of internationalization in the world economy (most notably by scholars of global and world cities such as John Friedmann, Saskia Sassen and Peter Taylor). This recent scholarship has revitalized the post-war tradition of studies on urban and regional development, but it has also gone beyond the established approaches in this literature, exploring the wider politics of place and space, and not just that related to economic development and spatial organization issues. Therefore, it is worth attempting to offer a definition of what is meant by 'politics of place and space' as a point of departure for this book.

Let's start from an identification of the substantive focus of research in urban political studies. A tentative list of issues and themes falling within this field of enquiry might include: the contradictory relationships between politico–economic elites and urban citizens (as showed by the case of Beijing); the role of culture in urban regeneration processes (as showed by the case of Bilbao); the transformations of public space and the struggles over the 'rights to the city' (enacted by subaltern actors such as migrants, sexual and gender minorities, the homeless); the politics taking shape around goals of sustainability and the management of environmental change; the evolution of the housing sector and related policy initiatives, institutional processes and social conflicts; the integration of ethnic and religious minorities within mainstream urban societies. Obviously, the list could be longer, covering a potentially countless set of issues and themes pertaining to the urban realm. Identifying a 'triad of urban politics' will help us to orient ourselves towards the complexities of city life. The spheres of this triad, which are at one and the same time autonomous, interrelated and antinomic, are the following: politics as representation, as government and as contestation.

I.2.1 Politics as representation

In the first instance, the politics of space can be dealt with in terms of representation. This line of interpretation draws inspiration from the writings of Michel Foucault on the 'dispositifs' (the devices) producing the 'order of discourse' as well as from those of Jacques Derrida on the critique of language and on deconstruction methodology within the literary work. These strands of thinking have led to the conviction that representations have an intrinsically performative potential, generating in our mental and cultural universes different modes of framing social phenomena and issues and thus opening the way for a variety of interventions and discursive tactics, as Foucault puts it.

This line of enquiry has been influential within the human and social sciences, especially after the publication of *Orientalism* by Edward Said (1978). In this book, the intellectual and literary critic of Palestinian origin famously showed that the

Orient should be regarded as a discursive category, which was constructed in the context of the project of Western civilization at the time of the European colonial rule in the Middle East. Representations, therefore, are capable of framing social phenomena in terms of negativity, inferiority or as sources of danger and threat, as recently experienced by Muslims in Western countries in the years following the 9/11 terrorist attacks.

The Other (social, cultural or geographical) is not only identified as a target of stigmatizing representations within contexts of colonial dominance and geopolitical conflicts. Annihilating the Other through the power of representations is a common practice also under 'ordinary' conditions. Today, for instance, cities are increasingly concerned with the position held in rankings assessing the attraction of investments and other indicators of economic growth. These rankings are formulated and presented against the background of the neoliberal discourse on competitiveness, which builds on the assumption that cities are homogeneous collective actors, behaving like individual agents and private firms. This representation draws a veil over uneven social formations and power relationships, which are distinguishing features of the urban experience. Existing socio-spatial contradictions are obfuscated not only by the conventional neoliberal rhetoric of competitiveness and entrepreneurialism. A related process of 'framing' takes into account also intrinsically positive goals and values such as the participation of citizens in public affairs, the equality of opportunities, the levels of social cohesion in liberal democracies, or the struggle against poverty in the developing countries. With regard to the latter, for instance, critical development studies have provocatively stressed the 'invention of poverty' associated with pro-Third World programmes: economic investments and anti-poverty initiatives have been supported by international organizations and Western countries in order to reinforce their cultural and economic hegemony on developing countries, rather than effectively empowering local populations and national economies (Escobar, 1995).

Those urban representations which implicitly prescribe the ways in which cities should act, regardless of their historical, political and socio-economic backgrounds, lead to the selection of specific policy recipes and thus end up imposing exogenous modes of conduct. For instance, cities are not really competing one with each other and cannot be considered 'collective actors' as such: the representations conveying these beliefs are instrumental in the reinforcement of hegemonic projects and related economic-political interests. From this point of view, it is worth drawing on the work of those critical political geographers that have offered a conceptual framework for the analysis of narratives, representations and metaphors uncovering the 'political unconscious' in the conduct of established spatial entities such as nation-states, cities and regions (Ó Tuathail, 1996). Even seemingly objective cartographic representations are associated with power relationships and specific visions of the world, as shown by European continental geographers who have discussed the rise and the subsequent crisis of 'cartographic reason' in the modern and contemporary ages (Farinelli et al., 1992).

Because of the importance of representations in the social consciousness, cities and larger metropolitan regions are faced with a complex and in many respects contested 'politics of translation', which is fostered by a variety of linguistic and cultural codes (see Mondada, 2000). Most typically, discursive and communicative practices and strategies selectively identify and target urban spaces, distinguishing between attractive neighbourhoods and those being stigmatized as 'deprived', 'unsafe', 'declining'. The representation process exerts an influence not only on public policies, but also on the conduct of private actors: take, for instance, the discrimination policy covertly adopted by banks and other financial institutions operating in the mortgage market in the United States, which are used to 'red-lining' off-limits neighbourhoods, where loans are considered too risky and are given at less convenient, even predatory rates and conditions. This example shows that representations wield an intrinsically performative power, which forges discursive objects, making a decisive contribution to the reproduction of existing socio-spatial inequalities in contemporary capitalist cities.

I.2.2 Politics as government

The politics of representation is intimately linked to the practice of governing cities. Within this sphere, the politics of space draws on a variety of intellectual technologies and practical tools which are created and used by local and national governments in order to improve the well-being of an urban community. Administering spatial entities such as a city or a neighbourhood requires the deployment of a wide range of technical and intellectual instruments (such as commissioned studies and reports, statistical indexes and the like) as well as regulations and policy tools (zoning laws, city and regional planning schemes, urban projects and initiatives, negotiation and consultation processes). Taken together, these measures and devices engender a 'governmental rationality', aiming to adapt the conduct of individuals and the whole citizenry to the government's moral imperatives and related institutional goals (Rose, 1999). The politics 'as government' draws on the combination of these politico-administrative procedures and tools, along with the related knowledge implications and moral imperatives.

An understanding of the 'politics as government' along these lines is heavily indebted to the analytics of power originally proposed by Michel Foucault (2004) and subsequently developed by 'governmentality' scholars, such as Nikolas Rose and Peter Miller above all. Geographers at the intersection of the Anglophone and Francophone academic 'traditions' have made important contributions to these debates and reflections, by dissecting the socio-spatial implications of this approach to the study of power relationships (Raffestin, 1980; Allen, 2003). The expanding Foucaldian literature, which has gone beyond the prevailingly philosophical and sociological focus of the beginning, touching upon a tremendous variety of research themes and disciplinary fields, illuminates the ways in which power relationships are exercised and reproduced by a multitude of collective and individual agents, which are not always affiliated with the established institutions and the state sector. The state itself should not be viewed as a static and monolithic entity, but as a mobile and contingent constellation of institutions, agents and social groups. As already anticipated, contemporary reflections focusing on the exercise of power and the art of government have converged on the discussion of 'governmentality'. This term has been used by those authors debating and scrutinizing the institutional and political processes giving rise to a governable space, through the deployment of government techniques, administrative procedures and discursive-ideological repertoires.

The government process does not consist, therefore, only in the execution of laws and other formal regulations, but is based also on specific techniques by which social and economic problems and issues are presented, governing bodies interact with the populace and with public and private actors, and by which societal advancement is understood. In the view of Nikolas Rose and the other theorists of 'governmentality', a distinguishing feature of globalization and the advanced liberal societies lies in the advent of an anatomy of power which replaces conventional patterns of political representation and social consensus (based on class consciousness and on the state provision of social services), turning individual citizens and local communities into increasingly responsible subjects in pursuit of their own well-being, as regards for instance issues of safety, social security and other fields in which the state once retained an exclusive role of regulation (Osborne and Rose, 1999).

Contemporary cities powerfully witness the shaping of the emerging 'governmental rationality'. Cities represent themselves as 'collective actors' and as such they are deemed responsible for the accomplishment of their own economic development goals. This is put into practice through the adoption of entrepreneurial modes of conduct dictating an attitude reconciling strategies of cooperation and competition with other cities at national and international levels. This new urban policy materializes in a wide array of initiatives: today, cities devise strategies aimed at the regeneration of the urban environment and the attraction of external investors, through the organization of hallmark events, the development of techno-poles, the invention of exhibition spaces for the arts and a host of other initiatives capable of enhancing the material and imaginary positionality of the city within the political and economic space of globalization.

I.2.3 Politics as contestation

Unlike Foucault and those authors whose work has followed in the wake of his intellectual legacy, for the French philosopher Jacques Rancière, one of the most distinguished exponents of today's critical thought, politics has not to do with the exercise of power, which is primarily an intellectual activity. In his view, one should distinguish between police ('la *police*') and politics ('la *politique*'): the former refers to the preservation of a pre-fixed social order and to the position 'naturally' assigned to the members of a polity, on the basis of a rational partition of the space of opportunities; on the other hand, the latter is fostered by the process of contestation of the order being imposed by the 'police', which is inherently controversial and modifiable, in the name of equality and social justice (Rancière, 1995, 1998). Therefore, according to Rancière, politics is not to be identified with the set of power relationships described by Foucault, but with the common space created by the contestation of the police order, which is produced by the existing government arrangement. The police thus creates an order which treats members of the community as governable subjects. The politics of contestation questions this relational and physical arrangement, in the name of an egalitarian and democratic city (Dikeç, 2005). This act of contestation produces a number of 'minor geographies' (Katz, 1996; Galluccio, 2007), which are made of – and nurtured by – a wide array of socio-spatial practices and invisible as well as visible claims. Despite their 'minor' status, this book argues that such geographies are expressions of a potential majority of subaltern actors prefiguring a horizon of 'absolute' democracy (see Virno, 1996).

The sphere of the 'politics as contestation' is qualitatively different from the other mentioned spheres in that it reintegrates an egalitarian and progressive view of urban politics (see Boltanski, 2009), which would be otherwise reduced merely to the capacity to represent and reproduce the dominant image (the 'politics as representation') or to govern and administer existing societies ('politics as government'). In addition, in concentrating on life-related issues (the main being housing, health care, the income, as well as citizenship and sexuality), through their politics of presence these movements shed light on a 'living politics of the city', which can be considered as the other face of the coin of the government-led urban biopolitics aiming to the control and the disciplining of bodies, urban spaces and social relationships, as well as of the conventional politics of urban economic development being driven by the goal of making cities more competitive and productive.

The space of contestation is commonly represented as a niche or an interstice by the mass media and wider public, because it is produced by apparently marginal and invisible actors, such as the angry young proletarians of the French banlieues, the international migrants struggling for citizenship, the students in authoritarian countries claiming access to civil and political rights, the 'irrepresentable' workers employed on casual bases identifying the urban field as a privileged terrain of struggle. In light of these struggles, contestation space appears in its foundational and constituent potential as a 'new beginning', one in which the emancipatory claims put forward by subaltern groups are recognized and accepted as sources of constitutional change and reform. The space of contestation gives rise, therefore, to a political sphere which is ontologically alternative to that produced by the 'politics as government', being the latter focused on the improvement of the relationships between governing entities and those being governed within the given political-spatial order. On the other hand, contestation space has an ambivalent relationship with the 'politics as representation': social movements constantly combine the refusal of mainstream representations of social and spatial processes with the elaboration of their own practices and strategies of expression and autonomous representation as a way of establishing their material and immaterial presence within the urban realm.

BOX 2	**KEY WORDS**

What is a city?

o Providing a definition of the city as a spatial entity is a difficult task, as the urban process can be observed from different points of view. Different aspects of urbanization can be identified along lines variously relating to the organization of the built environment (the high density of people and buildings), to cultural phenomena (the distinctiveness of urban cultures, its embodied symbolisms and meanings), to political processes (cities as sites of political action and representation), to economic issues (the economies of agglomeration and diversity generating at the urban level). Whereas in the last three decades or so critical geographers, sociologists and political scientists have placed the economic process at the centre of their interpretations of the evolution of cities, other logics underlying the development of the urban process can be identified. For instance, in his classic book Lewis Mumford (1961) related the culture of cities to the religious factor, the urban form being in his view the materialization of the perpetual dialectic between the human and the transcendental. From a more materialistic perspective, cities can be also understood as magnets attracting people, social relations and networks (Soja, 2000; see the concept of *synekism* in the next chapter).

o Broadly speaking, the city is a multifaceted physical, relational and governmental space. In purely geographical terms, there is no doubt that distinguishing features of the urban environment are those of 'density' and 'diversity' (Lèvy and Lussault, 2003). However, reducing urbanism to the idea of the physical clustering of human settlements and artefacts is misleading: as stressed by Soja (2000) in his account of the *exopolis* (see also Gottman's classic analysis of the *megalopolis*; Gottman, 1961), in contemporary cities the urban fabric is inherently fragmented and spatially discontinuous, comprising edge cities, sprawling regions, suburbs, outer cities, new towns. Moreover, even more significantly in a context of globalization, cities are re-shaped by relations developing under conditions of distance and non-proximity (Amin and Graham, 1997). Cities and metropolitan areas tend to become polycentric in their spatial form, multi-networked, stretched across transnational spaces and dispersed through a multitude of socio-economic flows. From this vantage point, cities are irrepresentable spatialities, taking the form of fluid and porous rather than bounded spaces, developing around relations of connectivity arising from persistently path-dependent development pathways (cf. Jones, 2009).

o As this book will show, urban political processes reflect the co-existence of contrasting spatial ontologies of the city. However, spatial determinism should be avoided in critical interpretations of urban politics, even in those formulated from the standpoint of human geography: urban politics is dependent on, but also relatively autonomous from, the contingent form and the spatial ontology of cities.

I.3 Overview of the book's structure

The structure of the book is organized on the basis of the three spheres of urban politics which have just been identified and briefly illustrated in conceptual terms. Part One begins with Chapter 1 introducing the reader to this theme by re-examining the overlapping imaginaries of the contemporary city in recent decades: from the post-Fordist and postmodern city to the global and entrepreneurial city. Chapter 2 unpacks one of the most influential urban narratives in the last decade: namely, the public discourse prescribing the requisites for a city to be 'creative' and more generally emphasizing the role of culture as an urban growth driver. As the latter example powerfully demonstrates, urban representations can be understood as discursive devices mobilized by urban elites in pursuit of strategies of urban development. These representational processes exert an important influence on the paths of urban development and most notably on the selection process that is behind the inclusion or the exclusion of issues and problems within the policy agenda of local governments. From this point of view, it can be concluded that representations offer major standpoints for understanding urban politics.

Part Two of the book deals with the sphere defined 'politics as government'. Chapter 3 offers a critical reconstruction of the trajectory of urban neoliberalism: from the apparently irresistible ascent in the late 1970s, passing through a stage of global circulation and expansion, until the recent regulatory and accumulation crises generated by the 2008–09 'credit crunch'. Urban entrepreneurialism, the imperative of growth and the strong emphasis placed on cities as self-governing entities and 'collective actors' competing with each other within the political and economic space of globalization are the 'pillars' of the urban politics that has taken shape around the rise of neoliberalism as a mode and style of regulation over the last three decades. Recent decades have witnessed, therefore, the shaping of an increasingly autonomous urban governmental realm, a process which has taken place in the broader context of the reconfiguration of the spatial scales of governance and regulation, particularly involving the nation-state as well as sub-national geographical entities such as the city and the region. Along with the entrepreneurial turn, the empowerment of cities as self-governing entities has also entailed devolving to local governments greater responsibilities concerning the regulation of violence and the public order: today, sovereignty and violence appear to be intimately interrelated spheres even at the urban scale. Chapter 4 thus describes the disturbing scenarios of contemporary 'urban geopolitics', most notably those related to the regulation of violence at the urban and metropolitan levels. The surveillance and militarization of urban spaces, the pre-emptive repression of the 'external enemies' of urban civilization, are the distinguishing features of an urban order increasingly regulated by the actual or only threatened use of force.

Part Three dwells on a dimension of urban politics which can be understood as the 'reverse' of the 'politics as government': the politics taking shape around claims of expanded democracy, substantive egalitarianism and deep recognition of cultural, ethnic and gender-sexual differences. The protagonists in this sphere of urban politics are social movements and 'organized' minorities committed to asserting their presence in the urban field. Chapter 5 engages with this theme from the point of view of the struggles arising around social and spatial justice. The 'urbanization of social justice' is a long-standing theme and matter of concern within urban critical scholarship, particularly since the 1970s in the wake of the diffusion of neo-Marxist and radical positions in the field, which explicitly politicized academic debates and related research programmes. Contemporary struggles for socio-spatial justice arise from conflicts and public controversies developing around a wide range of issues, such as: the regeneration and physical renewal of decayed neighbourhoods and the gentrification effects of these processes; the management of the urban environment and the ways in which existing socio-spatial inequalities are reflected into phenomena of environmental injustice; the grassroots demands for policies led by the principle of 'redistribution' rather than of growth, in contrast to the dominant neoliberal agenda.

As already anticipated, however, contemporary social movements and struggles do not mobilize only around issues of socio-spatial justice, but increasingly take form as a way of establishing a recognized 'presence' in the urban field. This important, in some contexts even prevailing, dimension of the 'politics as contestation' is examined in Chapter 6 of the book, which focuses on the 'politics of presence' from the standpoint of international migrants and dissident sexual minorities demanding access to citizenship, including urban citizenship. Subaltern or minority groups are protagonists of an ambivalent dialectic with the established authorities: they are invited to integrate into mainstream society preserving their identities and even to profit from their cultural diversity in economic terms, but on the other hand the radical manifestations of their claims and shifting positionalities are persistently marginalized. For this reason, the selected groups paradigmatically exemplify the complexity and ambiguity of citizenship politics in the neoliberal era.

Even though this book seeks to offer a broad view on the current state of affairs in urban politics, it would have been impossible to provide the reader with an all-encompassing account of the relevant themes and issues in the field. Indeed, the majority of social, economic and cultural aspects of human societies potentially fall within the field of urban politics to the extent in which they arise from the assertion and negotiation of material interests, geographical imaginaries and public discourses at the urban level. The realm of everyday life particularly comprises a wide variety of phenomena that can be investigated from a perspective of critical urban politics: from those relating to the ways in which individuals and communities interact with 'nature' and technologies to those throwing light on the dynamics of power associated with recurring and apparently meaningless actions, for instance when we eat, walk or even sleep. This book is not concerned, if not just peripherally, with the 'micro-political' dimension of socio-spatial life. Today, this dimension attracts the attention of increasingly numerous authors (poststructuralist geographers being at the forefront in this intellectual movement) embracing an expanded and radically pluralistic perspective on city politics, which emphasizes the importance of the 'small things' of everyday life and the unexplored spatio-temporal relationships between humans, technologies and other animated environments and entities (Amin and Thrift, 2002; Hinchliffe et al., 2005; for a recent philosophical account of this 'vitalistic neo-materialism' see Bennett, 2010). However, although these debates are fascinating, we will call attention mainly to those aspects of urban politics in which visible and organized (or deliberately invisible and disorganized) actors become involved.

While being aware of the inevitably selective character of the critical overview of urban politics offered in this text, we hope that this book will encourage readers to engage in a constantly creative deconstruction of the urban settings in which they happen to live or just occasionally spend part of their lifetime. In times in which economic and political issues and processes are commonly presented as 'natural' and 'inevitable' – from inter-urban competition to the privatization of public services, from the Westernization of the forms of urbanization to the entrepreneurialization of social behaviours – this may turn out to be an exercise less predictable in its outcomes than it would appear at a first glance.

part one

POLITICS AS REPRESENTATION

1

Urban Development and the Politics of Representation

Key Issues and Themes

The production of urban representations and narratives is intimately linked to capital accumulation and economic development strategies being pursued by the politico-economic elites in a postmodernized urban environment. The politics of representation, however, is a contested field, one in which conventional representations are challenged and contested 'from below'.

The crisis of Fordism as a mode of production has opened the way for the rise of a variety of representations and public discourses heralding the advent of the post-Fordist city in multiple forms.

The invention of the global city is at the heart of the globalization discourse. Over the years, this notion has travelled across the globe, being particularly successful in the East Asian context.

In recent years, the environmentalist discourse has been incorporated into the neo-liberal policy agenda, which emphasizes the link between sustainability and economic development. Urban resilience is the emerging policy catchword in this context.

A critical understanding of the politics of representation has to take into account the fact that conventional representations and narratives arise from a Eurocentric view of human civilization and socio-economic processes.

1.1 Introduction: towards a political economy of representation

The geographies of urban politics can be analysed drawing on a line of enquiry intimately linked to the poststructuralist turn in the social sciences. According to this theoretical perspective, the dynamics and forms of the urban process (like those in other realms of social life) are to be understood not only as phenomena that are empirically observable in the way in which they actually appear, but also as socially and culturally constructed 'discourses' from which a number of different meanings originate. Observing the urban experience from this point of view is not a merely intellectual exercise but should be regarded as a way of unpacking commonly held views on cities and the pathways of urban development. Today, it is commonly accepted that discourses and representations have a performative role (see Hall, 1997). In the field of urban studies, this means looking at the ways in which architects, urban designers, policymakers and planners discursively frame and represent urban spaces, through planning schemes and regeneration projects, shaping the conduct of citizens and the organized actors along the lines of the dominant rationalities of government and economic development.

Representations originate not only from official documents of urban policy, but also from the mass media and a number of cultural and popular outlets. The intimate relationship linking the political strategies of urban development to the dynamics of capitalist accumulation, through the power of representations, has led critical urban scholars to creatively draw on the 'tradition' of studies dealing with the political economy of city and regions (Harloe, 1977; see the section dedicated to Harvey and Castells in Chapter 3). Today, therefore, investigating the political economy of cities and regions entails coming to terms also with the importance acquired by the politics of representation within the urban realm. Advocates of urban political economy have thus engaged with poststructuralist social theory, advancing an innovative 'cultural political economy', which seeks to combine the established methodologies of historical (and geographical) materialism with critical discourse analysis (Jessop, 2004a; Ribera-Fumaz, 2009).

Far from resulting in a pluralistic depiction of the urban experience, representational strategies stem from a highly selective and politicized process. In order to build consensus among its citizenry around the dominant development strategy, urban elites confine the image of the city to monistic representations: the post-Fordist city, the postmodern city, the global and entrepreneurial city and, in more recent times, the sustainable and resilient city. This chapter will outline the social and cultural context in which hegemonic representations of contemporary cities take form, underlining their relationships with existing politico-economic strategies pursued by urban elites, nation-states and supra-national organizations. Prior to this analysis, the chapter will look at the ways in which the image of the city has become an explicit target of government initiative, particularly through the invention of the so-called city marketing.

1.2 Governing the image of the city

As will be shown in Part Two (Chapter 3), mainstream approaches to city government have changed over the last three decades, most notably within the framework of the shift from the public-managerial and redistributive policies of the Keynesian decades, focusing on land use regulation and the allocation of public services, to the entrepreneurial turn of the neoliberal era, emphasizing the role of cities and regions as economic growth drivers. The struggle over the production of captivating images of the contemporary city has followed in the wake of this epochal change within the philosophy of urban policy. The commonly held view behind the emerging policy rationale is that cities are compelled to compete within the global arena in the attraction of a variety of resources and 'competitive advantages', including direct investments by transnational firms, the inflow of international tourists, the organization of hallmark events, the localization of the headquarters of world organizations (Lever and Turok, 1999).

In this context, cities devise allegedly 'innovative' strategies aiming to assert or just to consolidate their competitive positionality within national and international arenas. In doing so, urban elites adopt entrepreneurial styles of action and communication, publicly selling the city's images and icons in the way private companies sell their commodities, even with regard to socially and environmentally relevant goals such as ecological development and social cohesion (Jessop and Sum, 2000). The production of images, discourses and urban representations thus offers a crucial point of observation for the analysis of contemporary strategies of urban development and related power relationships. Cities strive to re-connect themselves to the changing spatialities of global relationships and flows, making recourse to strategies of urban marketing and branding. Such efforts are intended to attract public and private investments and to infuse a dynamic mentality into local societies, open to competitive as well as collaborative relationships (Paddison, 1993; Kavaratzis and Ashworth, 2005).

What usually falls under the rubric of the 'image of the city' is a complex and variegated repertoire of representation devices, which includes: selected elements of the built environment (streets, monuments, buildings) being used as official urban brands; symbols and icons evoking the habits, routines, conventions and organizational structures regulating urban social relationships; the stereotypes associated with local culture as well as the popular accounts of city life featured in advertising campaigns of place marketing, in tourist guides, films and other cultural products. Although politico-economic elites tend to offer a monolithic image of the city, urban representations are constitutively plural, reflecting the different positionalities of social actors and groups and the uneven power relationships forging the urban political realm. There can be representations arising from the everyday experiences of those living in the poorer neighbourhoods of the city, which are usually confined to the status of 'imaginary geographies' of the city (Memoli, 2005); and there is, on the other hand, the production of dominant, allegedly shared, images of the city, which is the result of representations elaborated by the urban elites and imposed on city users and dwellers. Politico-economic elites propose optimistic representations of city life, downplaying weaknesses and contradictions, while emphasizing the competitive potentials of urban and regional economies and presenting urban communities as cohesive formations acting as 'collective actors' (Bagnasco and Le Galès, 1997; cf. the notion of 'locality as agent': Cox and Mair, 1991). The production of hegemonic representations of the image of the city, however, is likely to provoke the response of dissident voices and protest movements: for instance, popular coalitions in Denver and Toronto contested the image of the respective cities conveyed on the occasion of the Olympic candidature (in Toronto the slogan of the protestors was 'bread not circuses'); in Mexico City local citizens denounced the inequities and false promises emerging from government's discourse on efficiency and competitiveness at the time of the building of the new international airport (Levy and Bruhn, 2006).

1.2.1 Contested representations

Urban settings thus provide ideal conditions not only for the institutionalization of the representational process, in varying forms and modalities, but also for the development of grassroots movements contesting official representations in the name of 'absolute' democracy and a more egalitarian urban society (Part Three). The politics taking shape around the production of images and representations constitute a highly controversial and contested field. Energetic and optimistic visions are permeated by rhetoric and narrative devices opportunistically mobilized in order to assert a reassuring image of the city. This optimism can be expressed either in the form of banal slogans ('Los Angeles, city of the sun', 'Milan, capital of fashion') or through more sophisticated institutional processes, as occurs within contemporary strategic-relational planning initiatives based on accurate consultation and negotiation procedures involving organized actors and local communities (Jessop, 2001). The discursive tactics informing the planning processes are likely to appear even outrageous in the eyes of the powerless actors (the unemployed, the homeless, those living in deprived neighbourhoods, the unrepresented workers and undocumented migrants), in dictating a straightforward representation of the city as a place of opportunity, success, leisure, excluding what appears to stand in contrast to the reassuring picture of harmony and consensus. Nonetheless, despite expressions of dissent and resistance, the 'positive' representations of the city, and even of its problems and open questions, are assumed as being capable of generating a sense of community and civic pride (the so-called framing strategies theorized by Erving Goffman, 1974), which is crucial to the building of social consensus and the attraction of public as well as private sources of funding for megaprojects and hallmark events. This typically happens to be the case of those city councils presenting the candidature for the Olympic Games or as a European Capital of Culture (see Chapter 2), involving a wide variety of public and private stakeholders (Cochrane et al., 1996; Boyle, 1999).

The politics of representation frequently result in the generation and reproduction of seductive images reflecting the interests and the expectations of economic actors, particularly of those involved in the tourist sector. Conventional strategies of urban branding and the stereotypical images arising from them are aimed at attracting the global flows of tourists and those of other city users and visitors (Hoffmann et al., 2003). The representational process typically translates itself into a number of 'selective narratives' (Sandercock, 2003), targeting potential investors, visitors and occasional city users. This process, however, does not necessarily lead to the invention of ephemeral narratives: urban elites are usually committed to reinventing images and narratives which are already rooted in the social consciousness and the local everyday life. On the one hand, manifestly false representations are destined to fail; on the other hand, those characteristics of a locality which are unquestionably unattractive, such as polluting industrial plants and unsafe areas, are excluded from mainstream representations as they are regarded as unprofitable in terms of place marketing.

The politics of representation presupposes, therefore, a highly selective process aimed at identifying place qualities and potentials. This selective work entails a 'linguistic politics', which provides a discursive justification for the pursuit of regeneration policies in a variety of urban settings. For instance, Leela Fernandes (2004) has examined the ways in which the rise of an urban middle class in India has been accompanied by representations of the city praising the delights of consumerism and the irresistible attractiveness of city lifestyles, while a growing number of pubs, clubs, discos and fashionable shops have proliferated in the gentrifying areas of the large cities. In this context, the promotion of a vibrant and explicitly Westernized lifestyle has implied the adoption of a silent 'politics of forgetting', which has drawn a veil (or it has tried to do so) over an important dimension of the urban experience: the condition of the urban poor and particularly of slum dwellers. These embarrassing spaces and social groups are expelled from the urban experience not only at a symbolic level but also physically through the eviction of informal housing and the forced relocation of their dwellers outside of the boundaries of the city through projects of slum redevelopment. In some cases, these operations are presented as socially innovative initiatives, attempting to turn slum dwellers into active citizens and self-financed homeowners, even though the actual outcomes are rife with contradictions and unresolved problems (Mukhija, 2003). One of these slums, Dharavi in Mumbai, has been at the centre of lively public discussions in recent times, when the British film *Slumdog Millionaire*, directed by Danny Boyle (2008), proposed an image of the neighbourhood that some commentators (such as the famous writer Salman Rushdie, native of Mumbai) considered as unrealistic in telling the story of a young man of poor background becoming a 'millionaire' after participation in a TV quiz.

The politics of representation, in conclusion, is a controversial phenomenon, an aspect which is emphasized by the advent of globalization and the 'society of spectacle', where not only information circulates with increased rapidity and constantly changes in meaning, but where representations of local societies – as in the film just mentioned – can arise from the work of symbolic agents (filmmakers, novelists, journalists, essayists) originating from other contexts and 'local cultures'. In this sense, the critical scrutiny of the urban politics of representation illuminates the dynamics underlying the production of the contemporary urban imaginary on a global scale. What ultimately results from this contested politics of representation is that cities are not fixed entities but are constantly evolving discursive objects. For this reason, it is worth looking at the trajectory of urban representations in the last few decades, starting with the crisis of the Fordist city and showing how this crisis has opened the way for the reinvention of the dominant image of the contemporary capitalist city.

1.3 From Fordism to post-Fordism: reinventing cities in a context of economic transition

The 1970s and the 1980s have been described by scholars, politicians and major economic players as decades witnessing profound changes in the structure and organization of Western economies and societies: an era marked by the rise of technological, social and institutional forces that have appeared to be radically different from those dominating the world in previous years (Amin, 1994). The incipient sense of 'great transformation' has been accompanied by the increasingly widespread usage of seductive catchwords and locutions such as 'post-Fordism', 'post-industrial society' and 'new capitalism'.

1.3.1 Fordism and the golden age of the capitalist city

Cities and metropolitan areas have therefore played a central role in the recent process of economic and societal transition, experiencing structural changes in their spatial forms and socio-economic formations (Soja, 2000). In previous decades, Fordist capitalism had been the engine in the evolution of urban and regional processes. The rise of a regime of accumulation based on Tayloristic techniques of production (the assembly line), the generalization of a wage-based class structure, the diffusion of standardized patterns of mass consumption and production, the replacement of local cultures with commodified lifestyles, deeply transformed the dynamics and forms of urbanization, particularly in those cities in which urban economies were shaped by the presence of large industries. In the so-called golden age of Western capitalism, from the end of the Second World War to the economic crisis of the mid-1970s (Marglin and Schor, 1991), urban and regional spaces located in the 'central' areas of capitalist countries were organized so as to accommodate the needs of large industries (particularly in the automotive sector), to the detriment of agriculture and traditional manufacturing. The Fordist city has thus been shaped by economies of scale and agglomeration, by the homogenization of the built environment, by the prevalence of the nuclear family and by a strong urban–rural dualism. The diffusion of private mobility (through the expansion of car ownership) produced a marked differentiation of urban areas between spaces dedicated to manufacturing activities and those specializing in the residential function: intensified home-to-work commuting, unplanned urban growth in some regions (in Southern Europe, for instance) and middle-class suburbanization in other areas (such as in North America), along with the depopulation of inland rural regions, have been the socio-spatial manifestation of these processes. In this context, the nuclear family, the television and the car became key symbols of the societies of advanced capitalism in the twentieth century.

Even though the described processes have led to a general improvement in the living conditions of Western populations, they have not been exempt from contradictions and tensions. At the socio-spatial level, social conflicts of unprecedented intensity developed around the transformation of peripheral neighbourhoods into public housing complexes. However, even in the presence of tensions and contradictions, the image of the industrial city has been associated with positive values of prosperity and reassuring scenarios of unlimited wealth accumulation. In a historical context characterized by the optimism of the post-war era, Western societies were far from experiencing the anxieties and the concerns that would have been produced by the economic crisis in the 1970s, with an increasing awareness of the risks linked to mass production and Fordist industrialization. In Europe, living and working in large industrialized cities were regarded as desirable attainments by those emigrating from the less favoured regions (the Italian Mezzogiorno, Portugal, Greece, Spain) to the most prosperous ones in Germany, Belgium, France or Britain. In sum, despite the persistent generation of social tensions and injustices, at the time of the 'golden age of capitalism' city life became synonymous with progress, prosperity and civilization.

1.3.2 After Fordism: imagining and planning the informational city

The process leading to the transformation of advanced capitalist economies has exceeded the crisis of a merely economic paradigm, intersecting with broader societal, cultural, political and technological changes. The decline of Fordism is to be understood, therefore, within the broader context of globalization of contemporary economies and societies. The Fordist crisis has particularly influenced the production of the dominant urban imaginary: symbols and places of industrialization have shifted from being regarded in positive terms (as icons of prosperity and progress) to being explicitly stigmatized and associated with notions of crisis, structural decline and physical decay, with important policy implications (Short and Kim, 1998).

The reputation of cities basing their economies exclusively on the industrial sector has been undermined by these developments, and from the 1980s onwards urban elites have committed to formulating more seductive representations of urban economies and societies, generally labelled as 'post-industrial' or 'post-Fordist' (see, for instance, the change in the urban logo of the city of Syracuse in the State of New York, which previously reproduced an industrial landscape dominated by chimneys and since 1986 has replaced it with a postmodern skyline drawn within a sun-like circle; as an example of a post-industrial town in Europe see the case of Turin: Vanolo, 2008).

The identification of captivating and environmentally friendly images, in contrast to the legacies of the Fordist times, has been a crucial terrain of struggle and confrontation amongst local actors, considering the ephemeral character of cultural fashions and social attitudes. To put it very simply, it is far from being taken for granted that what is deemed attractive today it will be so also in the days to come. For instance, theme-parks (with the reproduction of historical heritage artefacts, the arrangement of fake safaris and the invention of exotic places) attracted growing amounts of visitors in the 1980s, while in recent years their popularity has constantly decreased, at least in Western countries after the rise of critical approaches to tourism, such as eco-tourism and cultural tourism.

In the 1980s and the 1990s, capitalist societies – those in the forefront of the socio-spatial restructuring experienced in the previous decade and commonly defined the 'crisis of Fordism' – have widely acclaimed the virtues of the technological and informational city in the wake of the worldwide success of the Silicon Valley in California (Castells and Hall, 1994). During the last three decades, a widespread belief held that cities proving to be capable of developing informational economies are more likely than others to become central places within the globalizing world. Examples of informational cities – urban and metropolitan regions promoting themselves as international hubs of ICT industries – are numerous and scattered around the world: from Osaka in Japan ('the intelligent city'), to Barcelona ('the telematic city'), Amsterdam ('the information city' and more recently 'the creative city') and Manchester ('the wired city') in Western Europe.

From being a terrain of economic and territorial experimentation in the 1980s (Castells, 1989), the economic-spatial model of the 'informational city' has become increasingly hegemonic in the subsequent years, being imitated and reproduced in a variety of geographical contexts, even by cities and metropolitan regions lacking basic economic and institutional qualities such as the integration of innovative economic activities with research laboratories and academic institutions, which has been one of the key factors behind Silicon Valley's celebrated success (Saxenian, 1994). Wannabe informational cities are expected to act as technopoles within wider regional complexes, also because this recognition attracts large amounts of public and private funding and investments.

Many authors have pointed to the illusions generated by the emerging technocratic era and the related high-tech fantasies (Massey et al., 1992) and techno-dreams

(Dobers, 2003). The process of imitation and emulation, however, has not always produced 'empty boxes' in terms of economic prospects and international competitiveness. In East Asia, in particular, the so-called Siliconization process has given rise to a number of internationally renowned urban success stories, such as that of the 'intelligent island' of the city-state of Singapore (Olds and Yeung, 2004). Other successful examples of Orientalization of the Silicon Valley model are the 'multimedia supercorridor' created in Cyberjaya in Malaysia and the technological pole of Zhongguancun near Beijing, usually advertised by Chinese authorities as the 'China's Silicon Valley'. These technological poles have been created through mega-projects in which national states have played a prominent role along with that of urban politico-economic elites, in the attempt to reproduce and adapt to local conditions the social and environmental factors that led to Silicon Valley's success. However, even in these apparently successful technological clusters, it has not been possible to reproduce all of the distinguishing features of the Californian model: the already mentioned role of research universities and laboratories, the supply of venture-capital, the uniquely American attitude towards entrepreneurial risk. In these 'peripheral' locales, the power of urban representations and the promise of a future of technological progress have been intended to counter-balance the limitations and deficiencies of the local urban-economic settings.

This section has tried to show how the crisis of Fordism has urged cities to experiment with innovative dynamics of post-Fordist revitalization in the attempt at reconnecting their economies to the global value chains. In the last two or three decades, cities have undergone profound changes in relation to the dynamics of capitalist accumulation, with an increasing emphasis being placed on knowledge, innovation and competitiveness. The effects of this process of cultural and technological change, however, have gone beyond the merely economic realm of cities and metropolitan regions. Broader understandings of the notions of urbanism and urbanization and their representations within the social consciousness have changed, inducing urban elites across the world to embark on innovative pathways of urban development and regeneration.

1.4 Postmodernizing the capitalist city

The economic transformations that have resulted in the shaping of a post-Fordist regime of accumulation are closely related to the broader cultural changes experienced by capitalist societies and most notably by urban societies in recent times. In his famous book dedicated to the condition of postmodernity, one of the most cited books within the social sciences over the last two decades, David Harvey (1989a) has shown that the economic and technological changes that have taken shape from the 1970s onwards have reconfigured the experience of space and time under the form of a spatio-temporal compression of social relations.

According to Harvey, these changes have had at least two important consequences on the urban experience.

The first relates to the growing emphasis being laid on the production of 'symbolic capital'. The forces of production and consumption (individual and collective) mobilize a variegated set of symbols: late-capitalist societies are increasingly dominated by the power of brands and by the prevalence of exchange values over use values in the way we consume things in our everyday life (cf. Patel, 2010). In this context, cities become central places in the production and regeneration of cultures, symbols, fashions and meanings transgressing the physical boundaries of the city itself and exerting an increasing influence on the broader cultural and economic practices in contemporary societies (Scott, 2000; Zukin, 1995). Urban phenomena make a distinctive contribution to this process of change: in so-called postmodern cities the changing built environment, the gentrification dynamics (the social upgrading of previously working class or socially mixed neighbourhoods), the reinvention of local identities and senses of spatialized belonging have their own codes of distinction and social determination (Wacquant, 2007).

The second effect, closely linked to the previous, concerns the role of 'spectacle' in the contemporary urban experience (Harvey, 1989a). Nowadays, the politics of urban development and change takes the form of a 'politics of spectacle', through the mobilization of iconographies, financial resources, relational capabilities, and local actors around the organization of hallmark events (festivals, concerts, sports events) and the production of places and sites of exhibition. These events and spaces inject enthusiasm and a renewed sense of belonging among city dwellers, even though these senses of belonging are admittedly ephemeral and dictated by contingent strategies of economic development. Shopping malls, commercialized pedestrian precincts, tourism-oriented ethnic districts (such as the countless number of Chinatowns scattered around the world), theme-parks, museums of contemporary art, and entire cities dedicated to entertainment and leisure (such as Las Vegas most famously), are the spatial manifestation of what is commonly identified as 'urban boosterism' (Boyle, 1999). Large portions of urban space are transformed into arenas of spectacle and play, making a distinction between those being able to enjoy these events and the commodified urban spaces and those that are not. The creation of organized spaces of spectacle and leisure shows how in postmodern times policies of local economic development concentrate not only on incentivation mechanisms for production and producer-service activities, but also on consumption per se (see Hudson, 2005).

The economic and cultural changes associated with postmodernity are not to be understood as a 'natural' evolution in the development trajectories of the contemporary city. Rather, these changes have arisen from deliberate strategies of urban regeneration and related projects of capital accumulation being pursued by politico-economic elites after the crisis of Fordism. More precisely, it can be argued that an intentional 'postmodernization' of the capitalist city has taken place from the 1980s onwards, initially in the United States and later in Europe, East Asia, Middle East and other regions across the world, including cities in the African continent (such as those in post-apartheid South Africa and in Northern Africa: see Box 1.1). In this context, the builders (administrators and policymakers, local and foreign investors, and national governments especially in non-Western contexts) of the 'postmetropolis' – to use the term suggested by Edward Soja (2000) – have re-shaped the contemporary urban experience around the overlapping of the real and the imaginary, turning consumption (of commodities, land, images) into a key factor behind the development of urban economies. Two examples will help us illustrate the variety of urban strategies of 'postmodernization' co-existing at the global scale: first, the pioneering pathway of urban regeneration that has led Baltimore to shift from an example of declining industrial and port city, affected by deep social tensions, to a sort of paradigm of ephemeral and consumption-led urbanism; second, the more recent case of Dubai, in the Middle East, which has come to represent a remarkable example of peripheral urban postmodernism, of its strengths and its weaknesses.

1.4.1 A pioneering pathway to postmodern urbanism: redeveloping Baltimore in the 1980s

Located on the Eastern coast of the United States, Baltimore is among the country's oldest cities and in the nineteenth century was a major destination for migrants coming from Europe. Until the Second World War, the city was among the most populated and industrialized centres nationally, specializing in steelworks, shipping, the automotive industry, and transportation. In the post-war decades, however, Baltimore underwent a process of deindustrialization and decline of its port economy and the related waterfront spaces. In the late 1960s, and notably in 1968 after the murder of Martin Luther King, racial riots exploded in the inner city, with devastating effects on some areas. During those years, port spaces were deteriorating, with derelict shipyards and warehouses scattered everywhere. In the mid-1970s, a newly formed public–private partnership, led by the Mayor and influential local businessmen, launched an ambitious plan for the renewal and the economic regeneration of Inner Harbor Place, the city's waterfront area. Within the space of few years, the regeneration process went so far, with shops, restaurants, museums and exhibition venues (such as the famous Aquarium) appearing all across the area, that Inner Harbor Place became one of the most popular tourist attractions in the United States and an icon of urban postmodernism (Harvey, 1989a). However, despite the success of Inner Harbor Place's renewal plan, the process of urban regeneration proved problematic in many respects: on the one hand, the social deprivation and the residential segregation of the African-American communities (70 per cent of the local population) remained strong; on the other hand, public and private financial resources were employed in urban-regeneration plans which benefitted business firms in the tourist and entertainment sector, while generating mostly temporary and low-paid jobs (Levine, 1987).

1.4.2 Urban postmodernism in the periphery: the Dubai experience

A geographically peripheral story of urban postmodernization that is worth recounting is that of Dubai in the United Arab Emirates. Dubai's urban economic development has been promoted by national political elites importing Western forms and dynamics of urbanization and economic growth, coming to represent an example of urban entrepreneurialism and postmodernism in a non-Western context. Urbanist Mike Davis (2006a) has associated Dubai's urban development pattern with the phenomenon of 'hyper-real' architecture described by Venturi, Brown and Izenour in their 1972 postmodern manifesto entitled *Learning from Las Vegas*. Originally, the strategy behind Dubai's redevelopment was to diversify the economy of the Emirates, which relied mainly on oil revenues and trade. Urban growth reached its peak during the expansion of real-estate markets experienced by the global economy across the world between 2004 and 2006, but like other regions and cities also Dubai was heavily affected by the major economic downturn caused by the bursting of the property bubble in 2008–09 (see Chapter 3).

A key actor in the strategy of accelerated economic development has been Sheikh Mohammed Al Maktoum, who was appointed Crown Prince of Dubai Emirate in 1995, promoting a number of ambitious real estate projects, the most famous being the construction of the Palm Islands, the Emirate Towers and the Burj Al Arab hotel, along with that of several other skyscrapers, shopping malls, business centres and technological districts. However, well before the economic downturn, Dubai's development path had already shown its dark side, even though this aspect was resolutely excluded from official representations: the multitude of exploited migrants of South Asian origin (Sri Lanka, India and Pakistan) employed in the construction projects, living in a state of semi-slavery (Sengupta, 2006). In any case, it has been the global credit crunch that has dealt an almost fatal blow to the economy of Dubai: several real-estate projects, including the spectacular Palm Islands, have been left unfinished, while property values have fallen precipitously. On 26 November 2009, on Thanksgiving Day in the United States, an enormous foreign debt weighing on Dubai Holding – an investment conglomerate owned by the Emirate's ruler – was disclosed, causing panic in international stock markets. Recent bankruptcy fears patently collide with the sense of excitement and optimism dominating just a few months earlier, when international investors and real estate firms were accustomed to portray Dubai as an example of unlimited growth and expansion. These concerns, however, have been promptly mitigated by the bailout deliberated by the Abu Dhabi government in December 2009, with an

Figure 1.1   Dubai's Palm Jumeirah (one of the three artificial Palm Islands)
Source: www.istockphoto.com

announced investment of ten billion dollars, which has attempted to keep the Dubai's dream alive.

1.5 Celebrating the global city

Dubai's story of success and subsequent risk of default is an example illustrative of the acceleration in the geographical circulation of urban neoliberalism over the last two or three decades. As already anticipated in the introduction to this book, globalization sets the scene for our observation of the dynamics of growth and development in contemporary capitalist cities. This derives from the close relationship linking globalization and the urban processes in recent times. A commonly held view within the social sciences, including human geography and the neighbouring socio-spatial disciplines, is that globalization has led to the development of economic-relational networks and related spatialities across the globe, being mutually interconnected thanks also to the role of a limited number of hegemonic urban agglomerations: the so-called global city-regions (Scott, 2001).

Since the 1960s the seminal contributions of geographers, planners and sociologists such as Peter Hall (1966), John Friedman (1986) and Saskia Sassen (1991 and 1995) have pointed to the crucial linkage between cities and the internationalization of the economy. In a world-economy being increasingly shaped by transnational flows and connections (of capitals, technologies, tourists, migrants, images, information), major urban agglomerations become favourite locations for multinational firms, financial institutions, international organizations, as well as centres of cultural and intellectual creativity, technological innovation and political leadership. Cities unevenly contribute to the making of this economic-political space of potentially global reach, participating in hierarchical cross-national networks in which a selected number of 'global cities' take the lead in the development of factors of production (material and immaterial) and competitive advantages for regions and nations. The small circle of global cities is not immutable, but is constantly subject to change. In his pioneering analysis, based on qualitative sources of information, planner John Friedmann (1986) distinguished between 'global financial articulations' (London, New York and Tokyo), 'multinational articulations' (Miami, Los Angeles, Frankfurt, Amsterdam, Singapore), 'national capitals' (Paris, Zurich, Madrid, Mexico City, São Paolo, Seoul, Sydney) and 'sub-national centres' (Osaka, San Francisco, Milan, Barcelona, etc.). Studies assessing the ranking of cities at a world scale have multiplied and methodologically evolved over the last two decades, elaborating increasingly more sophisticated models of analysis, based on statistical-quantitative data-sets (see in particular the achievements of the research group on 'Globalization and World Cities' directed by geographer Peter Taylor: http://www.lboro.ac.uk/gawc).

1.5.1 Wannabe global cities and the politics of becoming

Today, identifying existing global cities is no longer a merely academic and intellectual exercise, but it has become a terrain of struggle and competition among cities aspiring to this status: the so-called 'wannabe global cities'. It is not just a small number of powerful cities and metropolitan areas that aspire to become a global city, benefitting from integration into transnational spaces of flows, but potentially any large-sized city (over one million inhabitants, or even less) willing to devise strategies of urban boosterism and entrepreneurialism at an international level is entitled to compete for this recognition. This 'politics of becoming' is justified by reference to the idea that globalization has produced a proliferation of politico-geographical scales and spatialities, opening the way for the rise of emerging central localities, also in previously peripheral and even marginal geographical areas. East Asia has been at the forefront in this process: today, it is widely accepted within the scholarly community to consider Shanghai, Singapore, Hong Kong as world cities competing with established global cities such as Tokyo, London and New York (see, for instance, Olds and Yeung, 2004; Chen, 2009). In this context, local politico-economic elites have become acquainted with the idea that world cities are the most conspicuous manifestation of a global era that has transcended the centrality of the nation-state as an exclusive arena of politico-economic regulation (Taylor, 2000).

Globalization has reasserted, therefore, the importance of the urban scale in contemporary social, economic and political processes, leading commentators to emphasize the incipient 'urban revolution' in our civilization, not only in economic terms, as highlighted by global city scholars, but also in cultural and political ones (Bruggmann, 2009). Indeed, globalizing cities are not only sites of political leadership, economic innovation and intellectual primacy, but are also uniquely cosmopolitan spaces, being favourite destinations for international migrants, for instance (see Chapter 5). In the age of globalization, international migrants move not only to the major cities of North America and Western Europe, like their predecessors, but also to a number of medium and even small-sized cities located in a variety of regions across the world. Until recently, cities in China, the Middle East, Mediterranean Europe and South Africa were places of departure for people moving to wealthier regions of West Europe and the Americas, while now these cities have become destinations for international migrants and refugees. In addition, cities are a mirror of globalization because they tend to reproduce, within their own societies, contradictions and inequalities that are typical of the globalizing world: the gap between the rich and the poor, between millionaire professionals and low-paid workers, is persisting and has even widened over the last three decades, producing new forms of exclusion and marginality (Sassen, 2007). The interpretation of the latter phenomena has been debated: in the early 1990s urban scholars animatedly debated on whether globalization generates polarized forms of socio-spatial inequalities in large cities (Castells and Mollenkopf, 1991; van Kempen, 1994), or it produces a more diversified and stratified socio-professional structure (Hamnett, 1994). In any case, representational strategies tend to obfuscate the controversial aspects of globalization: acquiring the status of global city is a most seductive goal, which becomes imperative, particularly in cities in the global South, where urban politico-economic elites associate globalization with cosmopolitan culture, vibrant city life, revitalized neighbourhoods, challenging allegedly obsolete depictions of deprivation and despair.

In the last two decades, a heterogeneous set of 'wannabe global cities' have tried to establish a presence on the world scene: from Atlanta (defining itself as 'the next great international city') to Johannesburg ('an African world-class city') to Helsinki ('an international city') and Mumbai ('a truly global city') (Paul, 2005). This proliferation of global-city labels reveals a tendency already underlined by David Harvey in his path-breaking book on the postmodern condition (Harvey, 1989a): the loss of meaning and substance as a consequence of an overproduction of almost identical urban images, arising from the 'joining the world economy' rhetoric, which takes place in a world *already* deeply marked by the advent of globalization. Related forms of semantic commodification have affected other catchwords of the urban political lexicon in the era of globalization, such as the creative-city rhetoric most notably (see Chapter 2).

Even the iconography of urban success tends to homogenize at a global scale. For instance, urban planners and designers typically symbolize urban success in the form of a skyline in which shimmering skyscrapers stand out, especially in those cities in developing regions and countries where conventional representations are anchored in an image of physical decay. As Lily Kong puts it referring to Asian cities: 'the skyscraper is the architectural form that has dominated the imaginations of city-planners charged with ensuring that their cities come out well in the competition for global attention' (Kong, 2007, p. 386). Notorious examples are the Oriental Pearl Television Tower in Shanghai, the Petronas Twin Towers in Malaysia and the Burj Khalifa in Dubai. An architectural mega-project, such as the construction of luxury buildings, is crucial to the pursuit of a politics of representation, where the ambition is to celebrate a condition of connectedness overcoming previous peripheral posi-tionalities. In the post-Fordist era, and particularly in the post-industrial city, this role is played by emerging cultural icons: most famously, the Tate Modern, the new museum of contemporary art in London, which turned an abandoned power station into a venue for art exhibitions, being celebrated and imitated worldwide in the past ten years. Despite the promise of economic and cultural renaissance commonly associated with newly invented urban icons, architectural and broader urban mega-projects are manifestation of the hegemonic strategies devised by the most power-ful actors within the urban realm. Typical questions arising from discussions over the impact of mega-projects on local societies include: who is benefitting from these financially onerous initiatives? What are the direct advantages for local resi-dents? What is the impact on housing prices and on those of consumer goods in the target areas?

1.5.2 The spectacle of urban regeneration in post-Cold War Europe

An example of 'selective narrative' can be illustrative of the ambivalent significance of urban regeneration initiatives. In the aftermath of the fall of the Berlin Wall, local politico-economic elites enthusiastically committed to presenting Berlin as a global city situated at the crossroads between the East and the West of inner Europe (Cochrane and Jonas, 1996; Molnar, 2010). A series of spectacular events (such as the concerts of popular rock acts like Roger Waters and U2, and the Love Parade in 1995) have drawn attention from all over the world to the destiny of the German capital after the reunification. The redevelopment and redesign of Postdamer Platz have taken the form of a spectacular event itself, celebrated by artificial lightning, fireworks and music concerts. In the space of few years, however, critical commenta-tors have agreed on the fact that the new Postdamer Platz appears as a place void of

Figure 1.2   Berlin's Postdamer Platz (2008)

Source: photo © Alberto Vanolo

historical dimension, dedicated to the consumption of standardized commodities and events. The area once occupied by the Wall has been filled with pretentious buildings, many of them devoted to office space which have remained unused (Krätke, 2004). Dominant discourses and representations about the newly redesigned Postdamer Platz have erased disturbing legacies of the twentieth century, such as the presence of infamous institutions (the Gestapo prison) as well as the expropriation of land lots owned by Jews in the 1930s. The new high-rise buildings, used as exhibition and retail spaces by multinational firms such as Sony or as multiplex cinemas, configure a transnational urban space, which can be potentially accessed by everyone, provided that the visitor is interested in purchasing a technological product or a film ticket.

Powerful coalitions of public and private actors have taken the lead in programmes of physical renewal such as those that have been carried out in Berlin. Private actors are actively involved in these initiatives, being assigned with autonomous responsibilities also in the subsequent management of the regenerated spaces. The active involvement and empowerment of private actors, along with a strong emphasis laid on the 'general interest' of the urban community, are distinguishing features of the politics of urban development in neoliberal times, which will be analysed further in Chapter 3.

1.5.3 Religious icons and state-led urban reinvention

A non-Western example is illustrative of the controversial power implications in a politics of representation: the making of a new political capital in Ivory Coast, in West Africa. In 1983, President Félix Houphouët-Boigny transformed Yamoussoukro, a small rural village with only 15,000 inhabitants (and his birthplace), into the new political capital of the Republic, replacing the far more influential Abidjan. In the effort to build up the prestige of the new capital, Houphouët-Boigny allocated public resources to ambitious projects of urban regeneration, such as the construction of the Basilica of Our Lady of Peace, one of the largest churches in the world (with 7,000 seats and air-conditioned environments), which was built in a country where only one third of the population is Catholic. Consecrated in 1990 as a place of worship, and inspired by the Basilica of Saint Peter in the Vatican city, the project cost around 250 million euros, an exorbitant public investment in a country where the vast majority of inhabitants are far from enjoying the delights of Western modernity. Because of the huge amount of money allocated and the religious divisions within the country, the Basilica has been a matter of controversy since the inception of the project. However, despite the disagreements, twenty years later Yamoussoukro is experiencing an unprecedented housing boom and is finally taking the form of a capital city (Rice, 2008).

Whereas the Basilica of Our Lady of Peace has played a decisive role in the difficult and contested rise of Yamoussoukro as a capital city, in the more affluent Western Europe the Basilica of Saint Peter has been identified as the iconic building of the 2000 Jubilee in Rome: an event that Italian political elites portrayed as an opportunity for acquiring a global city status (McNeill, 2003). In conclusion, these different but also related examples show how a religious artefact like a basilica can be exploited by those governing capital cities in a variety of geographical contexts in order to support strategies of local economic development, urban competitiveness and place-making in a context of globalization.

BOX 1.1   CASE STUDY

THE RISE OF A GLOBAL CITY NARRATIVE IN AFRICA

Becoming a world-class city – the so-called 'wannabe global cities' or 'globalizing cities' (Yeoh, 1999) – is an imperative for a growing number of cities across the globe. African cities also contribute to this tendency, challenging the commonly held stereotype of Africa as a traditional, non-urbanized and non-globalized continent (Ferguson, 2006). As observed by geographer Jennifer Robinson (2002), the global-city literature has generally ignored African cities, confining them to the notion of urban marginality. However, cities like Cairo, Casablanca, Lagos, Nairobi, Johannesburg and Cape Town arguably reveal distinctive features of the global city (van der Merwe, 2004). In recent times, also Western popular outlets have called attention to 'how Africa is becoming the New Asia' thanks to the rapid growth (economic and demographic) of its big cities and the expansion of investment opportunities in technologically advanced sectors (*Newsweek*, 2010).

In the attempt at disrupting commonly held stigmatizing views, urban marketing campaigns in Africa have been conventionally aimed at disconnecting the image of cities from that of Africa as a whole through counter-stereotype messages. An interesting case of urban branding is that of Johannesburg, in South Africa. This country, whose conventional reputation was (and is) generally associated with problems of insecurity, socio-spatial segregation and with the apartheid legacies, has recently engaged in a massive marketing campaign, representing itself as an economic and financial hub at an international level. The City of Johannesburg started organizing an urban branding campaign in 2001, by setting an audit analysis in order to assess the commonly held perception of the city. The survey highlighted a generally negative attitude towards the city. As regards its tourist potential, for instance, it was found that Johannesburg was not regarded as an attractive destination, but just as a gateway being used by those willing to visit the rest of the country, and respondents did not associate the city with any remarkable cultural attraction and creative milieu. Broadly speaking, after the end of the apartheid era the city's identity was weak: it was not clear what identified Johannesburg as a city, apart from the skyscrapers in the downtown area; and also because the City of Johannesburg Metropolitan Municipality was organized in eleven administrative entities extending over a large region, with only about 10 per cent of the territory being definable as 'urban' in the strict sense of the term.

A path-breaking achievement in the pathway leading to the positioning of Johannesburg *on* the map of global cities has been the designation of South Africa as host country of the 2010 football World Cup. The designation urged urban and national elites to embark on an ambitious strategy of urban economic development, which was articulated along two lines: first, in 2002 the local government launched a long-term plan named 'Jo'burg 2030' aiming to transform Johannesburg into a 'world-class city'; second, between 2003 and 2007 the declining inner city was targeted by an urban regeneration initiative (the 'Inner City Regeneration Strategy'), based on the creation of Business Improvement Districts, with direct

(Continued)

(Continued)

gentrification effects (cf. Chapter 3). The branding of a more seductive name like Jo'burg (already used as a colloquial appellation) is indicative of urban elites' endeavour to convey enthusiasm and optimism among citizens and economic agents. The official name has remained the City of Johannesburg, but Jo' burg is now commonly used in marketing initiatives. The new logo (see the picture below) is intended to make sense of the renewed spirit and iconic consciousness of the city: the exclamation mark, which features a stylized b, represents Johannesburg's landmark, the Hillbrow tower, while the logo's golden point refers to its past identity as a gold-mining town (Rusch, 2003).

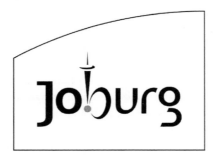

a world class African city

BOX 1.2   URBAN TV SERIES – *THE SIMPSONS*

BRANDING SPRINGFIELD

Even the world-wide famous TV series *The Simpsons* has explicitly touched on issues of urban branding and competition in a context of cultural and economic globalization, particularly in the *The Seven-Beer Snitch* episode, originally broadcast in 2005.

The episode starts with the Simpson family visiting Shelbyville, the rival city of Springfield (where the family resides) already appearing in other episodes. The way in which Shelbyville is marketed clearly evokes the stereotypes of neoliberal creative urbanism. Marge Simpson is irresistibly attracted by trendy designer shops, art venues and the city's cosmopolitan environment. The city celebrates itself through a spectacle (the Shelbyville song) emphasizing the beauties of the urban landscape, the available amenities, the opportunities for developing social relations and the openness to strangers. Overall, Shelbyville largely overcomes the rival Springfield in terms of attractiveness and vibrancy of city life.

In order to fill this gap, a newly appointed committee starts thinking about how to improve the image of Springfield. The 'think thank' decides to ask architect Frank Gehry to create a local version of the Guggenheim hosting a world-class-level auditorium. Initially, local citizens are enthusiastic, but when the building materializes they soon realize that this is just an empty container. Local citizens complain that the project has been finalized so quickly that they did not have the chance to assess the actual need for an auditorium. However, owing to a huge fiscal crisis caused by the financial investment in the auditorium project, the city council is soon forced to privatize the newly built music venue. The cultural icon ultimately loses its original purpose: it is sold to local capitalist Mr Burns, who turns it into a private prison.

A number of relevant urban issues are raised in the episode, most notably the increased inter-urban competition and the role of cultural icons and global archistars in postmodern and neoliberal urbanism. From a critical geographical perspective, it is also fascinating to look at the way in which debates on contemporary cities have been incorporated into a pop-cultural product like *The Simpsons*. The popularity of this television series is indeed so remarkable that Shelbyville was ranked tenth in 'The 10 Best Dystopias' in the December 2005 issue of *Wired* magazine (www.wired.com).

1.6 The environmentalization of the urban experience

As shown in the previous sections of this chapter, representations of pathways of urban development are constantly reinvented and negotiated by economic and social actors. Even though urban elites strive to assert a dominant image of the city, the urban imaginary is inevitably the result of the assemblage of a wide array of symbolic and discursive strategies and practices. From the 1980s to the mid-1990s narratives celebrating the shift to post-Fordism within the capitalist economy dominated public and scholarly debates over urban-regeneration processes, intersecting with those heralding the postmodern turn in the urban experience. In more recent years, these previous narratives have been set aside, being replaced by emerging narratives such as those about the creative city (analysed in detail in the next chapter) and the sustainable and resilient city.

Building sustainable cities is an institutional imperative that has become increasingly influential in contemporary urban politics and related discursive struggles over the last two decades. This book will deal with what is defined 'the environmentaliza-tion of the urban experience' from interrelated and also conflicting perspectives, testifying to the multifaceted and contradictory character of the urban public sphere. The present chapter looks at the production and circulation of normative discourses with strong institutional implications for contemporary cities, which are built on the mainstream narrative of sustainable development. Urban environmental politics, however, is also a highly controversial and contested field, as demonstrated by the grassroots struggles for environmental justice that have proliferated in contemporary cities around the world over the past two or three decades, which will be analysed in Chapter 5.

In the strict sense of the term, 'sustainable city' might sound like an oxymoron: cities are dependent on resources obtained from non-urban livelihoods (for example, food and water supplies drawn from rural environments); at the same time, urban communities are unrivalled producers of waste and pollution. The relationship between cities and the environment, however, should not be seen in a straightforward way: in many respects, the compact city (historically the ideal urban form) is far more sustainable than suburbanized and rural areas as its higher densities allow the optimization of the consumption of energy (Jenks et al., 1996). Even so, it is commonplace to associate urbanization with processes of environmental degradation. Even among critical urbanists, the city–environment nexus is generative of dystopian representations and metaphors of social life. Mike Davis's 'ecologies of fear', for instance, makes sense of the degeneration of contemporary social relations generated by the growing obsession for danger, crime, and safety issues in contemporary cities (Davis, 1999). The ecology of urban environments evokes apocalyptic visions, as it is closely related to the 'natural disasters' (floods, epidemics, hurricanes) that threaten the existence of cities and their residents (cf Kaika, 2005; Swyngedouw, 2007). Natural disasters have indeed a powerful discursive potential, which becomes pervasive of the urban experience as a whole. Such potential is amplified within the context of globalization, where the effects of environmental disasters occurring in the global South are not different from those in the global North, as the recent cases of the Asian Tsunami and the New Orleans flood have demonstrated.

1.6.1 The emotional politics of urban sustainability

Generating or alternatively suppressing fears and anxieties, while advancing or delaying policy initiatives, are complementary aspects of the highly emotional politics of pre-emption/oblivion, denial/recognition, interventionism/inertia taking shape around environmental emergencies in neoliberal times. The fear of annihilation associated with environmental disasters is used by those govern-ing the city to persuade the citizenry that there is no alternative to the develop-ment path commonly defined 'sustainable', if cities are to be rescued from a future of catastrophe and ecological degradation. A wide range of controversial urban policy schemes are thus proposed under a green umbrella, including infrastructure mega-projects (waste-to-energy plants, underground tunnels facilitating traffic flows, etc.), incentives for 'eco-efficient' automobiles, congestion charges, demolition of obsolete housing and even the construction of skyscrapers.

Since its appearance, leftist commentators have denounced the dangers of environmentalism as an ideology of nature. In the early 1970s, Italian polemicist Dario Paccino authored a pamphlet entitled *L'Imbroglio Ecologico* (or the Ecological Trick: Paccino, 1972); more recently philosopher Slavoj Žižek (2008) has provocatively contended that 'ecology is the new opium for the masses'. The scepticism of leftist writers arises from a substantial critique of the foundations of mainstream environmentalist discourse. Early Marxist critics have argued that there is no such thing called 'nature', which can be assumed as preceding the constitution of capitalist societies, demanding just to be preserved and eventually rehabilitated (N. Smith, 1984). Authors that have built on the Marxian critique of the ideology of nature warn that the environmentalist discourse has socially conservative implications, as it is concerned for example with reducing carbon emissions and limiting environmental degradation within a given economic framework, without aspiring to a more radical reconfiguration of capitalist societies and the underlying power relationships (Swyngedouw, 2007).

Embracing a critical stance on environmental politics does not entail dismissing the importance of city managers' growing concern over sustainability and climate change issues (Bulkeley and Betsill, 2005; Jonas and While, 2007). In this context, resilience has become the buzzword in the field of sustainable urban planning, understood as the institutional capacity to resist and recover from natural and human disasters (for example terrorist attacks), dissipating fears and anxieties (Newman et al., 2009). Within an increasingly neoliberalized public realm, however, the rising environmental consciousness has been strongly pervaded by a political and economic rationality emphasizing the link between sustainability and economic development. In particular, calls for a green economy based on alternative energy resources have become influential within the policy sphere at a variety of political-geographical scales, including the urban (Rifkin, 2003; Fitzgerald, 2010). From this perspective, the environment is presented not as a common good that should be protected from private interests, but as an opportunity for economic growth, which becomes even more imperative in times of global recession and stagnation of the conventional building industry like those that have followed the 2008–09 credit crunch. Despite their increasing influence, the consistency of commonly held propositions about the economic advantages of sustainable urbanism is dubious at least. Is it proven that green policies enhance competitiveness, and that green investments are profitable? Is it ethical to discursively justify a greener urbanism on the basis of utilitarian reasoning, persuading the wider public that sustainable development initiatives create novel opportunities for wealth accumulation? Are experiments of environmental

Figure 1.3 Sustainable housing in the Malmö Boo1 district, Sweden (2010)

Source: photo © Alberto Vanolo

design being undertaken in the affluent North, such as eco-friendly houses and condominiums, sustainable on a planetary scale (Davis, 2010)?

Whatever answer is given to these questions, there is no doubt that global anxieties about climate and wider environmental change have placed urban sustainability at the centre of contemporary discourses on the 'good city' (Amin, 2006) and related processes and practices of urban representation. As the modernist promise of urban prosperity unravelled (alongside beliefs in unlimited growth and infinite resources), the urban aesthetic has been modified accordingly, for instance confining physical infrastructures to a hidden presence. As highlighted by Maria Kaika and Erik Swyngedouw (2000), within the contemporary city pipes, cables and other infrastructures are located underneath, becoming invisible to urban dwellers, while until a few decades ago they were visible and monitored by citizens. Like urban infrastructures, also industrial buildings, warehouses, chimneys and larger manufacturing sites have disappeared from the urban scene, being either dismantled or displaced. At the same time, environmental iconographies have been incorporated into imaginaries of urban boosterism and place marketing, on the basis of a selective identification of those city spaces that should be included in urban representations and those being stigmatized and marginalized. While sanitized urban spaces such as gardens and public places in regenerated neighbourhoods are commonly portrayed as a materialization of ideals of sustainable urbanism, derelict spaces, wastelands and a variety of so-called 'urban voids' (that is, vacant land such as empty lots, closed industrial areas, disused harbours: see Doron, 2000) in cities in the North or slum settlements in those in the South are customarily represented as examples of disorderly and non-domesticated spaces, waiting to be 'redeveloped' and 'reconverted'. The socio-spatial selectiveness of an apparently progressive political discourse and practice such as environmentalism leads us to raise some final questions on the pattern of urban development arising from dominant but also from critical accounts of the contemporary city.

1.7 Concluding reflections: the Eurocentrism of urban scholarship

Understanding the evolution of the urban process against the backdrop of subsequent development stages (from Fordism to post-Fordism, from the industrial city to the informational and creative city) and regimes of regulation (from the Keyenesian city to the neoliberal city) reveals a 'political unconscious' (Jameson, 1981) rife with implications for the critical analysis of urban representations. In the first instance, conventional ways of representing cities are based on the typically Eurocentric assumption that the economy (the capitalist economy) is the driving force behind urban transformations. In his *Postmetropolis*, Edward Soja (2000) contended that the development of urbanization should not be understood in conventionally economic terms (the pursuit of economies of agglomeration and diversification), but as an intrinsic tendency of human societies to spatial concentration, which he defines as 'synekism'. In other words, the urban process is forged not only by externally generated forces and processes (of historical, social, and economic character), but is also the outcome of the human attitude to concentrate lives and social relations in one place. Soja's thesis stands in contrast to mainstream views of development, shared by both neo-classical and orthodox Marxist economists, which place an almost exclusive emphasis on market forces, and in particular on economic utilitarianism, as engines of socio-spatial evolution.

Consider the influence of an analytical tool such as that of global cities, deriving from the empirical observation of the economic and social transformations that have occurred in a selected circle of cities (only three in the first formulation provided by Saskia Sassen, 1991), which have been imitated by 'wannabe global cities' across the world, as shown in this chapter. In many geographical contexts, marginal or peripheral within the dominant circuits of capitalist accumulation, the politics of becoming on which local politico-economic elites have concentrated development strategies has distracted attention from the pursuit of goals that are far more closely related to the contextual specificities of cities and megacities in the global South (Robinson, 2002). Also within the context of cities in post-socialist Europe, it has been pointed out that the endeavours of urban elites are aimed not just at the expansion and accumulation of wealth, but also at the enhancement of their political position (Kulcsar and Domokos, 2005). The conduct of urban elites in other 'semi-peripheral' cities and regions, in Southern Europe or Northern Africa for instance, is not different from that described with reference to post-socialist countries in Europe. Academic theories are based on analytical and conceptual frameworks which have an appropriate meaning in specific spatial-temporal dimensions. As post-colonial scholars put it, Western dominance largely relies on the alleged universalism of knowledge and reason (Spivak, 1999).

Religion, for instance, is undoubtedly a key factor in several urban contexts, but is overlooked in contemporary scholarship conventionally referring to the West as the socio–historical ideal-type (see King, 2000). Even though it is now common to notice that in numerous cities in the West and elsewhere (Belfast, Jerusalem, Beirut, Teheran, Varanasi, Rome, Istanbul, North American and Latino-American cities) the public sphere is shaped by post-secular, faith-based movements (Beaumont, 2008), research efforts are still mostly concentrated on Christianity and lately also on the Islam, while there are few studies dealing with other religious affiliations and their urban cultures and spatialities (Hancock and Srinivas, 2008). That of faith and religion is just an example: what is worth underlining – also in a self-critical vein (this chapter began by advocating a 'political economy of representation') – is the partial view offered by an approach that is focused on an economic explanation of the urban process, even of its immaterial and representational dynamics. Moreover, representing the pathways of urban development in terms of subsequent and linear stages reinforces the idea that cities are bound to reach a supposedly final stage that is commonly labelled as 'modernity'. From this perspective, there are cities lagging 'behind' and others that have already moved 'forward'. It is no surprise, therefore, that cities facing an economic and political situation which is substantially different from that of their counterparts in the Western countries, but diverges also from the conventional pattern of 'developing' economies, are customarily defined 'in transition' (typically those in post-socialist Europe). This definition presupposes the idea that sooner or later 'transitional cities' will experience postmodern lifestyles (imported from the United States) and will develop modes of economic and social regulation largely derived from the Western political and economic thought (Wu, 2003).

In a controversial essay envisaging 'the end of history', political scientist Francis Fukuyama (1989) famously argued that capitalism and liberal democracy were the only viable alternatives after the collapse of the Soviet Union. Despite the triumph of Eurocentrism in the form of neoliberalism in the following two decades, however, ongoing economic turbulences have called into question conventional beliefs about urban development and human civilization. In sum, what is 'modern' 'now' and 'here' is likely to have different meanings and translations in other spatialities and temporalities: colonial modernity differs from post-colonial (post-)modernity, Islamic civilization diverges from that prevailing in predominantly Catholic and Protestant countries, whereas the socio-economic modernization of cities in the global North can be radically different from that of cities in the South.

2
Making Culture Work: The Rise of the Creative City

Key Issues and Themes

Culture and creativity play a pivotal role in contemporary strategies of urban economic development. The transition to a post-Fordist mode of production is at the origin of the 'culturalization' of the urban process under conditions of globalization and heightened inter-urban competition.

Richard Florida's creative-class theory and discourse have served as a 'governmental technology' easily adapting to a variety of geographical contexts across the world.

Urban processes of culture-led regeneration are qualitatively differentiated across the world: in North America growth-oriented approaches are predominant; in Europe, multi-level governance is the distinctive feature of urban cultural strategies; in Asia, the developmental state customarily takes the lead in cultural projects.

2.1 Introduction: urban development in a knowledge-based capitalism

As already mentioned in this book, the joint effect of the post–Fordist transition in the capitalist economy and the 'postmodernization' of social relations and urban

spaces has led urban scholars and policymakers alike to place renewed emphasis on
the role of 'culture' within existing trajectories of economic and territorial development. In this context, the re-making of urban spaces as dynamic socio-cultural
milieux, assembling a variety of art venues, exhibition spaces and spectacular events,
has become a key goal of contemporary urban policies and broader strategies of
socio-economic development. This approach has been embraced by both local–
national elites and supranational organizations operating in the affluent North as
well as in the emerging global South (OECD, 2005; UNESCO 1998).

The growingly inextricable link between cities, culture and economic development goes even beyond the conventional assimilation of cultural symbols within the
logic of profit and the circuits of capital accumulation, through sectors with strong
impact on collective consciousness such as fashion, design, cinema and literature.
The commodification of culture in contemporary capitalism has been interpreted
along these lines by critics of postmodernity such as David Harvey (1989c) and
Sharon Zukin (1991), who have drawn on classic Marxist reflections on popular
culture and the 'cultural industry' (Adorno and Horkheimer, 1947; Gramsci, 1948–
51; Williams, 1958). However, the further development of a knowledge-based capitalism demands this critical approach being amended and expanded. It can be
argued, in particular, that post-Fordist capitalism has witnessed not just a subordina-
tion of culture to the dictates of the market and the spatio-temporal circulation of
capital. Rather, 'culture' – in the multiple forms of immaterial labour, tacit and
codified knowledge, creative innovation, invention economies, and the like – has
been incorporated into capitalism as a mode of production and reproduction (Hardt
and Negri, 2000; Virno, 2004; Thrift, 2005). Put it another way, social and spatial
phenomena are increasingly relying on cultural processes within a knowledge-based
form of capitalism. The capitalist firm, on the one hand, draws on a variety of immaterial resources such as knowledge, conventions, rituals locally generated but also
fostered by global networks of collaboration and exchange (Faulconbridge, 2006).
On the other hand, cities as institutional entities are committed not only to creating
novel opportunities for wealth accumulation through the exploitation of cultural
capital assets, but also to acting as cohesive subjects asserting their presence at
national and international levels, through a process of 'subjectification' (the city itself
becomes a relatively autonomous subject) and re-scaling (the constitution of cities
as collective subjects takes place through the encounter with other political entities
at varying geographical scales).

In light of this context, it is no surprise to notice the success encountered among
the wider public and policymakers alike by Richard Florida's theorization of the
intimate relationship linking the rise of the 'creative class' to urban development
(Florida, 2002 and 2005). Although Florida's work has not been exempt from criticism within the scholarly community (see below in this chapter), the creative class
discourse has served as a powerful intellectual technology being appropriated by
urban elites around the world, mainly in North America and Western Europe but
also in Australia and East Asia (Ponzini and Rossi, 2010). The apparently irresistible

rise of the creative-class discourse also shows that within contemporary capitalist societies characterized by an over-production of images and representations the success of an urban theory – particularly in terms of practical application – depends not just on its scientific value, but rather on its capacity to exert a significant impact on social consciousness, stimulating the formation of 'discursive strategies' aimed at justifying the adoption of urban regeneration initiatives.

2.2 Creative cities: economies of diversity and discursive strategies in North America

In 2002, Richard Florida, an interdisciplinary social scientist specializing in studies on urban and regional development, published a book entitled *The Rise of the Creative Class*, which was enormously successful, with sales far exceeding expectations. In his book, Florida provided an enticing account of the emergence of what he called the 'creative class' in post-industrial and post-Fordist societies. This class is composed of a variety of occupational and professional figures (Markusen, 2006), having in common the use of talent and creativity in the everyday life and the working place: scientists and engineers, poets and novelists, figurative and performative artists, designers and architects, knowledge workers and professionals employed in the informational economy. According to Florida's estimates, the creative class has experienced intense growth over the last three decades. In the United States, it comprises about 38 million people, amounting to approximately one third of the workforce, a figure that has constantly increased since the 1980s onwards, in the wake of the transition to a post-manufacturing economy based on the centrality of immaterial labour and knowledge. In Florida's view, creative-class members share a number of important social values, shaping their professional conduct, their behaviours and moral attitudes: a pluralistic ethics refusing particularistic affiliations and based on freedom of speech and thought; meritocracy as an essential requisite for the attainment of individual success and social mobility; and finally – quite importantly as more directly concerned with creative class members' urban experience – a positive attitude towards the diversity of ethnic belongings and the variety of cultural and sexual orientations.

2.2.1 The fortune of creative-class theory

As also Florida admits, some of his theses have been drawn from previous theorizations in the scholarly literature. In particular, he has drawn on a number of assumptions within existing theories of economic development and social modernization, adapting them to the present conditions of post-Fordist economies and societies: from the conceptualization of the role of human capital within processes of economic development (Lucas, 1988) to that of so-called diversity economies in large cities (Jacobs, 1969) and to an emphasis on the ethics of responsibility, a long-term concern within contemporary social theory since the publication of Max Weber's foundational study on the spirit of capitalism. It should be also noted that Richard Florida has not been the first urban and regional scholar to call attention to the notion of creativity. In previous years, particularly since the late 1980s onwards, a number of mostly European urban scholars had picked on this notion in order to stress the role of culture in deindustrializing and regenerating cities: the closure of manufacturing plants and the capital abandonment of sites of industrial production had given place to newly established cultural districts and art venues (Hall, 2000; Landry, 2000; see also the cases of Bilbao and Beijing presented in the introduction to this book). Earlier approaches to cultural and creative urbanism were not informed by the economic growth imperative, both in academic work and in policy practice. In Britain, for instance, initiatives of culture-led regeneration were initially undertaken within the framework of socialist approaches to municipal government, but since the 1980s onwards they became subordinated to the dictates of neoliberal urbanism (Peck, 2011). The progressive approach, however, still largely permeates urban cultural policies in some peripheral contexts of the world economy, most notably in Latin American cities like Buenos Aires and Mexico City, where in recent years culture-led regeneration has frequently taken the form of grassroots empowerment and democratization (Kanai and Ortega-Alcázar, 2009).

While urban communities in some peripheral countries have resisted a process of cultural commodification and homologation, in North America, in Europe and in many Asian regions the neoliberalization of urban public realms has imposed on local governments the incorporation of cultural issues into ongoing strategies of local economic development. In this context, Richard Florida's merit has been to provide a convincing explanation of the link between creativity and competitive urban development. In his view, this link stems from the relationship existing between the propensity towards technological innovation and the formation of an urban environment inclined to recognize social and cultural diversities and to stimulate creativity. The technology–creativity–urban development nexus identified by Florida has found a fertile terrain of investigation in the North-American context, where the 1980s had witnessed the rise of the so-called informational city (Castells, 1989; see Chapter 1). Moreover, in the United States ideas about cities and creativity had to be inevitably related to issues of urban growth, as in the US context urban policy is more clearly growth-oriented, particularly since the late 1970s onwards (Judd and Swanstrom, 1998; cf. Chapter 3). In Western Europe, only during the last two decades, with the shift towards a strategic approach to city and regional governance, economic development has become the driver of urban policies and planning schemes, previously mainly concerned with land use regulation (Healey, 2004). The shaping of a post-industrial environment, alongside the widespread adoption of growth-led policies in the United States as well as in Europe (and in

Asia, as we shall see), are key factors behind the global 'circulation' of Florida's ideas about creativity among urban policymakers and political elites.

The cross-national success of the creative-class theory and discourse is even more surprising considering that Florida has based his ideas on empirical evidence derived from the analysis of social and economic variables referred only to cities in the United States. Referring to these cities, Florida has contended:

> Places that are open and possess *low barriers to entry* for people gain creativity advantage from their ability to attract people from a wide range of backgrounds. All else being equal, more open and diverse places are likely to attract greater numbers of talented and creative people – the sort of people who power innovation and growth. (Florida, 2005: pp. 39–40)

According to Florida, those taking advantage of this social and cultural porosity are individuals whose contribution to urban economic development broadly conceived is overlooked in mainstream theories, such as those belonging to ethnic and sexual minorities, to artistic communities and to other creative communities of practice (symbolic analysts, architects and designers, etc.). Correlating a number of indexes in order to identify the link between technological innovation, the concentration of talented professionals and the recognition of social and cultural diversities, Florida has thus put forward the following thesis: an open and tolerant urban culture is an essential precondition for the achievement of technologically advanced development at the urban and regional levels. Cities and metropolitan areas in the United States such as San Francisco, Boston, Seattle, Washington, Dallas, Los Angeles, Chicago, Atlanta, Phoenix and New York, which occupy the first ten positions in the rankings based on the localization of high-technology firms, are also highly ranked in Richard Florida's *Gay Index* and *Bohemian Index*, measuring the positive attitude towards homosexual minorities and artists within urban communities. Florida's conclusion is that his analysis highlights 'a connection [...] between a metropolitan area's level of tolerance for a range of people, its ethnic and social diversity, and its success in attracting talented people, including high-technology workers' (ibid.: p. 130).

2.2.2 Creative cities for the few, not the many

As already anticipated, Florida's theory has been widely criticized within the scholarly community. In the first instance, many have pointed to the 'circularity' in the logical structure of his argumentation (for instance Storper and Scott, 2009). Cities are technologically and economically competitive to the extent in which they are able to be attractive for the creative class members. However, this should be the case also the other way around: only cities that are *already* competitive in technological and broader economic terms are able to attract creative individuals, as they offer a wider range of opportunities to highly skilled professionals. In the second instance, critics have noticed that Florida, albeit embracing an explicitly normative approach prescribing how cities should work and be organized, does not provide an analysis of the diversity of institutional conditions (local governance structures, institutional capacity, etc.) in those cities that in his view should experiment with creative-class policies (Scott, 2006). Ironically, this scant consideration of institutional issues has made the fortune of Florida's conceptual-discursive framework: being vaguely articulated in terms of concrete prescriptions, creative-class policy recommendations are applicable to the most varied geographical and socio-political contexts. For this reason, the creative class thesis can be understood as an example of postmodern urban theorization: on the one hand, emphasis is laid on how cities should be organized and which actors should be placed at the centre of city life; on the other hand, the theoretical framework sustaining this thesis appears to be versatile and flexible so as to be ready to travel from one place to another, adapting itself to the changing local conditions and thus serving as a 'mobile governmental technology' (Ong, 2007). These characteristics have allowed policymakers to improvise policies of creative urbanism in a variety of political and cultural contexts, mobilizing soft governance structures, as documented within the urban scholarship with reference to Baltimore in the United States (Ponzini and Rossi, 2010) and in Brisbane in Australia (Atkinson and Easthope, 2009) for instance. In these and other cities, policymakers and city officials have issued symbolic initiatives and strategies aimed at the building of the creative city, which in many cases have ended up simply aggregating pre-existing policies and plans of urban and cultural regeneration.

The social selectiveness of the proposed model of urban development is another critical point raised by commentators of Florida's work. While the previously mentioned critical observation – the institutional vagueness of the creative class discourse – points to the 'postmodern' flexibility of Florida's theory, this critique underlines its neoliberal bias. A number of critics, such as Jamie Peck (2005), have warned readers of Florida about the gentrifying effects connected with the influx of creative class individuals into regenerating neighbourhoods. Unlike suburbanized households of the middle and upper classes, creative-class members prefer to live in thriving neighbourhoods of the inner city: in particular, in those urban areas that are about to shift from a condition of decay and relative deprivation to one of cultural revitalization, which still have affordable housing prices. Residential mobility of this type is likely to lead to processes of gentrification, being presented in a positive light in terms of social and cultural mix within the framework of the creative-class narrative. From a related vantage point, other critical commentators have pointed out that in capitalist cities creativity is not a prerogative of affluent creative class members, but also of the poor and the marginalized pursuing creative survival strategies on a daily basis (Wilson and Keil, 2007). The representation and the identification of the actors producing a creative-city milieu are thus highly controversial terrains and sources of socio-political and discursive struggles and conflicts.

David Ley, a distinguished representative of the new social geography in Great Britain and North America, has provided one of the first critical accounts of the link between the culturalization of the urban realm and gentrification. Referring to

Vancouver, Ley has shown that since the 1960s and the 1970s there has been an acceleration in the circulation and accumulation of 'cultural capital', culminating with the rise of the creative-class discourse and related strategies of urban regeneration so readily embraced by policymakers across the world: 'There has been movement from festivals to festival markets' – Ley argues – 'to an intensified economic colonization of the cultural realm, to the representation of the creative city not as a means of redemption but as a means of economic accumulation' (2003: p. 2542). The fact that Ley's reflections were formulated against the backdrop of Vancouver's path of urban regeneration is not secondary. Vancouver, a city with a population of over 600,000 inhabitants located along the Pacific Coast in the state of British Columbia in Canada, has repeatedly found itself near the top, if not first, in rankings measuring the quality of life in large cities and metropolitan areas, published by prestigious consultancy firms such as the Economist Intelligence Unit and Mercer Human Resources Consulting. Vancouver shares top-ranking with recurring rivals such as the other Canadian city of Toronto, the Australian cities of Sydney, Melbourne and Perth, the Western European cities of Vienna, Geneva, Zurich and Helsinki, while African and Asian megacities such as Lagos in Nigeria, Harare in Zimbabwe, Karachi in Pakistan and Phnom Penh in Cambodia are regularly relegated to the bottom positions. For instance, in the 2005 survey on urban liveability, the Economist Intelligence Unit defined Vancouver 'the world's best place to live' in terms of infrastructures, public services, environmental protection, low perception of terrorist threats and of an exceptionally thriving cultural environment. In 2010 Vancouver had the opportunity even to enhance its already strong attractiveness hosting the Winter Olympic and Paralympic Games. On the other hand, however, according to Mercer Consulting, Vancouver is also among the most expensive cities in the world, as regards housing prices and living costs (transportation and consumption goods).

Liveability and attractiveness are achieved, therefore, at the cost of increased social selectiveness in Vancouver as well as in other 'creative cities' in North America. The example of Austin, Texas, is also illustrative of this tendency. Over the last two decades, this city has witnessed an intense technology-based development, which reached its peak in the years between 2000 and 2006, when Austin became the third most dynamic city in the United States in terms of growth rate. The accelerated growth pace, however, has been associated with a deepening of income inequalities between those employed in the information and technology industry and those working in other economic sectors, particularly the members of the Hispanic minority (McCann, 2007), amounting to about one third of the entire population in Austin (precisely 30 per cent in 2008, while it was 26 per cent in 2000: see Brookings Institute, 2010). Even though Richard Florida reassures critics that creative urbanism and social equity are not mutually contradictory objectives (see the paperback edition of Florida, 2002), empirical evidence from existing pathways of creative urban development shows that improved quality of life and enhanced place attractiveness are accompanied by increased social selectiveness in the absence of a government's will to deal with issues of socio-spatial inequality and injustice.

BOX 2.1   URBAN FILMS

CREATIVITY AND URBAN MARGINALITY IN THE DEINDUSTRIALIZING CITY – *8 MILE* (2002, USA, DIRECTED BY CURTIS HANSON)

8 mile is a film inspired by real-life events of the hip-hop star Eminem. The story is about the early stages of the career of Jimmy Smith (Eminem) in Detroit in the mid-1990s. The film shows the 'ordinary' life of the artists and practitioners of the hip-hop scene, taking place in the decaying environment of a declining industrial city in the United States. The protagonist – like other characters in the film – is socially deprived and forced to live with his mother in a trailer along the 8 mile, the highway surrounding the urban outskirts. From the beginning of the film, a number of shots draw attention to the deteriorating and deindustrializing urban landscape: disused buildings, empty lots, architectural ghosts evoking an affluent past (an abandoned golf club, for example). The film repeatedly stresses the inadequacy of government policies, particularly as concerns health care and issues of urban liveability. Mobility is still based on car ownership, while the use of public transportation is discouraged and even stigmatized (as a loser's practice), and the police is viewed as an 'enemy'. In a context of such a poor, violent and racialized environment (where being 'white' or 'nigga' is thought to make the difference), one of the characters says: 'How can you be proud of your neighbourhood?'

Despite the hardship conditions, many characters in the film show a strong sense of place belonging. Coping with marginality in the urban fringes is (also) regarded as a genuinely urban experience, particularly in relation to the generation of art and creativity. Hip-hop music (and street art in general) is viewed as an emancipatory practice, allowing self-made artists to get rid of a miserable social and urban environment. While working in a factory is refused as a personal failure, being creative (as a hip-hop artist) is considered a highly rewarding activity, as the music scene gives access to a wide range of codes of distinction: money, social respect, girls and celebrity, the latter being used also to denounce social injustices. In the film, artistic practices draw on a number of social ties, which often take shape within gang-like environments. A male-based stance on creativity emerges from the film, understood as the ability to appear 'stronger' than other artists, for instance challenging them in rhyme competitions. The native urban setting plays an important part in the narrative as the context in which creativity arises and artists are recognized as such (the final 'battle' is won by Eminem by virtue of his reputation as an authentic street artist), but also as a place of constrained opportunities and frustrated aspirations: the dream of the beautiful female protagonist, for example, is to leave Detroit and move to New York City.

2.3 Governmentalizing the cultural city in Europe and Asia

The previous section of this chapter has shown that in North America the nexus between urban governance and economic growth has opened the way for an instrumental use of culture as a stimulus to the local economy. The creative-class theory and discourse have provided city managers with a powerful justification for an approach to urban development based on the culture-growth dialectic. This largely explains Richard Florida's success within the policy sphere and the wider public alike in the United States and Canada. In North American cities, the pervasiveness of the capitalist imperative, particularly in the technological-immaterial variant prevailing in the post-Fordist era, has more clearly marked the 'culturalization' of urban strategies, compared with other contexts of advanced capitalism, as this section will show. Behind this process of 'culturalization' there is the widespread conviction that in order to enhance the competitiveness of cities and regions sector-specific policies (those individually confined to the industrial sector, tourism, infrastructures, etc.) no longer suffice, unless combining with a wider commitment to promoting the attractiveness of places and localities within the globalizing economic and political space (Scott, 1998).

2.3.1 Cultural entrepreneurialism and the developmental state in Asia

Even more influentially than in North America, which already recognizes itself as the centre of the world economy, globalization has been a crucial spatiality into which politico-economic elites of the most dynamic cities and regions in the global South have ventured. In these contexts, the 'culturalization' of urban development has been viewed as an opportunity for strengthening the ties that connect these socio-spatial entities with cross-national economic flows and value chains. East Asia, and particularly its Pacific Rim region, is illustrative of this approach. In this area, the national state has played a key role in the generation of cultural icons and artefacts, which are conceived as catalysts of urban change, particularly in cities and metropolitan areas having a special significance at the national level, such as Shanghai and Hong Kong in the People's Republic of China, and the city-state of Singapore (Olds, 1995; Kong, 2007).

Figure 2.1   Shanghai's waterfront (2004)

Source: photo © Federico Rota

Take the case of Shanghai: since the mid-1990s onwards, this city has been recipient of a growing amount of money invested by the national government and also by foreign firms in projects of cultural revitalization (museums and theatres) and reconversion of decaying urban areas (most famously the waterfront area that has become a 'zone of historical protection'). In doing so, local and national elites have intended to build a cosmopolitan reputation for Shanghai so as to compete with the already established global cities, not only in economic terms but also at a cultural level (W. Wu, 2004). The cultural-economic strategy of urban boosterism has culminated with the organization of the 2010 World Expo, on which around four billion dollars were invested – more than twice as much as Beijing did on the Olympic Games in 2008 – plus tens of billions on the improvement of the city's infrastructure as well as on related projects, the most grandiose being the planned construction of a Disneyland Resort, which has already forced thousands of local residents to leave their houses to make way for the theme-park's site *(The Economist,* 2010).

Related dynamics of urban renewal, for the role played by the state in the developmental process, have been observed in other emerging contexts of the Asian continent, such as the already mentioned Dubai (Chapter 1) and Abu Dhabi, the capital of the United Arab Emirates. The latter, founded and built from nothing in the 1970s, has attracted in recent years vast amounts of public investments aimed at turning the city into a cultural hub of the Middle East, challenging the historical

Figure 2.2   Saadiyat – aerial shot

Source: © Tourism Development & Investment Company (TDIC)

primacy of monumental cities in the Arab-Muslim world such as Jerusalem, Beirut, Cairo and the imperial towns of Morocco. The 'launch' of Abu Dhabi has been pursued through newly established cultural spaces and institutions. In particular, Sheikh Al Maktoum (the son of the founding sheikh of the city) conceived (and generously funded) the plan turning the desert island of Saadiyat into 'the greatest cultural heritage in the world' (named 'Saadiyat Cultural District'). A number of worldwide renowned architects have been involved in this plan, such as Frank Gehry, Jean Nouvel, Tadao Ando and Zaha Hadid. The cultural district has magnificent local versions of the Guggenheim (Figure 2.2) and the Louvre museums, a Performing Arts Centre (larger than the London's Royal Albert Hall) and an outstanding Maritime Museum. Ignoring the sarcastic remarks of those criticizing the artificial reproduction of Western museums, the Emirate's rulers have insisted on the importance of the Saadiyat District, not just in cultural terms but also in environmental terms. According to the Dutch urban planner and designer Rem Koolhas, who has collaborated with the project, these venues are likely to attract visitors from across the Middle East, ridding those living in this geographical area of the journeys to Europe and the United States with the related carbon emissions' burden (Buruma, 2008). In general, the pursuit of an environmentally friendly approach to urban development is a crucial concern among the Emirate's governing elites, as shown for instance by the construction of a massive hydrogen power plant that should start operating in 2014 after delays caused by the economic downturn in 2008–09.

2.3.2 The multi-level governance of culture-led regeneration in Europe

Whereas in North America and in different Asian regions (East Asia and the Middle East) public–private partnerships and the national state respectively have played a crucial role as drivers of culture-led urban development, in Europe this prominent role has been played by the European Union (and the European Community until 1992) in cooperation with municipalities and other local administrations. A crucial starting point in the 'culturalization' of urban-development strategies in Europe is to be found in the launch of the 'European City of Culture' programme in 1985, which in 2000 became an official action of the European Union, being renamed 'European Capital of Culture' programme. The launch and the subsequent institutionalization of this policy are illustrative of the EU's will to broaden its prerogatives and lines of action beyond the merely economic realm relating to the regulation of markets. In the 1980s, in particular, an increasing emphasis started to be placed on the formulation and implementation of policies and initiatives capable of regenerating the European identity along common lines of belonging. A decisive step in the pursuit of this goal has been the inclusion of culture among the primary objectives identified by the Maastricht Treaty, which created the European Union (Barnett, 2001).

The European Capital of Culture programme is, therefore, an important testing ground for the analysis of the role of culture as a catalyst for urban development initiatives and mega-projects. The 1990 edition, in particular, which designated Glasgow, attracted the attention of policymakers and urban scholars, spurring lively debates over culture and urban development. At the time of the designation Glasgow was known more as a manufacturing centre with a strong working-class identity, rather than as a cultural heritage site, while in previous years cities historically renowned for their cultural heritage, Athens, Florence, Amsterdam, West Berlin and Paris, had been designated (see Table 2.1). Nominating Glasgow as the 'city of culture' entailed that cultural heritage (historic centres, monuments, art works, theatre, opera, etc.) was not to be considered the sole criterion for the identification of European cultural capitals, but it was the institutional capacity of a municipality, in partnership with other economic and political actors, to devise strategies of urban planning and management of cultural

Figure 2.3   Glasgow's Clyde Waterfront (2007)

Source: photo © Alberto Vanolo

events which mattered to a considerable degree. This shows the ways in which since the early 1990s onwards, when the forces of globalization (and of Europeanization in this context) became more pervasive, strategies of cultural revitalization started to be increasingly dependent on mega-events and nominations awarded by supranational bodies, responding to institutional imperatives of urban entrepreneurialism and governance re-scaling (Cox, 1993; Hall and Hubbard, 1998). An entrepreneurialist approach to the governance of culture as a driver of urban competitiveness has thus gained ground even in European societies, which historically tended to preserve the integrity of culture from the pervasiveness of market forces. Looking back at the nomination of Glasgow, the effect of 'invention' appears to be so strong that these initiatives have been understood in terms of 'propaganda projects' (Boyle, 1999): the vivification of citizens' sense of urban belonging and pride has been openly instrumental in the pursuit of strategies of urban economic development and capitalist appropriation of culture (Tretter, 2009) (Figure 2.3).

In 2008 the designation of Liverpool as European Capital of Culture generated discussions recalling those that were sparked by Glasgow's nomination. Like its Scottish counterpart, until the 1980s Liverpool was known primarily for the difficult situation of structural decline affecting the local economy, particularly the port

Table 2.1 European cities and capitals of culture

European Cities of Culture

1985: Athens (Greece)
1986: Florence (Italy)
1987: Amsterdam (The Netherlands)
1988: West Berlin (Germany)
1989: Paris (France)
1990: Glasgow (Scotland)
1991: Dublin (Ireland)
1992: Madrid (Spain)
1993: Antwerp (Belgium)
1994: Lisbon (Portugal)
1995: Luxembourg (Luxembourg)
1996: Copenhagen (Denmark)
1997: Thessaloniki (Greece)
1998: Stockholm (Sweden)
1999: Weimar (Germany)

European Capitals of Culture

2000: Reykjavík (Iceland), Bergen (Norway), Helsinki (Finland), Brussels (Belgium), Prague (Czech
    Republic), Cracow (Poland), Santiago de Compostela (Spain), Avignon (France), Bologna (Italy)
2001: Rotterdam (The Netherlands), Porto (Portugal)
2002: Bruges (Belgium), Salamanca (Spain)
2003: Graz (Austria)
2004: Genoa (Italy), Lille (France)
2005: Cork (Ireland)
2006: Patras (Greece)
2007: Luxembourg (Luxembourg), Sibiu (Romania)
2008: Liverpool (United Kingdom), Stavanger (Norway)
2009: Linz (Austria), Vilnius (Lithuania)
2010: Essen (Germany), Pécs (Hungary), Istanbul (Turkey)
2011: Turku (Finland), Tallinn (Estonia)
2012: Guimarães (Portugal), Maribor (Slovenia)
2013: Marseille (France), Kosice (Slovakia)
2014: Umeå (Sweden), Riga (Latvia)

Source: based on http://www.ec.europa.eu/culture © European Commission

sector. The designation offered an opportunity to reinvent the image of the city, emphasizing unique qualities (such as being the pop-rock hotbed as the Beatles' native town) and disclosing the presence of ethnic–minority identities so as to build up a reputation as a multicultural and cosmopolitan city, expressed in the slogan, 'The World in One City' (Bunnell, 2008).

It is not only in the United Kingdom, known for having a stronger entrepreneurial governance culture compared to Continental countries in Europe, that city managers have sought to maximize the benefits of the European Capital of Culture nomination in terms of urban growth. Also in other European cities local administrators have striven to take advantage of what has been regarded as a unique opportunity to trigger processes of urban renaissance and physical renewal. In 2004,

Palmer-Rae Associates (a private consultancy firm based in Brussels) published on behalf of the European Union a detailed report evaluating the achievements of the European Capital of Culture programme. The report shows how designated cities' priority has been to raise their international profile as a cultural hub at the European level. In most cases, this objective has been pursued by concentrating efforts on attracting international tourists through the organization of spectacular architectural projects, exhibitions and events. On the other hand, however, the report points out that only a limited number of cities, generally either those of small and medium size or those previously lacking a tourist economy, have seen tourist flows growing on a long-term basis in the wake of the European designation (as occurred in Glasgow and in Weimar, Germany), while in larger cities and in those already drawing significant numbers of national and international tourists the increase has been barely noticeable. The report also notes that most of the attention has been drawn to spectacular events and architectural projects mostly located in central areas of the designated cities. This has implied that tourists usually limited their visit to a small number of urban areas, particularly neglecting peripheral neighbourhoods. For instance, in Thessaloniki in Greece (European City of Culture in 1997) a concert by U2 (for which about three million euros were spent) attracted the vast majority of city visitors, while tourists interested in museums and other art venues largely concentrated (more than half of them) on the Treasures of Mount Athos, which is also inscribed by UNESCO in the list of World Heritage Sites and thus already attracts visitors. The case of Graz, a medium-sized city in Austria (about 300,000 inhabitants) known for its well-preserved medieval historical centre, is also significant, as one million out of the overall 2.7 million of visitors reported that they had chosen to visit Graz as the 2003 European 'Capital of Culture' in order to admire the magnificent architectural creation named 'Island in the Mur', the European nomination's flagship project: an artificial island built in the river crossing the city, composed of various merging shells, symbolically linking the city to the surrounding environment (Figure 2.4).

As these examples show, the concentration of organizational energies and financial resources on mega-events and magnificent architectural projects reflects the place-marketing approach currently prevailing among European urban elites in an era of apparently unchallenged neoliberal urbanism and advanced postmodernity. Albeit positively assessing the programme on the whole, Palmer-Rae Associates' report concludes that imperatives of place marketing centred on the improvement of the image of the city have led to the so-called 'cultural instrumentalism' (the growth-led promotion of culture), which has ended up privileging the enhancement of urban attractiveness rather than that of cultural institutions firmly embedded in local societies, with ephemeral results over the long-term. In addition, issues of social and spatial inclusion have been overlooked by the majority of European capital cities. Only in a limited number of cases, most notably in Nordic, Dutch and Belgian cities (such as Rotterdam above all), local governments allocated significant portions of European funds in this domain. On the other hand, the other cities

Figure 2.4   Graz's Island in the Mur (Austria)

Source: www.istockphoto.com

involved in the programme have tried to remedy the manifest lack of interest in social issues by superficially including them within plans and initiatives of urban renewal.

BOX 2.2   URBAN FILMS

CREATIVITY, STATE REPRESSION AND URBAN DISSENT – *NO ONE KNOWS ABOUT PERSIAN CATS* (2009, IRAN, DIRECTED BY BHAMAN GHOBADI)

Whereas in capitalist countries in the global North culture as an urban-policy catchword has been increasingly subordinated to the dictates of economic growth, within non-democratic countries culture and creativity are deployed and appropriated by dissident groups contesting the established political order.

No One Knows About Persian Cats is a film shot in Tehran and directed by the Iranian-Kurdish filmmaker Bhaman Ghobadi, which was awarded the Special Jury

Prize at the 2009 Cannes Festival. The film tells the story of a young couple of aspiring musicians seeking to temporarily expatriate in order to escape the repression of the ruling regime in Iran and establish themselves as an emerging indie-rock band. The protagonists are looking for other members of the band and this leads them to explore the Tehran underground music scene before expatriating. However, in the preparation of their escape from Iran to London (imagined as a place of freedom and creativity as opposed to an authoritarian Tehran) they are faced with a number of difficulties, particularly those relating to obtaining visas and passports through illegal channels. The tragic end of the film raises serious concerns about the prospects for emancipation of a generation of cultural dissidents in Iran. However, in spite of the sad conclusion, the film retains an optimistic outlook on the future of the city and of the country as a whole. Challenging the repression of the regime, a multitude of rock bands proliferate in Tehran, even though they are forced to remain clandestine, practising music and performing private concerts in underground spaces of the city. Sometimes the young bands gather also on isolated hills around the city, where the police are less likely to monitor the music playing.

In Ghobadi's film Tehran appears to be a culturally thriving city, full of energy and creative potential, standing in stark contrast to the conservatism of the country's ruling elites. In conclusion, the film powerfully shows the political uses of contemporary popular culture in the urban settings of non-democratic countries in the global South.

2.4 Conclusion: culture beyond representation

As this chapter has shown, the promotion and the representation of 'culture' and 'creativity', the latter being understood as a more energetic and growth-led variant of the former, have become central objectives and imperatives within the politics of urban development in a context of globalization. The process of 'culturalization' of the urban public realm is pursued through a variety of policies and related discursive strategies, which include: regeneration plans targeting declining urban spaces (in both economic and cultural terms), spectacular architectural projects and mega-events, citywide initiatives of creative urbanism.

The politics of cultural and creative urbanism has been approached and understood in this chapter as a politics of representation, even though this topic can be analysed also from other perspectives, such as those focusing on 'government' and 'contestation' which will be taken into account in Parts Two and Three of this book respectively. Within neoliberal urbanism, the government of culture acts as a powerful ruling mechanism ordering urban spaces and regulating their communities through processes of enrolment within newly invented macro-actors such as the creative class (Ponzini and Rossi, 2010). Moreover, urban neoliberalism emphasizes the economic potential of culture, especially as regards real-estate revitalization. The simultaneous exploitation of cultural capital and of the urban environment, however, is not limited to the increased value of land rent: in symbolic terms, culture becomes instrumental in the enhancement of consensus over the political leadership of cities and metropolitan areas; in economic terms, culture is portrayed as an opportunity to incorporate cultural and social diversities into government strategies of urban 'creative' development.

On the other hand, however, the neoliberal and capitalist assimilation and monopolization of culture is likely to be contrasted by minorities and dissident groups refusing to be normalized and enrolled within dominant political-economic networks, as we shall see in Chapter 6 dedicated to the struggles over urban citizenship. This aspect throws renewed light on the historically distinctive role of culture within larger cities in terms of critique and contestation of the established sociospatial order, while neoliberal urbanism gives pre-eminence to its contribution to economic growth and urban development. However, as Part Two of this book will show (particularly Chapter 4), the contentious role of culture does not take shape only in progressive terms: cities and urban life are arenas where claims, discourses and mobilizations develop in the name of group identity and socio-cultural belonging, not only with the aim of attaining egalitarian emancipation, but also as an expression of inimical rivalry and an unspoken willingness to divide and segregate residential communities and urban spaces on particularistic bases.

part two

POLITICS AS GOVERNMENT

3

Urban Neoliberalism: Ascent and Crisis

Key Issues and Themes

Neoliberalism is a multifaceted process that can be observed and interpreted from intersected ideological, economic and political points of view.

Neoliberalism is a key force shaping contemporary relations between capitalism and the urban process. Manuel Castell's *The Urban Question* and David Harvey's *The Urban Experience* are foundational studies as regards the conceptualization of this relation in a context of advanced capitalism.

After the urban crisis in the 1970s and the general crisis of the Keynesian mode of regulation, capitalist cities in the United States and also other Western countries witnessed the formation of an entrepreneurialist regime of urban governance.

Neoliberalism is understood as a variegated governmental practice, which dynamically adapts to local socio-political contexts but leads also to eradicate existing socio-economic structures. The three decades between the 1980s and the 2000s have been the 'golden years of neoliberalism', characterized by its global circulation and expansion across the world in multiple forms and institutional arrangements.

The bursting of the housing bubble and the associated global economic crisis that began in 2008–09 can be read as the end of the illusion of a homeownership society intimately linked to the neoliberal hegemonic project.

3.1 Introduction: the irresistible rise of neoliberalism

This book has already touched on issues variously relating to the rise of neoliberalism as a dominant form of societal government in the North and in the global South since the late 1970s onwards, following in the wake of the irreversible decline of Keynesianism and Fordism. This chapter will analyse in greater detail the process of urban neoliberalization, as this process has been commonly defined in recent years. The notion of neoliberalism has become key to contemporary debates and empirical enquiries within the critical social sciences (and perhaps even more importantly in human geography compared to its neighbouring disciplines), even though in many ways this has remained a loosely defined category. Since the 1990s an increasingly expanding literature has developed around neoliberalism, approaching this theme from a number of different perspectives. Schematically, it is possible to identify three closely interrelated ways of understanding neoliberalism: ideological, economic, and political (Jessop, 2002; Cochrane, 2007).

At the ideological level, the neoliberal doctrine builds on the assumption that the efficiency of economic, political and societal relationships are optimized when individual actors are freed as much as possible from formal obligations, being allowed to rationally pursue their own interests within the framework of a minimum set of norms and regulations (sufficiently broad for the protection of individual freedom).

At the economic-normative level, neoliberalism as a policy toolkit favours the expansion of the market economy, both geographically (through the spreading of market conditions throughout the world) as well as in quantitative-sectoral terms, through the circulation of a wide set of productive factors and social relations in the form of exchangeable commodities (the process of 'commodification' involving social services, the workforce, and even knowledge and culture).

Finally, at the political-institutional level, neoliberalism (or 'advanced liberalism' as has been influentially defined by sociologist Nikolas Rose, 1999) presupposes that the collective rationality of actors individually responsible for the 'common good' and being in a position to attain their goals (such as the maximization of profit and of economic utility in general) is to be preferred to centralized and bureaucratic political systems ensuring the state intervention in the economic sector. Put it another way, individuals and social groups building coalitions and alliances in pursuit of their own goals (which are permitted as long as they are not prohibited by law) are more effective than any governmental regulation, being the latter organized either on national or local bases.

These ideas have been formulated by the leading exponents of orthodox liberalism in the twentieth century: the Austro-British philosopher and economist Friedrich von Hayek, an advocate of the self-regulating order of socio-economic systems and a critic of the collectivist ideal of 'social justice' (see Chapter 5); the US academic economist Milton Friedman, founder of the Chicago school of economic monetarism; and philosopher Robert Nozick, a heterodox ultra-liberal thinker widely known as the proponent of the 'minimal state' from a libertarian perspective. This heterogeneous strand of ultra-liberal thinking holds that state intervention in the economy should be limited as much as possible, as 'big government' constrains the initiative of economic agents and is inevitably prone to the pressures of lobbies and other organized groups within the public sphere.

Drawing inspiration from this variegated repertoire of philosophical ideas and politico-economic recommendations, during the 1980s British Prime Minister Margaret Thatcher – internationally known as the 'Iron Lady' – committed to dismantling Labour Party's social-democracy, accused of being costly and inefficient. To achieve this goal, the Conservative government implemented a set of policies aimed at the downsizing of the public sector, the liberalization of public utilities and the erosion of progressive taxation. The Conservative government supported the business sector, seeking to limit the power of trade unions, which was considered overwhelming and uncontrolled after the Labour governments in the 1970s (Cochrane, 2007). A vigorous governmental campaign presented the austerity policy as the only one ('there is no alternative', as Margaret Thatcher famously put it) allowing the country to resolve the fiscal crisis of the state and to protect market forces from the pervasive power of the trade unions.

In the Anglo-American world, the 1980s witnessed also the rise of Reaganism as a prominent neoliberal experiment. During the Reagan administration (from 1981 to 1989), the United States saw unprecedented tax cuts: within the space of a few years, private companies had the fiscal burden reduced by about 50 per cent on average. The decrease in state revenues and the consequent budget deficits generated by tax reductions inevitably led to the scaling down of governmental activity and the dismantling of the post-war welfare state (Blanchard, 1987). Complementing the withdrawal from an active economic policy, the US government devolved upon the Federal Reserve the responsibility to deal with the stimulation of the economic cycle through monetary policy (i.e. the lowering of interest rates and the expansion of money supply), in compliance with the recommendations of Milton Friedman and his fellow economists at the University of Chicago.

In conclusion, the economic policy that subsequently came to be known as neoliberalism has supported the development of free (or 'anarchical': Jessop, 2002) market relations led by an ideology of competitive individualism, combined with policies aimed at socializing the costs of deficits in the private sector through generous capital injections to firms and banks during recessions. The success of neoliberal policies, being dogmatically imposed in the 'post-Cold war' era as the only viable option (a 'new religion': Peet, 2003) after the decline of the Keynesian mode of regulation, has been concomitant with the globalization of the international economy, impinging upon economic development processes at a variety of geographical scales, including the urban and regional levels.

Figure 3.1   Street economy: fruit stall in Boston (2008)

Source: photo © Alberto Vanolo

3.2 At the origins of neoliberalism: the urban question in the 1970s

At the origins of the irresistible rise of neoliberalism there is the end of an era of intense and apparently unlimited economic growth known as the 'golden age of capitalism' (Marglin and Schor, 1991), beginning after the Second World War and ending with the economic and geopolitical turbulences of the 1970s (the end of the post-war Bretton Woods system of financial exchange and the 1973 oil crisis). US cities and metropolitan areas have been central places in this age of prosperity in economic but also cultural terms, as spaces for wealth accumulation, technological advancement and commodity consumption. From the late 1960s onwards, however, the surge of social and racial tensions leading to violent riots and uprisings in the ghettoes and the deprived neighbourhoods of the United States, alongside the shaping of a broader 'urban crisis' (characterized by large budget deficits at the local government level), highlighted the structural weaknesses of Fordist–Keynesian capitalism and the socio-spatial injustices and inequalities associated with the conventional pattern of economic development.

3.2.1 Manuel Castells and the urban process under Fordist–Keynesian capitalism

The difficult period of recession and transition stimulated the formation within the social sciences of a critical stream of thought coming to terms with the structural functioning of capitalist cities and their governmental institutions. The main exponents of this critical stream were sociologists, many of them based in Western Europe but with strong connections with the US academia, and human geographers, mostly working in Anglo-American universities. A leading founder of the so-called 'new urban sociology' was Manuel Castells, a scholar of Catalan origin who had fled the Franco dictatorship in the late 1960s, moving first to France where he obtained his doctorate and published the groundbreaking book, *The Urban Question* (originally written in French and then translated into English and several other languages) and in the late 1970s settled in the United States as a professor at the University of California, Berkeley (Rossi, 2010a). In geography, the leading figure of the emerging radical approach to urban geography was David Harvey, a British geographer who, like others of his generation, developed his academic career in the United States, in his case in the turbulent city of Baltimore, where he has been teaching for nearly thirty years at Johns Hopkins University. In Baltimore, David Harvey became a direct observer of the violent riots in the black ghettoes and of a number of social justice movements, and in this context he developed a critical stance towards cities and urban issues which had an enduring influence on his scientific production in the remainder of his career (Harvey, 1973; see also Chapter 5).

In *The Urban Question*, Castells (1972) offered a systematic theorization of the relationship between the urban process and contemporary capitalism, drawing on the tenets of the Marxist structuralist philosophy of Louis Althusser and his students (such as Etienne Balibar and Jacques Rancière), as well as also those of the theory of the capitalist state proposed by the French–Greek philosopher Nikos Poulantzas. According to Castells, in the capitalist city the economic system is organized around the dialectic between (1) production (resulting in goods and information generated by industries and offices), (2) consumption (measuring the individual and collective appropriation of the produced wealth) and the derived element of (3) exchange (commerce and transportation). This dialectic is regulated by the state apparatus through the double movement of integration/repression and domination/regulation. While recognizing the primacy of the economic instance along the lines of Althusser's structuralism, Castells conceptualized the state as a strategic actor and a crucial source of power, exercised through urban planning and the institutionalization of social conflict. In addition to the emphasis placed on the role of the state, Castells believed that consumption is the element functionally specific to the urban realm. His interpretation of the dynamic of the urban crisis took into account, therefore, the interplay between the following factors: the state as a guarantor of the capitalist process of development and social reproduction; consumption as a terrain of struggle and inter-class competition. Unlike David Harvey who explained the contradictions of urban capitalism as a crisis of capital accumulation, Castells argued that the decline of the post-war pattern of urban management arose out of the increasing difficulty of keeping the basic mechanisms for accomplishing the provision of urban services functioning smoothly in such basic realms as housing, transportation, education and health care. In particular, Castells maintained that the urban crisis of the 1970s had to be understood as a failure of the state in managing a crisis of collective consumption, as the state in many capitalist countries received pressures both from the grassroots in the form of social movements (struggling over the provision of services) and from the business sector (demanding the building of central business districts and the provision of subsidies). This twofold pressure on public expenditure ultimately induced to the fiscal crisis of local governments in the major cities and metropolitan areas in the United States, which were particularly hit by the contradiction between corporate needs, rising social demands, and the budget constraints of the state in a market-led economy (Rossi, 2010a).

3.2.2 David Harvey and the financialization of urban development

Whereas the capitalist city was understood by Castells as the scale of social reproduction and collective consumption, the other major contributor to the theorization of the urban process under capitalist conditions, geographer David Harvey, concentrated his analysis on the role of finance and particularly of land rent as drivers of urban economic development and socio-spatial transformations (see Rossi, 2010b). In his view, the capitalist city grows up as a consequence of investment in the built environment, which follows the rhythms of capital accumulation (given by the periodic devaluations of fixed capital) and at the same time is limited by the physical and economic lifetime of the elements within the built environment itself (Harvey, 1989b). Uneven socio-spatial development is the result of the cyclical evolution of capitalist societies at varying geographical scales, including that of the city. In capitalist cities the housing sector is managed and exploited by the ruling classes as a 'contra-cyclical' regulator of the wider accumulation process. This interpretation places strong emphasis on the role played by the financialization of the housing sector as an engine of urban economic development (and partly also of the wider national economy). For this reason, it has received major attention in recent years: first, in the context of the neoliberal economic growth led by the real-estate sector in the 2000s; subsequently, in the context of the economic downturn triggered by the crisis of the subprime mortgage sector in the United States (see the last paragraph in this chapter).

Harvey's Marxist understanding of the urban process substantially differs from that of Manuel Castells (for a comparative analysis see Zukin, 1980). While the latter interpreted urban politics as an institutionalized process dealing with the redistribution of public revenues among social classes, Harvey focused the attention on money supply and particularly on the role of land rent and mortgage loans in the urban capitalist economy. In doing so, Harvey offered an alternative theorization of the supply-side economics advocated by Chicago monetarist economists at that time, which inspired the subsequent neoliberal hegemony in the United States and the globalized economy as a whole. It is no surprise, therefore, that Harvey was the first urban scholar to clearly identify and theorize – as this chapter will show – the shift that took place over the 1980s from a redistributive-managerial approach to urban government to one driven by the imperative of economic growth (Harvey, 1989c).

Even though Harvey promptly identified and accurately scrutinized the epochal transition from Keynesian urban policy to neoliberal urban policies, outlining what became a widely accepted theorization within critical urban scholarship, also other authors writing at that time provided explanations of the urban process centred on the dictates of economic growth. One of these scholars was political scientist Paul Peterson (1981) who published a widely debated book entitled *City Limits*. In his view, in order to survive and expand their fiscal base, cities struggle over the attraction of firms and residents; in doing so, local governments are compelled to put policies aimed at the enhancement of growth competitiveness before those aimed at wealth redistribution. Despite their politico-ideological orientation, policymakers and city managers, therefore, cannot avoid embracing a growth-led governmental approach because of the limitations being imposed by the dynamics of inter-urban competitiveness on the autonomy of local government. Peterson believed that cities substantially differentiate from national states for the more limited autonomy allowed to their governments, a statement that sounds odd today in light of the subsequent budget constraints imposed on national states by neoliberal policies and international treaties across the world (for instance, the Maastricht Treaty for the European Union or the Structural Adjustment Programmes for low-income countries in the Global South).

3.3 The 'new urban politics'

Even though Peterson's book made an important contribution to the emerging literature on growth-led urban politics, with the benefit of hindsight there are at least two reservations about his central thesis: first, the idea of a pro-growth logic as an immanent quality of local dynamics under capitalist conditions expressed a rigidly structuralist (and deterministic) interpretation of the urban process, which overlooked the active role played by individuals and social groups – subsequently commonly known as 'actors' – in shaping the pathways of urban development, sometimes in contrast to goals of economic growth even in a context of increased inter-urban competitiveness. Secondly, Peterson's analysis did not grasp the fact that the rise of a pro-growth agenda should be understood as a consequence of the crisis of the Keynesian mode of regulation of capitalist economies and of the related shift to a supply-side macro-economic policy at the national level, which had led to the reduction of money transfers from the Federal government to the local states and the municipal administrations in the United States.

3.3.1 The city as a 'growth machine'

As the previous chapter has shown, since the late 1970s urban scholars gave rise to a strand of research and thinking which placed renewed emphasis on economic growth, understood not only as a source of wealth accumulation, but also as a driver of a widely conceived politics of urban and regional development, fostered by an intricate web of economic interests, claims, public discourses, and planning initiatives. In this respect, a crucial point of departure is to be found in the publication of a pathbreaking journal article authored by US sociologist Harvey Molotch, which suggested looking at the capitalist city as a 'growth machine', a definition destined to exert a notable influence on the field of urban studies in the following decades (Jonas and Wilson, 1999). In this essay Molotch argued that the imperative of urban economic growth attracts a number of competing interests and related conflicts and negotiations in the urban public sphere. As a result, coalitions and public-private partnerships take shape in support of projects of urban renewal and broader strategies of urban economic development. On the other hand, Molotch also pointed out that US cities witness the formation of 'anti-growth' coalitions, formed by citizens and social movements advocating an environmentally sustainable urban development. In the following years, the understanding of urban politics as a dispute between pro- and anti-growth coalitions was revealed to be a highly fruitful hypothesis inspiring many studies undertaken in the US context and elsewhere (see for instance DeLeon, 1992; Purcell, 2001). It is also worth noting that the rise of anti-growth coalitions focusing on environmental issues shows the ways in which urban movements started to put ecology and sustainability high on their agenda in the 1980s, whereas until the 1970s socio-economic issues (housing, health care, employment) were predominant in the urban public realm.

About ten years later, Molotch's pioneering reflections on 'the city as a growth machine' were further developed by Molotch himself along with his colleague John Logan in a book entitled *Urban Fortunes*, with the evocative subtitle *Towards a Political Economy of Place* (Logan and Molotch, 1987). Paraphrasing Robert Dahl's famous question 'Who governs?', which became the pluralistic leitmotif within urban political scholarship in the post-war decades (Dahl 1961), Molotch and Logan argued that urban scholars should investigate not only 'who governs' but also 'for what'. In order to understand the way in which urban power dynamics actually work, scholars should engage in a systematic analysis of the processes of coalition-making, which bring together public-private actors and social groups attempting to exert an influence on city and regional planning processes and the related pathways of local economic development.

The socio-political processes behind the formation of urban coalitions constitute what Logan and Molotch define 'the politics of growth', or 'politics of local economic development', according to a definition proposed by other prominent representatives of the 'new urban politics' thesis (Cox and Mair, 1988). Whatever definition is preferred, proponents of this thesis agree on the fact that the evolution of the urban political machine follows in the wake of processes of confrontation, negotiation and coalition-making, led by city administrators, public officials, local mass-media and public utilities providers (water, transportation etc.). According to Molotch and Logan, it is also important to look at the role assumed in urban growth politics by the so-called auxiliary actors, such as cultural and educational institutions (universities, museums, foundations, galleries etc.), which are in search of support from those leading the 'growth machine' (local politicians, the rentiers, and the mass media patrons). There are also other important actors such as the trade unions and the organizations representing large firms, service professionals and traders, which are less inclined to unconditionally support an ideology of urban growth, feeling impelled to intervene in local politics when their own interests are directly involved in the ongoing disputes.

As already anticipated in the previous paragraph of this chapter, economic growth became predominant within the political-economic agenda of the 1980s in Anglo-American countries and other regions and cities around the world. As previously said in this chapter, in the United States the 1980s witnessed the dominance of the so-called Reaganomics, the supply-side economic policy pursued by the Federal Administration during Reagan's mandate. According to the supply-side approach, in order to revitalize markets and attain higher rates of economic growth it is necessary to reduce the fiscal pressure on businesses and capital holders so as to stimulate private savings and investments. This economic policy stood in contrast to the Keynesian approach, prevailing since the New Deal, which maintains that the growth in productivity follows in the wake of an expansion in aggregate demand, to be attained through an increase in public expenditure. The conservative and entrepreneurialist turn changed in depth the way in which economies and societies were governed in the United States as well as in the United Kingdom, which at the time – as already anticipated – was undergoing a parallel neo-liberal '(counter)revolution' led by Prime Minister Margaret Thatcher: from the privatization of state corporations to the controversial Poll Tax (officially named Community Charge), which introduced a fixed tax per adult resident, leading to protests all over the country and in the city of London most intensely. While the controversy that developed around the so-called Poll Tax in Britain presaged the end of Margaret Thatcher's premiership (the 'iron lady' resigned few months after the approval of the tax), in the United States the adoption in 1978 of the 'Proposition 13' in the State of California – a constitutional amendment deliberating that the maximum amount of taxation on real property should not exceed 1 per cent of the property value – coincided with Ronald Reagan's ascent from the governorship of California to the Federal Presidency. Indeed, the adoption of the amendment inspired an anti-fiscal campaign known as 'taxpayers' revolt' throughout the country which prepared the ground for Ronald Reagan's successful Presidential election in 1980.

The neoliberal (counter)revolution of the Reagan–Thatcher era had strong repercussions at the urban scale, opening the way for an unprecedented deregulation of housing markets and generally for an irreversible shift to the entrepreneurialization of local government. The translation of this ideology into an instrumental and geographically mobile 'intellectual technology' was not automatic, but relied on a number of institutional intermediaries and local importers of 'ideas from elsewhere' (Ong, 2007). In the Unites States, in order to build the reputation of neoliberalism as the emerging common wisdom within the wider public, politico-economic elites have drawn on the contribution of existing or newly established consultancy agencies funded by public and private donors. In tracing back the origins of the rise of neoliberalism as a hegemonic governmental discourse, Jamie Peck (2006) has shown that the Manhattan Institute, an established right-leaning think tank, has played a

Figure 3.2   Anti-poll tax demonstration in London (1991)
Source: photo © Ian Macdonald

crucial role since the 1970s in the diffusion of an urban policy orthodoxy centred on the imperative of economic growth and based at the governance level on the involvement of private actors (particularly from the business sector) within processes and initiatives of urban regeneration. The neoliberal 'revolution' (or 'counter-revolution', according to its critics) has thus changed the way in which at one and the same time the economic base and the politico-institutional realm of cities are conceived and concretely organized. Regarding the latter, it is crucial to investigate the impact of the changing forms of capitalist regulation on socio-spatial relations embedded within established pathways of economic development.

3.3.2 Globalization and the emerging spaces of urban governance

In a path-breaking article published in 1989, David Harvey accurately illustrated the causes and the effects of the process of change in the sphere of local government, which he analysed in terms of a shift from the public-managerial approach prevailing until the urban crisis of the 1970s to the entrepreneurialization of urban governance associated with the advent of a neoliberal mode of regulation. In his article, Harvey distinguished between the 'government' and the 'governance' of cities and regions, anticipating a conceptualization that became widely accepted within the field of urban studies and the wider social sciences in the following years. In his account, the former (government) identifies a hierarchical and 'managerial' governing style, founded on the primacy of the public sector and aimed at redistributing city revenues through the provision of services to firms and households. On the other hand, the latter (governance) highlights the decentralization of governing procedures in a context of public sector's reduced institutional capacity and of rising importance of public–private partnerships and related processes of negotiated decision-making. At the time in which Harvey wrote his article, the role of public–private partnerships was also emphasized by proponents of the urban regime theory, such as political scientist Clarence Stone, who defined urban regimes as 'the informal arrangements by which public bodies and private interests function together in order to be able to make and carry out private governing decisions' (Stone, 1989, p. 6).

While acknowledging the important contribution of regime theorists, Harvey lamented the 'localism' in regime analysis and in the related literature on cities as growth machines, identifying four distinctive features of the changing governance dynamics originating from local as well as extra-local spaces:

1 The intensified competition at the international level among cities and regions struggling over competitive advantages and agglomeration economies in the industrial and manufacturing sector, and the related rise of 'new industrial spaces' such as the American Sun Belt, the Third Italy, the Île-de-France urban region and Baden-Württemberg in Germany (see also Scott, 1988).

2 The growing importance of post-manufacturing, consumption-led sectors in terms of attraction of public and private investments, such as tourism and cultural events.
3 The heightened inter-urban competition on issues relating to the creation and improvement of highly specialized infrastructures and services associated with the directional function of a city (finance, accounting and law firms, etc.).
4 The struggles among municipalities over state funding for infrastructure projects and landmark events.

To urban and regional scholars further expanding the conceptual framework elaborated by Harvey, entrepreneurial cities appeared to be crucial sites where politico-economic elites are in a position to experiment with innovative capital accumulation strategies, tending towards the immaterialization of the economic process (Hall and Hubbard, 1998). While Harvey verified these dynamics in light of the case study of Baltimore and its regenerating waterfront (see Chapter 1), related processes of socio-spatial restructuring were observed in a number of cities in the West and elsewhere. In Britain, the deindustrializing cities in the North of England (Newcastle upon Tyne, Leeds, Manchester, Liverpool) dealt with policies and plans of urban regeneration aimed at stimulating private businesses, especially small and medium-sized enterprises, and at revitalizing inner-city areas which were affected by economic and demographic decline (Ward, 1997). Related dynamics of urban regeneration and changing economic governance were also noticed in other large cities and smaller towns in North America and Western Europe (Judd and Parkinson, 1990).

Since the 1990s, the discursive and material forces of globalization exerted a growing influence on the evolution of urban entrepreneurialism and the trajectories of economic development and socio-spatial restructuring. As Harvey had explained, politico-economic elites across the world were urged to connect cities and regional spaces to economic, political and cultural relations of global reach. The localistic bias of the scholarship on urban growth machines and regimes in the 1980s, analysing in detail the dynamics of power at the urban level but overlooking the influence of external forces and the growing interplay of global and local spatialities, was left aside by embracing a stance towards urban governance processes which looked at what was defined 'the local politics of globalization' (Cochrane et al., 1996). The so-called 'new urban politics' becomes thereby a crucial terrain of investigation with reference primarily to Anglo-American cities and metropolitan areas but also to cities in other contexts of advanced capitalism. On the other hand, however, facing the danger of conceptual stretching, urban scholars have warned about straightfor-wardly importing theories and concepts elaborated in light of the US pattern of urbanism and economic growth (Wood, 2004).

In the 1990s, Europe increasingly attracted the attention of scholars concerned with issues broadly falling within the field of studies investigating the 'new urban politics'. In this context, the acceleration of the unification process, with the

founding of the European Union in 1992, had important effects on the reconfiguration of urban and regional governance. The emerging role played by the
European Union in the realm of urban affairs, leading European elites to propose
the contested representation of the 'Europe of the cities' (Harding, 1997), was
pursued in two ways: first, the EU's promotion and financial sponsorship of mega-
events, such as the European Capital of Culture programme previously analysed
in this book (see Chapter 2); second, the Europeanization of urban governance,
triggered by large EU-led initiatives such as the Urban Programme for the
regeneration of deprived neighbourhoods adopted in 1994–99 and in 2000–06
(involving 118 and 70 urban areas respectively), as well as other minor initiatives
such as the Urban Pilot Projects, focusing on urban innovation and socio-
economic experimentation. In the late 1990s, the European Union, through its
Commission, issued a document entitled 'Framework for Action for Sustainable
Urban Development', in which the following principles were identified as urban
governance pillars: *subsidiarity*, by which decision-making is devolved at the lowest
appropriate level; *integration*, demanding that urban issues be simultaneously
addressed in intersected policy realms (cultural, social, economic, environmental);
partnership, emphasizing the involvement of citizens and the private and community
sectors in the regeneration initiatives; *sustainability*, which puts environmental
concerns at the centre of the urban policy agenda; and *market efficiency*, using the
market mechanism in order to develop the economic potential of cities (European
Commission, 1999). Observing these institutional processes, the 'Europe of the
cities' has been associated with the rise of territorialized forms of governance,
referring to the institutional capacity to integrate organizations, social groups and
contrasting interests into processes of urban and regional planning (Le Galès,
1998; Pinson, 2009). The emphasis on the integration of collective structures of
human agency and social integration has led some commentators to identify
corporatism as the distinguishing feature of the European model of urban governance,
which brings together different and even contrasting goals, such as economic
growth, social inclusion and participatory democracy, whereas according to this
view the Anglo-American model of urban governance is characterized by a
mono-directional pro-growth agenda, based on the formation of public–private
actions boosting the local economy, as the literature on urban-growth machines
has shown (Pierre, 1999).

Whatever understanding of the models of urban governance is provided, the last
two decades have witnessed the increased importance of globalization for urban
elites and coalitions across the world. This has led to the 'de-provincializing' of inter-
urban competition with the rise of new players within the globalizing world
economy. In responding to the challenges of globalization, cities located in a wide
range of world areas – from East Asia to the Middle East but also South America
and some African regions – have devised urban-development strategies aimed at the
creation of incubator spaces for technologically advanced firms and at the attraction
of foreign direct investment. In the academic debate, the advent of globalization and

its influence on the strategies of urban development and governance has induced scholars to embrace an analytical perspective exceeding the boundaries conventionally associated with the local scale of social, political and economic relations. This broader scope of analysis has led to a rediscovery and critical reappraisal of the concept of geographical scale within urban scholarship as well as within other domains of socio-spatial enquiry.

3.3.3 The deterritorialization of urban politics

In his book on 'the urban question', Manuel Castells associated the specificity of the urban and metropolitan scale with the contentious social movements claiming access to collective consumption and the related processes of institutionalized conflict and social integration. As has been noted previously in this chapter, this interpretation of the urban process is intimately linked to the Fordist–Keynesian stage of Western capitalism. This chapter has already discussed the way in which the crisis of this model of capitalism and the subsequent neoliberal turn in the policy sphere have led to a deep restructuring of urban and regional economies, along with the reconfiguration of the spatialities of governance. The latter tend to exceed the dimension of place-based (or local) territoriality, reaching a wider variety of closely interconnected geographical scales.

As already anticipated, the political-administrative space of the European Union has been widely investigated in studies dealing with the 're-scaling' of urban governance in a context of globalization (Brenner, 1999). In the European Union, this process has occurred in the following ways: first, the inflow of Structural Funds has deeply re-shaped the ways in which pathways of spatial development and restructuring are being pursued in the less-favoured regions of the EU and their urban and metropolitan areas; second, through its projects of urban regeneration (such as the previously mentioned Urban Programmes) the European Union has prepared the ground for the rise of cross-national interurban networks in which collaborative relationships among cities of different sizes and economic wealth have developed and through which the neoliberal agenda has been disseminated (Leitner and Sheppard, 2002); third, inter-urban competition has been encouraged by popular EU initiatives such as the European Capital of Culture programme; finally, far from losing relevance, the national state has re-positioned itself as an interconnecting site and a strategic spatiality between the supra-national institutional scale and the urban and regional spaces of governance (Brenner, 2004).

The described changes have opened the way for the rethinking of a key concept in the tradition of geographical disciplines, namely that of 'scale', which had been already reappraised and brought to light by French-speaking geographers in previous years (Raffestin, 1980; Lévy, 1994). In the early 1990s, an important contribution to this conceptual reappraisal came from the foundational debates on globalization in human geography, looking at the local–global dialectic as a crucial determinant of urban and regional processes, particularly in the context of post-Fordism and the related shift towards flexible specialization regimes in the 'new industrial spaces'. In that context, Flemish geographer Erik Swyngedouw (1992) famously suggested using the term 'glocalization' to make sense of the growing interplay of global and local forces and of the emerging dynamics of economic development. Building on these lively debates, an important scholarship has developed around the concept of geographical scale. A crucial source of inspiration has been the neo-Marxist philosopher Henri Lefebvre and his theorization of social space as a complex overlapping of social practices, spatial representations and politico-ideological elaborations (Lefebvre, 1974; Soja, 1989).

This discussion has brought increased awareness of the political, social and relational significance and relevance of geographical scale. Even though they are hierarchically ordered, geographical scales are neither entities whose status and positioning are pre-given nor fixed spatial containers, but are the outcome of material and discursive strategies and practices as well as of conflicts and contentions among unevenly empowered actors and spatialities. Geographical scales are thereby contingent and constantly changing socio-spatial formations, whose

Figure 3.3   City life and street vending in Delhi (2009)

Source: photo © Alberto Vanolo

features, potentials, spheres of influence and hierarchical order considerably vary in space and in time (Swyngedouw, 1992; Brenner, 2000; Marston, 2000). In operational terms, the concept of geographical scale is a highly useful tool in the analysis of cities acting as 'collective actors' (Bagnasco and Le Galès, 1997). The pressing demand on cities for acting and representing themselves as competitive actors within the increasingly globalizing politico-economic arenas has imposed the strengthening of the identities of cities as unitary agents (Scott, 1998; cf. Chapter 1). In this context, urban politics is the realm in which the urban macro-actor takes shape, whose profile cannot be taken-for-granted, but is the outcome of cultural-economic practices and strategies of economic development devised by urban elites and supported by a variety of local actors. Such practices and strategies draw on an increasingly variegated and sophisticated repertoire of public policies and multi-scalar initiatives of urban planning, altogether giving rise to a complex 'transnational governmentality' of cities and their actors. Neoliberalism has provided the analytical, discursive and operational tools for such hegemonic strategies of urban economic development.

3.4 The practice of urban neoliberalism

Due to its geographical expansion as well as to its characteristically pragmatic attitude, urban neoliberalism appears to be an inherently contradictory phenomenon, which constantly reinvents itself through the assemblage and repositioning of its distinctive features under changing institutional conditions. In this paragraph we identify two sets of contrasting features helping us understand the variegated practices of urban neoliberalism across the world.

3.4.1 Adapting and eradicating: urban neoliberalism in the global South

Understanding the contemporary politics of urban and regional development against the backdrop of neoliberalism has become a widespread approach within contemporary critical scholarship. However, despite a tendency to overemphasize the globalizing effects of neoliberalism, one should not be led to think through this category as a monolithic entity, uniform in time and space. As anthropologist Aiwha Ong (2007) has pointed out, the neoliberal regime of institutional governance and capitalist accumulation should be viewed as a mobile governmental technology, constantly travelling through a variety of geographical contexts and related socio-political cultures. For instance, the Chinese experience, with its unique combination of authoritarian state and unregulated market, reads as an example diverging from the Anglo-American ideal-type of neoliberalism. By approaching neoliberalism as a political-economic practice it will be evident that the neoliberal mode of regulation relies on existing socio-cultural institutions, producing a wide range of hybrid formations.

At the same time, however, the hybridization of political and institutional forms should not lead us to believe that the transition to urban neoliberalism is linear and compatible with local values and socio-cultural diversities. In the vast majority of cities in the South of the world, the effects of neoliberal policies have been pervasive, eradicating existing cultural, economic and socio-political institutions. In the 1980s and the early 1990s, the Washington-based financial institutions (essentially the International Monetary Fund and the World Bank) recommended a set of economic and social policies (the so-called Structural Adjustment Programs) which were approved and implemented without negotiating decisions with the local citizens, with strong repercussions on the most deprived urban areas (Peet, 2003). Adjustment programmes were forcefully adopted by those countries receiving financial aid and re-scheduling debt payments (on the basis of the so-called conditionality principle). These plans were deeply informed by neoliberalism as an ideology and policy rhetoric, under the banner of the so-called Washington Consensus Decalogue, which prescribed allegedly universal recipes for the recovery of national and urban-regional economies, including:

- the reduced role of the state and the downsizing of public administration;
- the depreciation of the local currency, so as to make imports less convenient and to boost the export of nationally produced goods;
- the liberalization of trade, in line with conventional free-market theories;
- the elimination of subsidies for low-income households, a social assistance policy widely adopted by national governments in the South of the world (particularly in Africa) in order to allow access to commodities and social services to the poorer residents, but considered too onerous for the public budget;
- the investment in export-led sectors of the economy balancing the state budget.

Such macro-economic and sector-specific policies, mainly elaborated at the national level, have had deep implications for cities in the South of the world. The joint effect induced by the privatization of important public services, the closure of a number of state-owned corporations, and the bankruptcy of manufacturing industries that previously benefitted from public subsidies, has had serious consequences on local societies, leading to rising unemployment rates and generating novel forms of exclusion from the labour market (Riddel, 1997). These processes have also led to the expansion of the informal, underground economy. Job losses, the shrinkage of the state sector, the fall in living standards, have forced city dwellers to rely on a variety of sources of experimentation and commonality (Simone, 2004): shared relational capital, unused land converted into community gardens (cf. Box 3.1), informal trading and street-vending are common responses to poverty and deprivation in the cities of the global South.

BOX. 3.1   URBAN FILMS

CONTENTIOUS COMMUNITY-BASED ECONOMIES IN LOS ANGELES – *THE GARDEN* (2008, USA, DIRECTED BY SCOTT HAMILTON KENNEDY)

Community-based urban agriculture (also known as 'community gardening') is an increasingly widespread phenomenon in cities all over the world. Urban farming takes place in a variety of societal contexts: it is commonly associated with environmental activism (its radical version being the so-called 'guerrilla gardening'), it can be practised as a hobby by elderly and middle-class people, or it can be used as a source of food and income by the poor and the jobless in deprived urban environments of the global South and North (from African cities to the racially segregated neighbourhoods in the United States).

The Garden is a 2008 documentary film presenting the largest experiment of community gardening in the United States: a 14-acre area in South Los Angeles known as South Central Farm (see Irazábal and Punja, 2009). Started as a do-the-right-thing initiative after the 1992 riots in Los Angeles, the LA Harbor Department subsequently authorized local inhabitants to occupy and use the site as a community garden. Since 1994 the cultivated area has constantly expanded, giving rise to a sort of environmental miracle within a peripheral and marginalized area of the city. Run mostly by poor Latino immigrants, the urban farm provided fresh food for about 350 families involved in the farming experiment.

The film describes the legal and political struggles against real-estate speculators and in defence of the farm and the related social dramas taking shape between 2004 and 2006, concluding with the eviction of farmers and the area bulldozing. The forced closure of South Central Farm occurred despite the strenuous local community resistance and a massive fund-raising campaign led by American celebrities (such as Danny Glover, Joan Baez and Zack de la Rocha) along with urban activists. In a context of deeply neoliberalized urban environment like that of Los Angeles in California (the state being known for the adoption of Proposition 13 and for having paved the way for Reagan's political ascent – see section 3.3.1), this documentary shows that the appropriation of urban vacant land becomes a battlefield opposing community-based coalitions to powerful economic actors and related political supporters.

In this context, existing welfare states have been restructured and widely dismantled: educational and health-care services have been drastically reduced, the already scarce supply of social housing has been halved on average, the price of imported food has considerably increased as a consequence of the devaluation of local currencies, while large portions of fertile land have been reconverted to export-oriented productions. These processes of socio-economic restructuring have led to the expansion not just of the informal economy but also of the illegal, criminal economies: newly formed street gangs and urban mafias have proliferated, engaging in large-scale organized theft and drug trade through increasingly transnational networks. In a context of increased poverty and hardship, large cities in the South indeed tend to become less safe places to live in. In the face of perceived or actual threats, the so-called 'transnational capitalists' (Sklair, 2002) – those involved in the most profitable sectors of the economy (the oil industry for instance) and well-linked to local politicians – respond to this situation by tightening security systems and militarizing their residential spaces (see Chapter 4). In general, social disadvantage has intensified in large cities and metropolitan areas, particularly affecting migrants and the ethnic minorities. The ambivalent effects of neoliberal urbanism are highly visible in the most dynamic city-regions (such as the industrial coastal cities of South China, the fast-developing cities in the Middle East, such as Dubai most famously, as well as established global cities in the West like London and Los Angeles), where migrants are employed on casual bases in the industrial and the service sectors under conditions of unbearable workloads, low wages, uncertain contractual status and precarious housing.

On a transnational scale, global economic elites of Western origin have been those that have most benefited from the deregulation and liberalization of market economies in the South: transnational firms with headquarters located in global cities in the North have opened new branches internationally, with significant economic returns (Dicken, 2007). The North–South relationships and most notably the transnational governance of development processes in the South have also evolved over time: the normative and straightforward approach to economic restructuring characterizing the Structural Adjustment Programmes in the 1980s has become softer in many respects. The International Monetary Fund (IMF) and the World Bank alike have indeed taken into account the critical views of those stressing the contradictions of their programmes and policy recommendations based on the received wisdom of orthodox neoliberalism, partially modifying their orientations accordingly. The basic logic underlying development programmes, however, appears to be immutable: for instance, despite the asserted good intentions, the financial aids provided in order to attain the Millennium Development Goals identified by the United Nations (from poverty alleviation to the reduction of infantile mortality rates, from the pursuit of an environmentalist agenda to the promotion of inter-state and supranational agreements for international development) are persistently subject to IMF conditionality, which dictates the transition towards modes of social and economic organization and development based on the neoliberal agenda (Amin, 2006).

Figure 3.4   Semi-abandoned central railway station in Dakar, Senegal (2010)

Source: photo © Alberto Vanolo

Note: The railway system in Senegal has been severely reduced as a consequence of the structural adjustment plans dictated by the IMF.

3.4.2 Dismantling and reconstructing: urban neoliberalism in the global North

Whereas economic development policies adopted in poorer and emerging countries in the South have gradually abandoned the shocking therapies of first-generation neoliberalism, the 'original' forms of neoliberalism (those elaborated and commonly practised in the West) have changed over the years, and they will certainly change in the future, without losing their distinguishing features, relating to the emphasis laid on goals of economic growth to the detriment of those of social justice and wealth redistribution. After the rise and the triumph of ultra-liberal approaches during the Reagan–Thatcher decade, the 1990s and the first half of the 2000s have seen the reformulation and the re-framing on novel discursive bases of neoliberalism as a politico-economic discourse and as a policy practice. In the attempt to conceptualize the recent evolution of neoliberalism, geographers Jamie Peck and Adam Tickell (2002) have provided an influential interpretation of the shift from an unconditionally deregulatory policy rationale, definable as 'roll-back neoliberalism', which characterised the Reagan–Thatcher era, aiming to extinguish the social-democratic legacies created by the Keynesian regulation of capitalism, to a renewed neoliberal approach, more positive and 'constructive', aimed at rebuilding the capitalist state on entrepreneurial bases and at re-shaping in innovative ways the relationships between business interests and the public sector. The latter approach (defined as 'roll-out' stage of neoliberalism in Peck and Tickell's terminology) was advocated during the 1990s by the New Democrats and the New Labour Party led by Bill Clinton and Tony Blair in the United States and Great Britain respectively (but also by the post-social-democratic governments led by Gerhard Schröder in Germany and by the more unstable centre-left government coalitions in Italy between the late 1990s and the early 2000s).

Neo-progressive parties have taken the lead, therefore, in the second stage of the neoliberal 'revolution', replacing the conservative parties dominating the first stage, in the United States as well as in their most influential allied countries – notably those belonging to the Atlantic Alliance, which has remained unchallenged after the collapse of the Soviet Union. Having assumed this role, the progressive parties have engaged in a vast endeavour of self-legitimization in the eyes of business actors, by precipitously converting to the basic tenets of the neoliberal orthodoxy: the obsession for budget rigour (leading in Europe to the adoption of a restrictive fiscal and monetary policy as the distinguishing trait of the newly founded European Union in 1992), the reduction of public spending in social assistance and, finally, most importantly in the context of post-Fordist capitalism, the flexibilization of the workforce. Unlike the conservatives, refusing the idea itself of society as a collectively organized entity and embracing the purest free-market ideology, the centre-left governments have sought to reconcile objectives which were considered mutually antithetic until a recent past: combining the enhancement of social cohesion with the stimulation of economic competitiveness and turning the public sector into a more entrepreneurial and accountable organization have been distinguishing features of the so-called 'new liberal formulation' (Harloe, 2001). The 'Third Way' publicly announced by British Prime Minister Tony Blair, and theorized by sociologist Anthony Giddens (1998), came to represent the most consistent example of neoliberal formulation being proposed on the progressive side of the political spectrum as an alternative to the ultra-liberalism advocated by the conservatives: the emphasis placed on 'global governance' and transnational civil society, in contrast to the neoliberal aversion to 'big government' and social justice, alongside the attention paid to issues of environmental sustainability and cultural pluralism, in lieu of the conservative predilection for the integrity of the family and the nation, have been the essential principles of Giddens–Blair's Third Way.

Within the sphere of urban government, apparently indissoluble beliefs and taboos received from the past shattered in the face of local and nation-wide campaigns against petty and organized crime and the variety of phenomena of social deviance (homelessness, drug abuse and even 'art crimes' such as graffiti and writing). While urban administrations led by conservative mayors gave rise to highly mediatized repression campaigns against urban crime, such as most famously the 'zero tolerance' initiative adopted in the 1990s by the Mayor of New York Rudolph Giuliani, the centre-left governments sought to restore their credibility in security policies; a field in which progressive parties were still conventionally associated with tolerant attitudes. In this vein, Prime Minister Tony Blair announced, in the political manifesto of New Labour in 1997, a new course of action against crime under the banner of the slogan: '*tough on crime and tough on the causes of crime*', which explicitly attempted to reconcile policies addressing issues of social exclusion and urban deprivation with measures to combat crime and deviance.

Broadly speaking, the second stage of neoliberalism in the 1990s testifies to an important re-definition of the ways in which capitalist cities are governed and administered. In the unified European space, these changes have taken form through institutional dynamics of multi-level governance, in which cities and regions play a crucial role, after the hollowing out of the state and of the institutions gravitating within its sphere (Jessop, 2004b). In the service sector, local and regional governments assume key roles in the governance process; on the other hand, however, they externalize their prerogatives to other subjects of private or not-for-profit status, in line with the general trend of contractualization of social services, by which services are delivered on the basis of a contract signed between the providers (either within or outside the formal public sector) and welfare recipients: job centres sub-contracted to private companies or quasi-public agencies replace the old state-led employment bureaus, while similar processes of outsourcing occur in the health-care services and other social assistance sectors organized at the local level with a view to achieving a modernized local welfare state based on dynamic local–central and public–private relationships (Cochrane, 2004). In times in which economic and financial flows appear to be increasingly out of juridical and political control and in which the strategies of transnational firms and other 'foreign' investors are caught in a hardly decipherable chaos, large cities and metropolitan areas – in their capacity to foster internationally competitive economies of agglomeration and diversity – are assumed to be crucial institutional arenas in the regulation (i.e. the de-regulation and re-regulation) of capitalist economies and societies (Brenner and Theodore, 2002). At the same time, however, owing to the reduced government spending and the fierce competition in obtaining public and private funds for economic regeneration policies and particularly for costly infrastructural projects, urban governments are compelled to devise a wide range of local economic development strategies: place marketing and promotion campaigns, mega-events, company subsidies and the creation of free economic zones (cf. Chapter 1).

3.5 Neoliberalizing urban economic spaces

In the described context of hegemonic and at the same time spatio-temporally variegated neoliberalism, two local economic regeneration schemes are particularly illustrative of the dominant approach to urban development: the 'Urban Enterprise Zones' policy, which was first carried out at the time of the Thatcher premiership, and the Business Improvement Districts initiatives. The former, based on fiscal incentives and ambitious infrastructure projects, is designed to trigger economic development dynamics in declining and peripheral urban areas. In neo-capitalist China, the creation of 'economic special zones' in the 1980s made a decisive contribution to the booming of its export-led economy, particularly in the Southern coastal regions which have become the drivers of China's path of economic development: the industrial cities of Shenzhen, Dongguan and Canton in the rampant Pearl River Delta region (Cartier, 2001). The Business Improvement Districts policy, on the other hand, which has been embraced by local governments in a number of countries including Britain, Germany, New Zealand and South Africa since the 1970s onwards, focuses on the physical renewal and the aesthetic amelioration of attractive and potentially profitable urban districts (usually shopping and entertainment precincts located in downtown areas), using funds obtained from the self-taxation of local private firms, whose financial efforts are rewarded with the assignment of autonomous responsibilities in the management of the regenerated spaces (Ward, 2006).

As these examples show, contemporary processes of urban and regional governance highlight the rise of relatively autonomous scales of economic and spatial regulation at the local level, but also the persistent influence of the national state in this realm, particularly in the East Asian context (China), but in different ways also in Western liberal democracies. In the unified European space, the last two decades have indeed seen the national state repositioning itself as a key actor in the coordination and the material structuring of the complex multi-level governance structure regulating the processes of urban and regional development (Brenner, 2004). This institutional context demands attention being paid to the ways in which neoliberal imperatives dictated by international and national politico-economic elites become incorporated into economic development strategies at the urban and regional levels, particularly in the form of public–private partnerships aimed at revitalizing local economies through the creation of technological districts, the abatement of local taxes, the demolition of obsolete housing, the redesign of residential spaces, the mega-projects of downtown and waterfront regeneration, the construction of iconic buildings, the invention of luxury and mass-consumption spaces, the adoption of surveillance devices guaranteeing the safety of inhabitants and city users (Asian,

European and North American case studies are available in: Olds, 1995; Moulaert, Rodriguez and Swyngedouw, 2005; Orueta and Fainstein, 2008).

Outside the Western world, powerful think tanks and supranational institutions have made a decisive contribution to the diffusion of the approach to urban policy that has been described above. At the global scale, a crucial role has been played by the World Bank and the Organization for Economic Cooperation and Development (OECD). The World Bank's 'corporate goals of reducing poverty, promoting market-based growth, building durable institutions, and protecting the environment' (World Bank, 2000, p. 40; see also World Bank, 1991) stem from a conventionally neoliberal understanding of economic development issues. From the standpoint of the Washington-based organization, cities are not to be considered as containers of social problems, let alone places where socio-spatial inequalities have to be addressed, but as 'engines' of economic growth, more precisely as centrepieces for processes of economic-relational networking reconnecting local economies to the global flows of capitals, commodities, information and policy discourses. In the emerging economies of the global South, as a result, local elites are pressed with demands from international organizations for turning the major urban agglomerations into global-izing cities competing with their Western counterparts (see Chapter 1). Even in cities located in what was previously labelled as 'Third World' the 'urban question' is no longer concentrated on housing issues and the allocation of adequate services for the local population, but on the optimization of local economic productivity. The currently common wisdom on development issues holds that even anti-poverty initiatives – which used to have priority in the urban-policy agenda until a recent past – have to be combined with strategies of economic growth.

The link between anti-poverty and economic growth policies is justified not only along 'ideological' lines (for instance as a way to avoid parasitic social assistance), but also by reference to structural changes within urban-development dynamics. In the cities and metropolitan areas in the global South, economic growth processes and the regeneration of large urban areas have been accompanied by the proliferation of informal settlements (variously defined slums, favelas, bidonvilles, shantytowns, depending on the geographical–linguistic context). This 'planet of slums' (Davis, 2006b) has taken shape also as an indirect consequence of selective and elitist strategies of urban development, concentrated on a limited set of 'competitive' urban spaces. In the discursive politics of neoliberalism, even slums and favelas are portrayed as 'opportunities' for economic development, waiting to exploit the potential of their entrepreneurial talents. In spite of such optimistic representations, the link between economic growth and poverty reduction appears to be questioned by empirical evidence: for instance, in recent years the city of Luanda – the capital of Angola in Africa – has showed rising growth rates, which have benefitted mostly local and foreign potentates involved in the oil industry, while the city on the whole has remained one of the most deprived places in the world (Pitcher and Graham, 2006).

The Organization for Economic Cooperation and Development (OECD) advo-cates an approach to urban-development issues which is closely related to that of the World Bank, even though it is more concentrated on wealthier countries.

In portraying cities as 'engines' of economic development, OECD recommends to its member countries the adoption of policies aimed at the generation of entrepreneurship within the framework of a sustainable pattern of economic development (see, for example, OECD, 2002). Social cohesion, environmental sustainability and economic-spatial competitiveness are considered interrelated objectives. From this standpoint, cohesion and sustainability are not understood within broader notions of social and environmental justice, but are instrumental in the pursuit of economic growth (see Harloe, 2001; Gordon and Buck, 2005).

A related view on economic policy and urban development issues emerges also from the European Union's 'Territorial Agenda' (EU, 2007). The document stresses the interdependence between economic competitiveness and 'territorial cohesion' (a broader but also vaguely articulated variation of the notion of social cohesion). This interdependence is pursued through the identification of objectives such as the creation of job opportunities, the promotion of a knowledge-based society, the improvement of governance mechanisms (Vanolo, 2010). The socio-political implications underlying the adoption of such objectives are evident: for instance, concentrating public spending on the promotion of knowledge-based activities may have the effect of marginalizing low-skilled workers, while professional training programmes alone are not sufficient to address this issue. At the same time, regeneration initiatives embracing place-marketing approaches, such as the already mentioned European Capital of Culture programme, highlight the influence within the European Union's policy field of the strategic framework of urban entrepreneurialism, in a context in which the EU itself does not assume an explicitly direct role in the field of urban planning (which remains under the control of the member-states).

3.5.1 Contingency, mobility and the 'politics of the mime'

A result of the dynamics that have been described and analysed in the previous section has been the global expansion and circulation of neoliberalism, which has adapted to the varying (geographically and historically) configurations of post-Fordist urban capitalism in the central, peripheral and marginal regions of the world. Many authors have approached the urbanization of neoliberalism through the lens of the 'new urban politics' originally identified by Kevin Cox and other critical urban geographers (Cox, 1993; Cochrane, 2007). The characteristic, and the ambiguity, of urban neoliberalism rests on its ambivalent relationship with the public sector and the state in particular: on the one hand, in line with the tenets of classic liberalism and its more recent formulations in the last quarter of the twentieth century, supporters of urban neoliberalism postulate the retreat of the state from the socio-economic realm, advocating an involvement of private actors within the institutions of urban and regional governance; on the other hand, supporters of neoliberal policies do not hesitate to exert pressure on national governments when it comes to obtaining financial support for megaprojects and international events capable of fostering the so-called urban boosterism (Harvey, 1989c).

The ambivalent relationship between the state, the market forces and urban politico-economic elites is particularly exemplified by pathways of urban economic development and restructuring taking place in countries that have embraced neoliberalism in more recent times (the so-called 'late-comers', as the conventional lexicon in development studies puts it). These countries, on the one hand, have committed to reproducing the key factors lying behind the success of the Anglo-American pattern of capitalism and local economic development; on the other hand, however, they have inevitably based their development pathways on specific socio-economic features and modes of institutional regulation, embracing the imperative of economic growth as a fundamental driver of the politics of urban and regional development. This is the case of two important national states in East Asia: China and the Republic of South Korea. In both countries, the political-economic reforms implemented in the late 1980s (in China, the liberalization of the economy; in Korea, the democratic transition and the technological upgrading of its industrial base) have been accompanied by an increased role of cities within economic development processes, which has been achieved through the devolution of power from central to local administrations. In China, the national government committed to enhancing, or creating ex nihilo, the economic (industrial, financial and commercial) potential of coastal towns, resulting in unprecedented economic and demographic growth rates, which attracted multitudes of migrants from the rural regions. In Korea, the end of the authoritarian regime in 1987 led to crucial institutional and economic-spatial changes, with the introduction of elected mayors and the decentralization of functions and economic activities in smaller towns, reducing the country's dependence on Seoul (a new-towns policy inspired by the related planning programme pursued in post-war Britain).

In both countries, the state has been a central actor, though in varying modalities. In Korea, state prerogatives have been devolved to local administrations and particularly to elected mayors, whose leadership has been catalyst for the formation of public–private coalitions and partnerships taking the lead in the processes of urban development (Bae and Sellers, 2007). In China, the national state has been more reluctant to devolve its prerogatives to local actors and institutions: in the property sector, it has retained the ownership of land, conceding to private economic agents only the right to exploit limited portions of urbanized space, even though under the pressure of growing global competition and the organization of global events such as the Expo 2010 in Shanghai national elites have assigned to local governments stronger responsibilities and the power to concede demolition and redevelopment rights to private investors (He and Wu, 2009). As already anticipated in the previous paragraph with reference to the adaptive capacity of neoliberalism as a governmental technology (specifically, section 3.4.1), the example of China (and partly also that of South Korea), with its distinguishing features and evolutionary paths, points to the way in which neoliberalism should be regarded not only as a government-led economic regime imposed on cities and regions by state agencies and international organizations, but also as a constantly changing mode of economic governance and regulation, depending on the historical and institutional factors under which development pathways evolve and contingent opportunities for economic growth and wealth accumulation take shape (Wilson, 2004).

Apart from internal contradictions as well as the relentless attempts to mediate between conflicting interests, the strength of urban neoliberalism rests on its capacity to incorporate all sorts of urban problems and issues (social, economic and environmental) into the seductive domain of spatial competitiveness and economic growth, proposing policies flexibly adapting to a variety of geographical contexts. What can be defined the 'politics of the mime' – namely, the alternatively passive or creative imitation of successful models of urban growth – has expanded across the globe, albeit this process has occurred in varying forms and with contrasting outcomes; a phenomenon that has been analysed in this book with reference to the so-called 'wannabe' global and creative cities. As soon as the depressive effects of the geopolitical and monetary crises of the 1970s vanished and the Japanese challenge to the Western hegemony on technology and business management unravelled, 'ideas from America' became again predominant (cf. Box. 3.2). As a result, the 1980s strategies of urban economic development and restructuring in the United States have since acquired a renewed leading role, offering success stories of innovation and entrepreneurship in a number of advanced sectors such as finance, business administration, information and communication technologies. In an increasingly competitive and interconnected environment such as that of the globalizing capitalist economy, the rapidity and intensity of economic and spatial changes being observed in the North American context have forced those governing cities and regions in other contexts to accelerate the implementation of regeneration policies and broader projects of urban development. As Peck and Tickell have underlined (2002), the length of time covering the manifestation of an urban issue, the selection of objectives and priorities, the mobilization of institutions and financial sources, the organization of projects and urban-planning initiatives and, finally, their implementation has increasingly shortened, inducing local elites to rely on ready-made policy recipes ('imitations from the shelf' as the two authors put it), more easily implementable and less likely to be contested by the local population in comparison to strategies formulated at the local level.

For the reasons explained above, neoliberalism has succeeded in reproducing and 'territorializing' itself in apparently efficient and even creative ways, rapidly migrating from one place to another across the globe. In doing so, it has drawn on the contribution of a variety of powerful agents and intermediaries: technocratic elites, think tanks, global consultants, political networks, development gurus (such as the aforementioned Richard Florida and before him economist Michael Porter, the theorist of 'competitive advantages'). The planetary circulation of presumably winning ideas and policy solutions is conventionally labelled as 'policy transfer' within the mainstream political sciences, while it is alternatively understood in terms of 'policy mobility' by critical urbanists pointing to the effect of reinvention associated with the process of circulation (McCann, 2010). The phenomenon of policy mobility and transfer is related not only to strategies of growth-led development and governance (such as in the cases of the Special Economic Zones and the Business Improvement Districts policies), but also to issues and problems firmly anchored in local and institutional specificities, such as poverty, deviance, social marginality and urban criminality (Wacquant, 1999). Using a metaphor drawn from evolutionary sociobiology, it can be observed what happens when an intrinsically complex system (such as the city or the world economy) reduces its own 'political biodiversity' (consisting in the variety of conceptual and operational tools normally used in order to identify policy issues and formulate appropriate strategies to tackle them), becoming more vulnerable and exposed to the risks associated with the reduction of viable options for action (the selection mechanisms in the evolutionary terminology: Simmie and Martin, 2010). An illuminating example of the dangers associated with the reduction of complexity generated by the global expansion of neoliberal urbanism is that of the structural financial crisis that hit the world economy in 2008 and 2009. Owing to the role played by the housing finance sector in triggering an economic recession in the United States that has rapidly travelled towards other advanced capitalist economies, today's cities appear to be crucial sites ('the geographical scale of experience' as Peter Taylor put it in 1982) in which the limits and the contradictions of neoliberal capitalism and globalization can be observed and critically scrutinized.

BOX 3.2   URBAN FILMS

THE POLITICS OF THE MIME IN SANTIAGO UNDER PINOCHET – *TONY MANERO* (CHILE, 2008, DIRECTED BY PABLO LARRAÍN)

Under Pinochet's dictatorship (1973–1990), neoliberalism became the dominant economic doctrine in Chile. The ideas of neoliberal gurus like Milton Friedman and Friedrich von Hayek were imported in Santiago by economists trained at the Chicago school of economics (the so-called 'Chicago boys') who recommended the privatization of state-owned companies and of a number of public services. After a period of economic growth (the alleged 'Chilean miracle', according to Milton Friedman's judgement) socio-economic inequalities expanded substantially, particularly as a consequence of the international debt crisis of 1982.

Tony Manero is a film shot in Santiago, the capital of Chile, which provides a fascinating, embodied depiction of what in this book has been defined as 'the politics of the mime'. The protagonist is Raúl, a man obsessed with John Travolta's famous character in *Saturday Night Fever*, a popular cult film set in New York City in the late 1970s (just after the urban crisis and before the 'neoliberal revolution'). Living in the outskirts of Santiago, the man has to cope with a decaying and scary urban environment, where the informal economy and illegal activities proliferate, and where social ties and forms of solidarity appear to be absent. In this context,

Raúl practises on an everyday basis the bodily imitation of his American hero, of his ways of dancing and dressing, his monologues, paying attention to every detail as a sort of catechistic practice, where the metaphor of neoliberal 'religion' becomes evident. The protagonist is vividly described in his violence and lack of humanity, much like the representation of the city of Santiago as a whole, a place where people shelter in doorways at any sign of trouble and are constantly afraid of being spied upon. The residual dream keeping Raúl alive is the experience of New York's dance floor, the only way to leave the miseries of Chilean society behind.

3.6 The expected unforeseen: the housing bubble and the global recession

The intimate relationship linking capitalism, the housing sector and processes of urban development has come to the fore in an extraordinarily visible fashion over the last three decades or so: first, the so-called financialization of the global economy (the steady increase in financial transactions at a world scale and their autonomization from the real economy) has played a key role in the ascent of established or emerging global cities, such as London and New York in the West, and Shanghai, Hong Kong and Singapore in East Asia; in addition, in more recent times, the housing boom has been the engine of economic growth during the first half of the 2000s, precisely between 2002 and 2006, after the end of the short period of contraction that followed the bursting of the New Economy bubble (the economy based on 'dotcoms' firms which expanded between 1995 and 1999). The noticeable but also virtual profits linked to the financialization of the economy, alongside the precipitous rise of property values, have generated – during the relatively short golden age of post-Cold-War neoliberalism, the two decades between the mid-1980s and the first half of the 2000s – widespread illusions and expectations of unlimited wealth accumulation until the 2008–09 financial crisis.

The financialization of the economy, which has been brought about by neoliberal globalization and the dismissal of Keynesian economic policies, is at the origin of the economic trajectory that has eventually led to the economic downturn in 2008–09. The term 'financialization' refers to the process that has led in those countries whose financial systems have been heavily deregulated (in particular the United States and the United Kingdom, but also countries in continental Europe and in East Asia) to the creation of financial assets having an overall value four or five times greater than that of the gross national product of each national economy. This phenomenon has produced an unprecedented availability of capitals, which have been partly reinvested in the mortgage market, resulting in the growing expansion of the real estate sector. In the early 2000s, the United States, and particularly the

Southern and Western states (the Sun Belt which had been at the forefront of the post-Fordist transition and is particularly attractive in environmental terms), such as California, Texas and Florida, witnessed a steady rise in house prices, as a consequence of the expansion of homeownership due to the illusory increase in mortgage opportunities.[1] Related phenomena of rising demand in the housing market have been observed in those European countries that have laid out permissive regulatory frameworks on financial services and consumer credit, such as Spain, Ireland, Britain and Iceland. These countries, along with the American states that were in the forefront of the housing bubble, have been those that most have suffered the consequences of the 'credit crunch' that hit the world economy in 2008–09. A variety of social groups have been affected by the economic downturn, especially those that had the illusion of attaining a higher standard of life thanks to easier access to homeownership and to a number of goods (not always strictly necessary) purchased through consumer credit.

The push for homeownership has been actively encouraged by the deregulation of mortgage markets in the United States and in many European countries as well. Since the early 1990s, the acceptance policies of banks have become increasingly lenient, and credit limits (i.e. the maximum amount that can be borrowed through a mortgage) have expanded (Aalbers, 2008). The illusion of an ever-expanding homeownership is, therefore, at the origin of the subprime mortgages crisis in the United States. Subprime mortgages are riskier loans – in many cases, re-finances – offered at higher ('predatory', according to its critics) interest rates to economically vulnerable and potentially insolvent clients: low-income individuals belonging to ethnic minorities and other disadvantaged groups, frequently employed on a casual basis and with a background of credit default (Wyly et al., 2007; Sidaway, 2008). High-risk, 'predatory' loans were introduced in the 1990s, preparing the ground for the housing bubble of the subsequent decade (estimates report that subprime mortgages amount to one fifth of the mortgage market in the United States). In 2006 the apparently unlimited expansion of the mortgage market started slowing down, giving rise to a set of interrelated negative phenomena, eventually leading to a downward spiral: growing insolvencies by mortgage borrowers, foreclosure proceedings, increase in housing abandonment at the neighbourhood level, crisis and in some cases bankruptcy of credit institutions, fall of house prices and depreciation of property values. In September 2008, the bankruptcy of Lehman Brothers, one of the largest and oldest financial firms in the United States, triggered by the subprime mortgage crisis, created a banking panic which was followed by the global economic recession.

The economies of cities and metropolitan regions that in previous years had taken the lead in the process of globalization and neoliberalization have been seriously affected by the credit crunch, the crisis of the housing market and of the wider economy: from established global cities (New York, Los Angeles, London) to globalizing cities (Dubai, Shanghai, Singapore) where spectacular megaprojects were under way when the crisis began, to the new capitals of urban Europe such as Dublin, Barcelona, Manchester and even the quiet and peripheral Reykjavik, have faced a deep depression of the economy, with the closure of several firms and commercial activities, the generation of new reserves of unemployed and working poor, while a number of urban megaprojects have been suspended. In the United States, which has been the epicentre of the global economic shock – after having been at the core of the organizational and technological 'revolution' of post-Fordism (see Chapter 1) and of the process of financialization – it is not only the private sector that has suffered the consequences of the downturn: with increasingly passive local budgets owing to the risky investment operations undertaken in the years of the financial boom, the administrators of several US cities have been forced to drastically reduce the supply of important services (transportation, health care, cultural events) so as to manage to repay the debts.[2] This situation recalls the terrible fiscal crisis that hit New York and other cities in the United States in the 1970s. There is substantial difference, however, between that crisis and the recent one: in the 1970s the budget deficit was the result of the increase in public spending and the fiscal crisis of the state (and of the related Keynesian mode of regulation), while recent collapses of municipal budgets arise from public sector's financial dependence on bank loans and financial investments, in line with the neoliberal mode of economic (de)regulation and financialization. Are not only the municipal administrations that have become involved in the credit crunch in the US, but even more importantly the 'real economy' has been heavily affected by the downturn at the local state level: for instance, the state of California, whose technology-led pathway of economic development had been widely celebrated and imitated in previous years, had to face an unprecedented reduction of public investments in higher education and applied research.

Whereas orthodox economists are blamed for not having predicted the economic and financial crisis, but also for having actively contributed to foster the belief in self-regulating markets, the expansion and the subsequent cataclysm of urban capitalism in the neoliberal era were somehow prophesied by David Harvey and those sociologists, geographers and critical economists who, drawing on his pioneering studies, have analysed in detail and at the same time have denounced the destructive link between finance, capitalism and urban development (Harvey, 1989b; cf. Aalbers, 2009). In his work, Harvey applied Marxian theory to the study of urban development dynamics, pointing to the ways in which the capitalist city grows as a consequence of investment cycles in the built environment, which are linked to capital accumulation, on the one hand, and are regulated by the limited physical and economic lifetime of the elements constituting the built environment itself, on the other hand. In this context – Harvey concluded – the real-estate sector is exploited by the ruling classes as a contra-cyclical regulator of the wider accumulation process and thus as a crucial sector in the stages of economic growth, as happened at the time of the so-called golden age of post-war capitalism, until the 1973 crisis, and has happened more recently with the flourishing of the globalized financial capitalism and the subsequent downturn in 2008–09.

It is clearly hard to predict whether, and to what extent, the still ongoing crisis will lead to the rethinking of the neoliberal model of economic and spatial development which had become hegemonic in previous years, both in its neoconservative and ultra-liberal variants and in those vaguely progressive. In any case, the fact that the wider public has become increasingly aware of the structural pitfalls inherent in this socioeconomic model might urge politico-economic elites with governmental responsibilities at the local scale to question the unconditional primacy of the imperative of economic growth, drawing attention – also for reasons of consensus building – to existing claims of wealth redistribution and social and environmental justice, as the next chapter will show (see Keil, 2009). An alternative to the redistributive and democratic turn is represented by the intensification of authoritarian and hyper-individualistic tendencies within the urban realm, fomented by an increased sense of economic insecurity and uncertainty. The future of contemporary cities appears to be, therefore, at a crossroads: the coming years will show whether inimical or egalitarian stances towards city life will prevail among city managers, policymakers and the wider public alike.

Notes

1   The expansion of homeownership was at the heart of George W. Bush's mission to build an 'ownership society'. In a speech given to the Republican National Convention in September 2004, just two months before his second Presidential Election, Bush famously declared: 'Another priority for a new term is to build an ownership society, because ownership brings security, and dignity, and independence. Thanks to our policies, homeownership in America is at an all-time high. Tonight we set a new goal: seven million more affordable homes in the next 10 years so more American families will be able to open the door and say welcome to my home.' A similar statement was made in December 2006 by France's prospective President Nicolas Sarkozy, who referred to his objective of turning France into 'un pays de propriétaires' (a nation of homeowners) as a basis for a renewed national cohesion and sense of the Republic: 'Mon premier projet en matière de logement est de faire de la France un pays de propriétaires car la propriété est un élément de stabilité de la République, de la Démocratie et de la Nation.'

2   *Businessweek* magazine ('The new threat from Wall Street', 19 November 2009) has reported that the most indebted municipalities in the US are Detroit, Indianapolis and the major cities of the state of Tennessee such as Nashville and Memphis. At the beginning of 2009 also Chicago – among many other things, the city where President Barack Obama politically grew up as a lawyer and community advocate – publicly announced its serious budget crisis. *Businessweek* observes that the debt crisis has hit cities in those states that have enacted permissive legislation regulating the allocation of credit among public and private uses.

4
Urban Geopolitics: Legitimate Violence, Terrorism, Urbicide

Key Issues and Themes

The field of geopolitics has expanded beyond the national scale of enquiry to which it was conventionally confined, being applied to the study of social-spatial relations regulated by violence 'in the last instance' also at the urban scale, under the banner of the newly established 'urban geopolitics'.

The global era is commonly portrayed as the age of insecurity in multiple forms. Zygmunt Bauman's distinction between 'security', 'certainty' and 'safety' provides an interpretative framework for the understanding of the multifaceted 'politics of fear' taking shape in contemporary cities across the world.

The home and the residential community are settings in which the urbanization of fear is particularly evident. The global expansion of the so-called gated communities, reflecting local residential cultures and other socio-spatial features (including ethnic and religious divisions), testifies to the growing demand for safety understood as community self-defence in a variety of geographical contexts.

Violence is not only exercised but also evoked or just exhibited as a capacity to act by the established authorities. In the 2000s, terrorist threats have fostered a complex politics of pre-emption leading to an increasingly pervasive surveillance of urban spaces, which has intersected with the effects of the process of transfiguration of public space already brought about by the advent of neoliberal urbanism in previous decades.

In some contexts and historical circumstances, cities become explicit targets of institutionalized violence and acts of war. Urbicide is understood as the deliberate destruction of the urban built environment and the annihilation of related socio-cultural relations.

4.1 Introduction: the governmentalization of the urban experience

As the previous chapter has shown, the neoliberal shift has had a number of important consequences on the urban experience, such as the rise of entrepreneurialist
governance, the privatization of public services, the commodification of socio-
spatial relations and the shaping of growth-led urban strategies. In addition to these
changes triggered by the capitalist imperative of creative destruction and restructuring, neoliberalism as a governmental technology has reshaped on novel bases the
relationships between politico-administrative authorities, on the one side, and citizens and urban communities, on the other side, at a variety of geographical scales.
Put simply, neoliberalism should be viewed not only as an economic policy, but also
as a mode of societal and moral regulation. This chapter deals with the latter dimension of neoliberalism at the urban scale.

  Whereas in the past local governments were concerned mainly with issues of land
use regulation and with those relating to the allocation and distribution of public
services, today an increasingly larger number of aspects of city life become subsumed within the sphere of urban government and administration. Using the conceptualization originally proposed by French historian and philosopher Michel
Foucault (1979), which has inspired the work of many scholars across the human
and social sciences (sociologists, political theorists, anthropologists and geographers),
it can be argued that the era of 'advanced liberalism' is marked by a growingly pervasive governmentalization of the urban experience: from cultural events to initiatives of spatial and economic regeneration, from policies tackling issues of social
deviance and crime to those concerned with the surveillance of urban spaces, cities
have witnessed the deployment of a variegated set of governmental tools, where
'government' means at one and the same time disciplining, control, ordering or
'putting in relation' actors, discourses, and socio-spatial practices (Rose, 1999).

  Whereas Foucault identified the 'population' as the target of the rising governmental rationality in the modern age, in societies of advanced liberalism this role is
assumed by the 'citizen', who is asked to be increasingly aware not only of rights
and entitlements – as occurred at the time of the Keynesian state – but also of duties
and responsibilities, leading to the generation of a self-governing society (Imrie and
Raco, 2000; Marinetto, 2003). The emphasis placed on the link between rights and
responsibilities has a wide range of consequences, which can be viewed either as
complementary or contradictory to each other (see also Chapter 6 on citizenship).
On the one hand, building on the influential communitarist line of thought led by
sociologist Amitai Etzioni (1993), a great deal of attention has been drawn to
the nurturing of a collaborative ethos within a revitalized civil society, one in which
the 'responsible' citizen contributes to the generation of a sense of belonging to the
urban community through membership of non-profit associations and other forms
of active citizenship (Amin, 2005). On the other hand, as this chapter will show,

there is the 'authoritarian' side of the 'responsibility turn', which is evidenced by the devolvement to selected and 'reliable' citizens and communities of important pre-rogatives concerning the management of security devices and anti-crime measures (Raco, 2007). Albeit partly contradictory, these phenomena shed light on the increasingly moral connotation of urban government in advanced liberal societies. The idea of citizen participation in the public sphere and the related ideal of the 'active citizen' are pursued through the mobilization of a variegated repertoire of policies and regulations orientating the moral conduct of the urban community (understood as a collective entity and as a complex of individuals), while classic goals of socio-economic emancipation and justice appear to be marginalized from the urban policy agenda despite persistent struggles making reference to them (see Chapter 5).

The chapter that follows will deal with these issues from the point of view of 'urban geopolitics' (Graham, 2004a). In many respects, this definition is unusual, as the discipline of geopolitics conventionally confines itself to the realm of inter-state relationships, particularly those concerned with processes of expansion, consolida-tion and delimitation of national boundaries, both in times of peace and of war. Even a heterodox political geographer like Jacques Lévy (1997, Italian edition, p. 342) has recently defined geopolitics as 'the spatial dimension of inter-state rela-tionships (...) regulated by violence in the last instance'. As this definition shows, violence is conventionally considered to be the distinguishing feature of geopolitics in relation to the field of political geography in which it is comprised, sharing with its 'mother' discipline the focus on the state as the political spatiality par excellence. In more recent years, however, it has become commonly accepted that not only political geography broadly conceived, but also geopolitics should expand the scope of analysis beyond the spatiality of the nation state, taking into account the role played by other politico-geographical entities of supra-national, macro-regional, regional and local levels (Painter, 1995; Agnew, 2002). In this context, the contem-porary city is an example of emerging politico-geographical spatiality, tending to assume an explicitly 'geopolitical' significance. As Jan Pieterse (2002) explains, the national state no longer retains an exclusive and pre-eminent position in matters relating to the exercise of violence (as it no longer has an exclusive role in political and economic affairs). For instance, conventional inter-state wars, historically linked to nationalist ambitions, today increasingly take the form of unconventional, asym-metrical, low-intensity conflicts and of 'civil wars' (Kaldor, 1999; Graham, 2004a). Despite this evolution, however, one should not expect that national states are losing their military powers within and outside of their borders. On the one hand, at a global scale recent years (especially the first decade of the 2000s) have witnessed the resurgence of ambitions of imperial hegemony pursued by established or rising national powers (the United States, above all, but also emerging countries such as China, Russia and also Brazil and India). On the other hand, at the national level epochal events deeply marked by violence have fostered an increasingly pervasive obsession for issues relating to the safety of citizens and urban communities: from the Seattle revolt in 1999 to the protests in Genoa over the G8 summit in 2001 and, of course, the terror attacks on the Twin Towers on 11 September 2001. Following in the wake of these 'exceptional' events, security and safety issues have become prominent within public discourses, becoming 'the basic principle of state agency', and this has occurred in a historical context characterized by the hollowing out of major state functions (social protection, education, fiscal policy) and their devolution to other governmental entities (Agamben, 1995 and 2002).

The obsession for measures of control and surveillance guaranteeing the safety of citizens finds fertile ground in exceptional spatio-temporal circumstances, such as New York City after the 11 September attacks, the Gaza Strip, Bombay facing the bloody clashes between Muslims and Hindus in 1992–93, the Bosnian cities at the time of the ethnic cleansing in 1992–95. Such spatio-temporal occurrences led to the shaping of what Carl Schmitt (in the 1920s) and more recently Giorgio Agamben (2003) have called 'states of exception': apparently contingent situations that are at the threshold of, or even beyond, the sphere normally regulated by law, authorizing the established authorities to transgress the existing jurisprudence (and, at the same time, giving rise to an opposite movement claiming the 'right to resist'). History, however, shows that policies originally aimed at disciplining 'exceptional' spaces and individuals (such as the 'suspected aliens') end up being extended to the majority of citizens, becoming the 'norm' rather than the 'exception'. Moreover, when the established authorities arbitrarily acquire control over the body of the citizen, this can lead to the 'animalization' of the human species, as envisaged by Michel Foucault (1976). The brutal experiment of the camp of Guantánamo for international detainees suspected of being involved in terrorist activities, which was explicitly presented as an 'exceptional' suspension of human rights, can be seen as a normalized 'state of exception' (Minca, 2005; Gregory, 2006a).

In more ordinary contexts, the obsession for security is used as a pretext for the limitation of free expression in the public sphere by dissident movements, undermining an essential requisite of liberal democracies. Peter Marcuse (2006) has shown how at the time of the second war in Iraq the US legislation against terrorism was instrumental in the attempt at silencing political dissent with the limitation of the freedom of assembly which affected also peaceful demonstrations such as the rally in which approximately 400,000 people gathered in Union Square and Central Park in August 2004 protesting over Bush's war campaign (Figure 4.1). A basic right – the democratic expression of political dissent in public space – was questioned by using the pretext of 'exceptional' circumstances, even in the absence of terrorist threats and other concrete dangers. The approach to issues of national security that has taken shape in the wake of these events and as a consequence of more structural transformations of the public sphere has important effects on the urban experience. As this chapter will show, decisions concerned with the regulation and the repression of violence tend indeed to pervade the entire everyday life of city dwellers, well beyond 'exceptional' spatio-temporal conditions.

Figure 4.1 Anti-war protest in New York (August 2004)

Source: www.unitedforpeace.org (accessed September 2010) © united for peace and justice

4.2 The politics of fear

At the beginning of his *In Search of Politics*, Zygmunt Bauman (1999) recounts what happened in the small town of Yeovil in England when a paedophile was released from prison. Emotionally reacting to the event, local people gathered in a public space to call for the lynching of the former detainee, even without being sure of the crime he had committed. What is surprising in such ordinary stories is the fact that those that take to the street demanding the punishment of the suspect are individuals that are not accustomed to actively participate in the public sphere. In Bauman's view, this story shows how it is possible to hate someone in public, with absolute impunity, while behaving like a good, decent and responsible citizen willing to contribute to a sentiment of collective indignation that revitalizes a sense of community which appears to be lost in an era of globalization. In his classic book *Civilization and Its Discontents*, originally published in 1930, which is a source of inspiration for Bauman, Sigmund Freud famously put forward the thesis that modern societies create structures limiting personal freedom (for instance, in the expression of individual instincts, frequently generating neurosis and hysteria) in the search of 'security', thus giving the illusion of being emancipated from fears commonly associated with the nature, the body, and the actions of other humans.

4.2.1 The age of insecurity

In a previous work, the highly influential *Postmodernity and Its Discontents*, Bauman (1997) argued that the relationship between freedom and security has become increasingly problematic within globalizing societies. He develops his argument by identifying different meanings of the notion of security (and specifically of the German term *Sicherheit* originally used by Freud).

First, there is a notion of 'security', understood in purely existential terms, based on the commonly held perception that the world is stable and reliable, as are the skills allowing us to cope with its challenges. This is a form of security which is currently threatened by the increase in casual and low-paid jobs, by the reduction of social protection and by the rapid obsolescence of individual abilities.

Second, security is understood as 'certainty', namely as the capacity to predict and devise plans for the future. Nowadays, this capacity increasingly exceeds the powers of national governments (and indirectly those of citizens), being appropriated by 'exogenous' forces and organizations: the International Monetary Fund, the World Trade Organization, the large transnational firms. What kind of certainty can be achieved when it comes to dealing with the 'structural violence' of a threat like being excluded from the labour market, a matter which is largely out of reach for politico-economic elites (Bourdieu, 2000)?

Third, security can be understood in terms of 'safety', which means being protected from the dangers commonly associated with everyday life. The sense of fear derives from the fact that the postmodern individual lacks adequate responses to the eternal mystery of human contingency: heteronomous strategies, such as those arising from religion, are suited only to believers (based on the conviction that, whatever will happen, behaving in a certain way will ensure life after death), whereas the search for eternity through personal contribution to the reproduction of the family and the nation (the so-called 'heteronomous/autonomous' strategies) appears to be increasingly less reassuring, owing to the weakness of these institutions and the related social values (what does belonging to a national community mean in times of globalization?) as well as to the individualistic culture prevailing today (will the marriage last 'till death do us part'?). As it is impossible to give definitive answers to these dilemmas, a growing number of people adopt neurotic behaviours in the attempt to remove the spectre of uncertainty: by making sense of life through the purchase of useless goods and engagement in ephemeral experiences; by obsessively contrasting the decay of the body; by taking a number of practical precautions as a way of making everyday life more reassuring and secure, like continually checking the oscillations of body weight, avoiding passive smoke and learning self-defence techniques.

In the three ways of approaching the issue of security outlined by Bauman, the terrains of globalization and postmodernity appear to be inherently mobile and unstable, signalling a widespread sense of loss of control and imminent danger. The only domain in which it seems possible to have chances of survival is that of personal security, understood merely in terms of physical safety. This phenomenon is particularly visible in the private sphere (the obsession for video surveillance and other security devices protecting the domestic space), but also in the public realm, as political elites tend to devolve the responsibility for the solving of the problems generating anxiety, which are relegated to the more manageable domain of physical integrity and security. Indeed, the established authorities exert limited influence on other forms of insecurity: the promised improvement of life conditions stands in contrast to actually existing policies increasing the flexibility of the labour force, reducing social protection and privatizing public services. In this context, to those wielding the political power in Western democracies the most rewarding way for building consensus amongst their constituencies is to concentrate efforts on security and safety issues by adopting severe legislations towards marginal actors: for instance, by making it more difficult for international migrants and asylum seekers to enter the national territory without permit and obtain the status of refugees; and by launching 'zero tolerance' campaigns against urban crime and social deviance. Being unable to guarantee or just promise a future of prosperity to their citizens, national and local governments seek to remove the factors of disorders that are presumably behind collective anxiety, exhibiting an ability to suppress phenomena threatening the security of citizens. In this context, common phenomena of social deviance – speed excess by car, smoking in public and a wide range of immoral behaviours – not only are stigmatized as a violation of the law, but are presented as threats against the security of the citizen, the body, and the individual properties (Foucault, 1975; Wacquant, 2008).

4.2.2 Globalizing urban fear

This chapter uses the notion of 'politics of fear' in order to understand the ways in which social issues, important or ephemeral, actual or perceived, are addressed at the urban scale within the framework of security policies and the related mobilization of private interests, discursive practices, and government tools. Fear is a powerful force behind socio-spatial transformations. A typical example is the aftermath of the 9/11 attacks: in the United States and other Western countries, the emotional reaction to the event led to widespread prejudice against individuals belonging to specific ethnic and religious groups (particularly, the South Asians, the Arabs and the Muslims widely conceived); moreover, as a direct consequence, the policing of key sites, such as airports and public places, was intensified. The contemporary 'politics of fear', however, has significant historical antecedents: in the 1950s, at the time of the Cold War, in the United States city and regional planning agencies actively supported processes of urban sprawl, as compact cities were believed to be unsafe, being more exposed to atomic threats from the Soviet Union (Farish, 2004). The post-war politics of fear was a major force behind the American myth of suburban life, of a quasi-rural community escaping the dangers of urban environments.

The neoliberal regime of urban governance has generated its own 'geographies of fear', as a reaction to 'uncontrollable' phenomena such as epidemics and 'natural' catastrophes (floods, earthquakes, etc.) which have served as opportunities for the experimentation with innovative procedures of societal government (Davis, 1999; Kaika, 2005). French sociologist Loïc Wacquant (2007) has examined the way in which poverty is currently approached on novel practical and discursive bases as a social problem falling within the field of deviance and crime issues. The tension between welfare policies tackling issues of poverty and indigence (as a way of addressing wider inequalities, drawing on ideals of justice and solidarity) and their transmutation into penal categories (as evidenced by the rise in imprisonment rates, particularly affecting the most disadvantaged groups) is increasingly oriented towards criminalization in the context of neoliberal governance. These processes have been analysed with reference to the Americas, particularly to the United States and to South American countries (Brazil, Argentina, Columbia, Venezuela), but are detectable in other regions and countries across the globe.

The ambivalent management of poverty finds evidence in the contrasting ways in which marginalized spaces of cities and metropolitan areas around the world are governed: from the favelas in Brazil to the French banlieues and bidonvilles, and the slums in Asian and African megacities. On the one hand, local administrations, autonomously or in collaboration with national governments and international organizations, devise 'innovative' planning strategies designed to normalize unauthorized settlements through the demolition of indecent housing and the rebuilding of residential spaces, in some cases pursuing strategies of slum dwellers' involvement and empowerment, albeit with contrasting outcomes (Mukhija, 2003). On the other hand, when troubles arise (riots, acts of violence, etc.), youth groups and other supposedly turbulent inhabitants of these neighbourhoods are criminalized, being labelled, for instance, as *bande de racailles* (the term used by French President Sarkozy during the uprisings of banlieues in 2005) and even as 'enemies

Figure 4.2   The exhibition of police as a deterrent against criminality, São Paolo, Brazil (2009)

Source: photo © Alberto Vanolo

of the nation' (Dikeç, 2006).The criminalization approach ends up fostering violent attitudes and behaviours, particularly in those contexts – such as the segregated neighbourhoods of metropolitan areas in Western countries and the bidonvilles of the megacities in the South – where the police is not viewed as an 'independent

agent' (willing 'to solve the problem'), but as 'part of the problem', because its conduct is conditioned by social and ethnic prejudice (as happens in the French banlieues) or because police officers are involved in acts of corruption, violence and
torture, creating an atmosphere of terror, as occurs in cities in South America and
the United States.

The criminalization of social deviance and marginality has contributed to changing the ways in which the police deploy repressive measures against street gangs and
organized crime. Geographer and criminologist Steve Herbert (2001, 2006) has
analysed the rise in the United States of the so-called 'broken windows' approach
to police service. In a context of urban neoliberalism, previous views emphasizing
the embeddedness of police within local communities (understood as actors being
part of the same social entity) have been replaced by approaches distinguishing the
role of police from that of community. Proponents of the latter view argue that the
police should be committed to combating all forms of crime, including those apparently less dangerous for mainstream society, so as to discourage the diffusion of
illegal behaviour.[1] The approach briefly outlined here has inspired the 'zero tolerance' policy embraced by the Mayor of New York, Rudolph Giuliani, between 1994
and 2001 (N. Smith, 1998). This policy approach maintains that a variety of marginal
individuals, including those without permanent housing (the homeless and the
urban nomads), those selling their bodies (the prostitutes), those appropriating abandoned houses (the squatters) and those using street art as a form of expression (the
graffiti writers), are examples of deviant conduct and disorderly behaviours, which
should not be tolerated by the established authorities. Such attitudes are at the origin of the rise of the so-called 'revanchist city', as the phenomenon has been defined
using a term borrowed from the French populist movement in the late nineteenth
century (N. Smith, 1996).

According to Steve Herbert, local politicians and city managers are in favour of
adopting the punitive approach to social deviance and crime, because it is popular
amongst the middle and the upper classes and also because it is more easily implementable, compared with approaches seeking to address the structural causes of
deviance, prescribing the reintegration of deviant individuals into local communities, recommending measures of risk prevention and trying to strengthen the link
between local societies and the police in deprived urban areas (the so-called community policing). On the other hand, the 'revanchist' approach to police service
does not exclude the adoption of violent behaviours by the police. Rather, as the
police are authorized to arrest individuals merely on the basis of suspicion, it is likely
that the members of socially disadvantaged groups and ethnic minorities and those
residing in stigmatized neighbourhoods are targeted by large-scale campaigns of
repression. The identification of individuals and social groups supposedly more
inclined to become involved in phenomena of crime and deviance is the main
objective driving contemporary anti-crime campaigns, which do not hesitate to
adopt explicitly military techniques of repression (police and army round-ups in
low-income housing complexes, the use of helicopters, the evacuation of schools

and shopping areas). When one thinks of the (in)applicability in wealthier social areas of repressive measures that have become common in deprived urban settings, this shows that the currently dominant approach to the management of police operations reflects and reproduces existing social inequalities and place-based forms of discrimination.

The other side of the coin is that socially and residentially marginalized groups can react to these processes by re-organizing themselves in violent forms. As already pointed out in this and the previous chapters, within the neoliberal regime of societal governance the management of poverty increasingly falls within the sphere of individual responsibility. The public sector has undergone a structural process of decline and restructuring: government spending on social programmes and institutions has reduced, while the management of education and health care has been devolved to private and quasi-public actors: the liberty '*to go to a doctor of my choice at a time of my choice*', as Margaret Thatcher famously put it (quoted in Bauman, 1997, p. 72). In advanced capitalist countries, the United States being the precursor as this issue has long been at the centre of political debates since the last century, adult citizens have to purchase health insurance and, in doing so, are subject to the dictates of private companies while dealing with health problems.

The privatization and marketization of public services has intersected with the process of financialization (see Chapter 3). In an age of 'casino capitalism' (Strange, 1997) the entire sphere of social reproduction tends to be subsumed within the circuits of financial markets, through the financialization of the social-security system most notably, but also of other crucial services within the post-Fordist knowledge-based economy such as those relating to professional training and technical updating (the process of 'life-long learning': Rizvi, 2007), considered essential in an increasingly competitive labour market. The individualization of social relations (through the interrelated forces of privatization, marketization and financialization) reinforces old prejudices against the poor (and particularly the low-income ethnic minorities such as the African-Americans in the United States) for being responsible for their deprived condition. Feeling abandoned and isolated, the weakest groups reorganize their survival strategies through the informal/criminal economy channels (see Box 4.1). In the US cities most hit by rising unemployment and industrial decline (such as Detroit, the former capital of the automobile industry), the spectre of insecurity and impoverishment pushes social outcasts to engage in networks of criminal affiliation, becoming members of urban gangs. Related examples in other geographical contexts are those of the *commandos* of drug-traffickers in Latin America or those of the private armies organized by the 'war landlords' in Africa. Such institutionalization of violence and urban fear can be understood in terms of communitarian self-defence, which takes a variety of forms, including those that will be discussed in the next section of this chapter in relation to practices of dwelling and partition of urban residential spaces.

BOX 4.1   URBAN FILMS

SOCIAL REGULATION AND MONOPOLY ON VIOLENCE IN THE CITY OF CRIME – *GOMORRAH* (ITALY, 2008, DIRECTED BY MATTEO GARRONE)

Based on the best-selling homonymous book by Roberto Saviano, *Gomorrah* is a film describing the everyday life of people involved in organized (and disorganized) crime (the so-called Camorra) in the metropolitan area of Naples in Italy. Appealingly acted by a mostly non-professional cast, namely 'real' people (the arrest of the actor playing *Zi Bernardino* has drawn the attention of mass media in Italy) speaking the local dialect (subtitles are provided also for the Italian audience), the film presents 'ordinary' stories of crime taking place in a variety of socio-spatial settings: from the segregated and highly deprived public-housing complex in the district of Scampia (known for being one of the largest illicit drug markets in Europe), in the northern outskirts of Naples, to the densely and chaotically urbanized countryside between Naples and Caserta.

Much like the book, the film offers a vivid account of the social regulation of organized crime in an age of globalization of economic flows, including those falling under the control of mafia-like organizations. The book indeed famously begins by describing the trafficking of dead human bodies hidden in containers being handled in an area of the port of Naples managed by Chinese government-owned shipping companies. The five stories selected in the film deal with the vicissitudes of individuals happening to live in a highly criminalized environment, where the state (and the related welfare system) is not only absent but is commonly viewed as an enemy. The stories are centred on a haute couture tailor working in an informal economy in which local and Chinese entrepreneurs compete against each other by using all necessary means (including violence and murders); on two young wannabe gangsters who end up being killed by established criminals; on a *mesata* distributor (an income provided by Camorra gangs to the close relatives of their affiliates who are dead or have been imprisoned); on a child dreaming of becoming a member of Camorra; and on an employee of a North Italian company involved in the illegal dumping of hazardous wastes and, in doing so, profiteering from the garbage crisis that has been plaguing the metropolitan area of Naples for many years.

While the young author of Gomorrah now lives under police protection following a series of anonymous death threats, both the book and the film have raised a great deal of controversy within the public debate (even Silvio Berlusconi, the Italian Prime Minister, has criticized the work of Saviano) for having depicted an urban environment in which there appears to be no room for a sense of civicness and respect for law and thus for reproducing an image of the Italian South as a hopeless region in which not only the criminal monopoly on violence but also the wider social, cultural and economic influence exerted by mafia-like organizations remain unchallenged.

4.3 From fear to communitarian self-defence

In socio-spatial terms, the forces of fear and individualization, which have been described in the previous section, take the form of an increasing segregation of residential spaces within closed, self-contained, homogenous, guarded communities.

The phenomenon of 'gated communities' has become widely known to the scholarly community after the publication of Mike Davis's successful book on Los Angeles (Davis, 1990). The so-called 'fortified communities', which are now scattered all over the world (even though they are still relatively rare in Europe), are characterized by the self-financing of the material infrastructures (the maintenance of streets and public spaces) and the services specifically dedicated to the members of the residential community (from security to leisure). In order to prevent unauthorized access, residential spaces are rigorously controlled and the perimeter of the communities is delimited by walls or wires. Originating in the United States and quickly spreading to other countries in the world (cf. Caldeira, 2001), the phenomenon of socio-residential segregation on a voluntary basis has arisen from demands for safety posed by the medium-upper classes, concerned about the growth of crime in large urban areas.

In more recent times, not only the members of the affluent classes, but also those belonging to a variety of social groups organizing on the basis of age (e.g. elderly people), ethnicity or of shared hobbies and lifestyles (such as the passion for golf) have created fortified communities (Blakely and Snyder, 1997), where concerns over 'safety' combine with the willingness to remove the 'alien' from the dwelling space. Paraphrasing the definition of geopolitics proposed at the beginning of this chapter, it can be argued that gated communities are examples of socio-spatial relations (of dwelling and propinquity) regulated by violence in the last instance. In terms of land-use regulation, the transformation of urban spaces into marketable entities and spaces of self-representation for exclusionary communities of city dwellers leads not only to the privatization of large portions of urban space, but even more importantly to the annihilation of urban democracy, which is constitutively founded on principles of coexistence and recognition of difference (Rossi, 2008). When the living place is organized as a self-segregated space of inimical defence from individuals belonging to other social, ethnic and religious groups, the prophesied advent of 'post-political' (or post-democratic) societies is likely to materialize, as even the possibility of social conflict vanishes (Rancière, 1990).

As already anticipated, having originally appeared in the United States, gated communities have quickly spread across the world. The global expansion of gated communities, however, should not be interpreted merely in terms of an 'Americanization' of lifestyles. Within an increasingly cross-national literature on this subject, it has been shown that in post-socialist countries such as Russia and Bulgaria the formation of 'closed' residential communities is linked to previously existing practices of socio-spatial separateness pursued by the Soviet elites, from the Communist party's *apparatchiks* to the intellectuals and the artists supporting the political establishment. In Soviet times, the members of political and cultural elites resided in affluent houses, called *dacha*, which were located in suburbs surrounded by natural environment and accessible only through private or semi-private streets carefully watched by the army (Blinnikov et al., 2006; Stoyanov and Frantz, 2006). The subsequent collapse of the Soviet regime gave rise to significant changes in the social configuration of elite groups, whereby previous political leaders and the supporting intellectuals were replaced by the so-called 'new rich', mainly businessmen and financial investors desiring to experience luxurious lifestyles. In many emerging and also low-income countries, living in a gated community has become customary for local elites and most notably for the communities of expatriates. This has important consequences on the conventional pattern of urban dwelling, as diplomats and businessmen view residential communities as temporary living places rather than as their 'homes': a 'state of residential exception', to paraphrase Carl Schmitt and Giorgio Agamben. Foreign 'guests' choose to reside in separate communities as these are more comfortable and safe and also because it is easier for them to meet other expatriates while shopping and having a stroll.

In the global South residential segregation happens to be closely linked to business interests. In African countries where mineral and energy resources are copious and highly remunerative (such as oil, natural gas, gold, diamonds, amongst the most profitable), extraction industries are confined to isolated enclaves, militarily controlled and disconnected from the local society, which does not benefit in substantial ways from their presence. Western technicians are forced to reside in these areas, in order to avoid being kidnapped by autonomist organizations claiming the right of indigenous population to the appropriation of local resources, as has repeatedly occurred in the Niger Delta in Nigeria (Watts, 2004; Ferguson, 2006). Without facing dangers comparable to those threatening their colleagues in Africa, also in the Arab cities of the Middle East technicians of Western origin reside in separate communities, called 'compounds'. In Saudi Arabia, which has attracted a considerable number of technicians and specialists from Asia and the Western countries, 'fortified communities' serve as spaces of protection for expatriate women looking for safe living places (Glasze, 2006). In cities in the South, socio-spatial segregation is also related to ethno-religious divisions. In Indonesia, ethno-religious divisions, which have generated forms of residential segregation since the times of Dutch colonization, are reflected in contemporary gated communities, reproducing the traditional separation between the Chinese and the Christians, on the one side, and the native Muslim population, on the other side (Leisch, 2002).

In ethnically divided urban settings, phenomena of residential separateness and segregation do not arise only from demands for pleasing living environments and personal safety, but are tied to needs of mutual assistance within communities experiencing social exclusion and political marginalization. The fragmentation of urban space along ethnic lines is tragically exemplified by the case of Beirut, the capital of Lebanon, a city with a historically lively and multicultural urban environment, in which neighbourhoods are identified on an ethno-religious basis. In the 34 days of siege between July and August 2006, the hostilities between Israel and Hezbollah militants provoked several deaths and the massive destruction of al-Dahiya, a district in the Southern area of Beirut, inhabited by a majority of Shiite-Muslims: it is estimated that at least 500,000 people remained homeless after the bombings. The destruction was intentionally circumscribed to the Muslim district (other areas in the city were untouched), hitting everyone who was in the target area, including civilians not affiliated with the political-military organization of Hezbollah. After the end of the war, Hezbollah efficiently helped the civilians in the process of recovery: when the ceasefire had been just proclaimed, Hezbollah's volunteers were already visiting local residents needing help, planning the reconstruction of the houses and the infrastructure destroyed by the Israeli raids. In that context of emergency, the Lebanese government proved to be unable to devise an efficient reconstruction plan, despite the considerable amount of money invested. Government's institutional inertia led to widespread gratitude towards Hezbollah, which was regarded not only as 'a state within a state', but even as 'a state within a non-state' (Arif, 2008). Today, Hezbollah has a recognized role in Lebanon, not only in politico-military terms, but also as regards informal initiatives addressing housing issues and other social problems. The fact that the national government has left Hezbollah alone dealing with the process of reconstruction has had the consequence of making neighbourhoods even more isolated and ethnically segregated. The case of Lebanon, like that of Israel (see below in this chapter), shows how existing ethno-religious divisions and their spatialization are deepened by communitarian disputes and political struggles. In these contexts, however, even though 'fundamentalist' and anti-democratic forces like Hezbollah in Lebanon and Hamas in Palestine are conventionally blamed for irresponsible conduct, governmental ruling elites (both 'national' and 'colonial') make a decisive contribution to the reproduction of ethno-religious divisions in two interrelated ways: first, through spatially selective military operations, targeting specific groups and residential areas; second, avoiding any direct commitment to helping and assisting the marginalized ethno-cultural minorities.

However, not only cities in the Middle East have to cope with issues of ethnic separatism, communitarian politics and the related conflicts. The case of the slaughter of the Sikh population in Delhi in 1984 is also illustrative of the politics of ethno-religious conflict at the urban scale: in the space of few days – after the murder of Prime Minister Indira Gandhi committed by a Sikh guard – approximately 4,000 people were brutally killed by armed mobs affiliated with the Indian National Congress. As a response to these events, communities of widows formed in several areas of the city in order to help the victims and to create a sense of solidarity and commonality amongst people sharing the experience of ethnic persecution (Legg, 2007). Like that of Lebanon, this case shows, on the one hand, the failure of the state in preventing ethno-religious conflicts and effectively dealing with its consequences (Indian authorities failed to identify those responsible for mass executions) and, on the other hand, it shows the subsidiary role played by local communities in the provision of assistance and aid to the population.

BOX 4.2　URBAN FILMS

GATED COMMUNITIES AND THE URBANIZATION OF THE 'US VERSUS THEM' OPPOSITION – *LA ZONA* (MEXICO, 2007, DIRECTED BY RODRIGO PLÁ)

Like other megacities in the global South, Mexico city has witnessed the rise of a growing number of gated residential communities. *La zona* is an independent Mexican–Spanish co-production exploring the anthropological consequences of this phenomenon.

The story takes place in a wealthy residential neighbourhood called *La zona*. Surrounded by a wall, the area is guarded by private police and constantly monitored through cameras, in order to keep it safe and physically isolated from the neighbouring *favela*. The state of apparent calm is interrupted, though, when in the middle of the night, during a storm, three boys living in the favela decide to sneak into the gated community hoping luck will be on their side. However, something goes wrong, as during the robbery an elderly woman is shot to death. As a consequence, guards intervene, killing two of the housebreakers. The story then concentrates on the third one, Miguel, who becomes the object of a ruthless manhunt by the inhabitants of the gated community.

The film emphasizes the deep divide between *La zona* and the neighbouring areas. The division of urban space is based not only on income and infrastructure differentials: the gated community is also a sort of 'state within a state', having its own rules, institutions and moral order (cf. the role of autonomist organizations like Hezbollah in Lebanon described in this section). The killing of the woman triggers a state of emergency, authorizing the suspension of the law as a justification for self-defence. In contrast to this rather gloomy picture, there is still room for hope in the film, given by the covert friendship between Miguel and an affluent teenager, Alejandro, living in the gated community. In the eyes of Alejandro, Miguel is not regarded through the lens of the 'us' and 'them' dichotomy, i.e. as a dangerous and deviant boy, a poor inhabitant whose destiny is to become a professional criminal, but as just a boy of the same age.

4.4 The use of force as a threat: terrorism, urban marginality and the politics of pre-emption

There is one further manifestation of urban geopolitics, one in which the city is identified as a potential target of violence both by anti-systemic actors (such as terrorist and other armed groups) and by government authorities through policies of pre-emption. At the global as well as the urban scale, the events of 11 September 2001 sparked widespread concern about threats against local communities originating from unknown actors and places and for this reason being perceived as uncontrollable and unpredictable. This led to an equally widespread demand for the militarization of urban spaces. The increased surveillance of public places is one of the most debated consequences of the 'authoritarian turn' that has taken shape as a reaction to these events. Critical scholars and other progressive commentators have drawn attention to the subtle distinction existing between 'acceptable' security devices and restrictions (e.g. metal detectors in the airports and the limitations to the ownership of weapons) and those being 'unacceptable' for violating human rights and civil liberties.

With regard to the latter, Peter Marcuse (2006) has referred to the alarm messages propagated by the mass media, in the form of the so-called ethnic profiling (which associates perceived dangers and threats to specific ethnic groups, such as the Arabs in recent years), the keyword detection in telephone messages and emails, the monitoring of library books and a number of other surveillance procedures threatening personal privacy (particularly those authorized by the Patriot Act in the post-9/11 United States). While ordinary security devices are viewed as an evolution and an updating of existing surveillance techniques, exceptional procedures have an unprecedented impact on social life. In the United States, the terrorist threat has justified the construction of the US–Mexico border fence, hypothesizing linkages between illegal immigration and terrorism. At the same time, along with the use of increasingly sophisticated technical devices and the deployment of army and police troops across international borders and in sensitive urban sites, state authorities pursue the goal of national security by inviting local communities to play a responsible role in terrorism and crime prevention, with the risk of generating 'do-it-yourself justice' responses (see Figure 4.3, where the police authority praises the benefits of video surveillance as a deterrant against terrorist attacks, encouraging citizens to report any suspicious activity and behaviour).

The described 'emergency' policies have contributed to the furthering of the process of annihilation of public space, which started with the advent of neoliberal urbanism in the United States and other Western countries. In fact, prior to the occurrence of the notorious terrorist attacks at the beginning of the new century, previous years had witnessed a silent but equally effective 'annihilation of space by law' (Mitchell, 1997). The victims of this process of space annihilation have been particularly those surviving on the margins of society – such as beggars

A bomb won't go off here
because weeks before a shopper reported
someone studying the CCTV cameras.

Don't rely on others.
If you suspect it, report it.

Confidential Anti-Terrorist Hotline
Call 0800 789 321

Figure 4.3   Involvement of local population in terrorism prevention in United Kingdom

Source: http://www.dorset.police.uk (accessed June 2010)

and homeless people – regarded as a threat against urban 'civilization'. In the United States, the legislation has particularly concentrated on the homeless: punishing someone for sleeping in public (as municipal ordinances have done in Santa Cruz, California, and in Phoenix, Arizona), a practice that is not 'dangerous' per se, reduces the chances of survival for the homeless, dispossessing them of the space – the public space – in which sleep as a vital function is performed (the homeless having no private space by definition: Blomley, 2004). Another example is related to the marginal practice of urinating on the street: punishing the act of street urination without providing public restrooms is consistent with the rise of a biopolitical order willing to purify the urban public space (Brown, 2009), by removing the homeless and all those that escape sanitary control from the street. It should be noted also that the purification and the annihilation of public space is pursued not only through state law and municipal ordinances, but also by making recourse to sophisticated, apparently unpolitical technical tools such as those of urban design and planning. Steven Flusty (1997) has provided a variety of examples throwing light on the dark side of urban design practices: park benches that cannot be used as sleeping places; automatic irrigation systems suddenly turning on so as to discourage the homeless from sleeping in public places; public restrooms located in shopping malls that only customers can use. These planning regulations and design techniques are illustrative of a 'micro-politics of pre-emption' which has the effect of transfiguring the public character of urban spaces, paving the way for a regime of informal privatization and unaccountable surveillance.

Broadly speaking, the transfiguration of public space is a distinguishing feature of the neoliberal city. Under conditions of neoliberal urbanism, there is not only a reduction of public space in terms of physical size and opportunities for free access, but city dwellers increasingly rely on privately owned spaces for socialization and interaction. In Western cities, for instance, the use of chain cafés like Starbucks as places of encounter, relaxation and reflection has become customary, while in the past these activities were conducted in open public spaces (typically, the Italian piazza) or in locally owned café shops (such as those analysed by Jürgen Habermas in his influential account of the rise of the bourgeois public sphere during the nineteenth century in Europe: Habermas, 1962). Contemporary café chains owned by multinational companies are inclined to adopt policies of selective admission (getting rid of unwanted customers), to impose strict rules of behaviour, to obsessively propagate advertisement messages and at the same to forbid those containing political content. It is, therefore, at least dubious to consider the time spent in a café like Starbucks or in a shopping mall as a truly public, democratic, convivial experience, and the fact that these spaces are generally perceived as public places demonstrates that social consciousness is infused with neoliberal values of privatization and commodification (MacLeod, 2002). Moreover, the variety of planning regulations and design practices undermining the vitality of urban life and generating feelings of fear and persecution ('is the person walking behind me a terrorist?') throw light on the pervasive governmentalization of the urban experience in the context of advanced neoliberalism. In an age of turbulent globalization and fluctuating geopolitical order, neoliberal governmentality, and the underlying disciplinary regime, draws on the conviction that governing elites are entitled to control and monitor whatever is being done or said for the sake of national security, even beyond existing constitutional principles.

In this context, albeit officially conflicting, the effects of 'global' terrorism on public space complement those generated by the processes of societal government. On the one hand, terrorist groups take advantage of the described 'politics of fear', which contributes to popularizing the effects of their actions, including those less spectacular and even those bound to fail. On the other hand, these groups are able to exploit communication and transportation technologies (Luke, 2004). An intrinsically 'open' transportation system like that of air transportation can be manipulated and turned into a weapon of mass destruction, as happened in New York on 11 September 2001, with effects immediately resonating across the globe thanks to the instantaneous circulation of the information allowed by contemporary communication technologies. Terrorists opportunistically mobilize whatever technologies and socio-economic resources at their disposal: the Internet, world finance, civic and religious associations, and the tourist industry can be instrumental in pursuing terror strategies. This leads to a distorted political use of communication technologies, civil infrastructures and socio-economic institutions, undermining important foundations of city life. In this context, urban settings are central not only to the enactment of neoliberal techniques of social control and moral regulation, but also to the experimentation with symbolic and material strategies of terror.

In the last instance, the ambivalent politics of fear that has been described in this section has the effect of obfuscating the role of protest movements, questioning the legitimacy of their presence within the urban public sphere (Graham, 2006). Social movements opposing environmentally unsustainable infrastructural projects (such as the planned high-speed rail line between Turin in Italy and Lyon in France) or contesting the summits of undemocratic international organizations such as the G8 and the WTO are said to be fertile ground for terrorist propaganda (Warren, 2004). In belligerent areas, the label 'terrorism' is used to describe also armed liberation movements. In Baghdad and other cities in Iraq, an armed uprising took place in May 2003, when the occupying forces announced the official end of the military operations (and the transition to a state of 'peace'). The attacks organized by the armed civilians were presented by the Bush Administration in terms of guerrilla terrorist actions, in an attempt to discredit the resistance movement, despite the fact that the attacks were explicitly directed against military targets (also because within an occupied country there are no foreign civilians that can be identified as targets).

4.5 Cities at war/the war against cities

The concluding observation in the previous section drives us to deal with the purest manifestation of urban geopolitics, one in which cities are explicit theatres of war, albeit in varied and even contradictory forms. As already said, the age of globalization witnesses, on the one hand, the proliferation of a wide range of low-intensity conflicts taking place at the urban scale (youth gangs, terrorist groups, inter-ethnic tensions, slum riots, commonly represented and dealt with in military terms) but, on the other hand, it also reproduces the historical role of cities as key sites and crucial targets for conventional wars. Historically, control of cities has been vital to military success, as proved by common phrases such as 'the fall of Paris' and 'the siege of Berlin'. Today, the intimate link between cities and wars becomes even stronger. Urban spaces are exposed to forces of destruction and physical annihilation that are more intense than ever. There is no fortification protecting cities from the 'new invaders', while war instruments like guided-missile cruisers or biological and chemical 'weapons of mass destruction' (whose presumed but unproven possession has been used as a pretext for the invasion of Iraq by the US army and its allied countries) expose cities to unpredictable dangers which in the twentieth century were confined to exceptional circumstances (such as the atomic bombing of Hiroshima and Nagasaki at the end of the Second World War) (Bishop and Clancey, 2004).

In recent years, the relationship between cities and war has been 'normalized' so as to make the violence of military operations more acceptable. In areas of endemic conflict, the loss of innocent lives and the destruction of homes, factories and civilian infrastructures (schools, hospitals, etc.) are portrayed as 'accidental events' and 'side effects', caused by technical errors (like the misleading information provided by satellite maps). In their reports on the 'global war against terrorism', mainstream mass media avoid specifying that a cruise missile in Kabul or Baghdad is hitting an urban environment that has been already affected by previous attacks, with dilapidated buildings and a traumatized local population (Gregory, 2006b). In addition, the fact that military operations become increasingly deterritorialized – with the use of guided missiles and other technological devices (such as the Predator aircraft) allowing members of armed forces to keep physical distance from war targets – is at the origin of the 'inhumanization of war', which makes the experience of war similar to that of a virtual game.

Obviously, military conflicts are not confined to urbanized areas. There are several examples of acts of war against rural population during the modern and contemporary ages, as happened with the devastation of the Chinese countryside perpetrated by the Japanese army, with the Nazis' invasion of the Russian rural regions, or with the US bombing of the Vietnamese countryside in the attempt to defeat the resistance in Ho Chi Minh (at the time known as Saigon). However, the destruction of cities, of their human capital and of their built environment and iconic monuments, is key to the annihilation of the enemy. In recent years, the emphasis placed on the inextricable link between cities and war has led urban scholars to use the notion of 'urbicide' (originally advanced by Marshall Berman, 1996), referring to the deliberate destruction of the built environment by belligerent armies and paramilitary groups (Coward, 2009). Shaw (2004) has used this concept in his study dealing with the conflict in Bosnia-Herzegovina in 1992–95: Serbian military and paramilitary forces annihilated not only the Bosnian-Muslims (perpetrating a genocide) but the entire urban community of Sarajevo, suppressing the historically plural, multi-religious and multicultural identity of the city. Urbicide and genocide, therefore, are two facets of the same ferocious reality. On the other hand, however, the notion of genocide is ambivalent and only partly interchangeable with that of urbicide: identified for the first time as a specific type of war crime in the Nuremberg trial of Nazi officials, being understood as an extermination of entire ethno-national and religious communities (such as the Holocaust), the notion of genocide thereby differs from the broader notion of war crime. In light of this commonly held distinction, several commentators believe that the restricted meaning of genocide contributes to downplaying the importance of epochal destructions such as those of Hiroshima and Nagasaki, where mass extermination was not limited to a specific ethno-religious group. It is no surprise, therefore, that such war crimes have never been explicitly stigmatized by international courts and other supranational institutions.

In dealing with urban geopolitics one cannot avoid referring to the permanent Israeli–Palestinian conflict, which has an inevitably strong urban dimension in the context of a small and densely populated territory like that of Israel and the Palestinian Territories. The urban implications of this conflict powerfully emerge by taking into account the implementation of the so-called 'road map': the peace process started in 2002 and supported by the United States, the European Union, the Russian Federation and the United Nations. In the official documentation, the violence of Israeli spatial planning is compared to the brutality of Palestinian terrorism. The text explicitly recommends that Israel should stop the process of planning, construction and enlargement, while dismantling existing settlements in the occupied territories (the Israeli 'colonies'). This position was formulated at the time in which the Israeli government, led by Prime Minister Sharon, was erecting several hundred metres of protective concrete barrier separating Israeli territories from the Palestinian zones, such as the West Bank, giving rise to a de facto apartheid regime justified by reference to objectives of national security and defence (Weizman, 2007). However, prior to this stage of formalized segregation of Palestinian areas, the Israeli state had already laid the material foundations of its politico-territorial hegemony: first, by expanding the colonial settlements, officially in order to decrease the density of Israeli cities, but actually with the effect of enlarging its sphere of influence; second, by building new motorways so as to improve inter-urban transport networks and to provide the military with more efficient infrastructure (Figure 4.4). Therefore, in time of 'peace' the process of spatial planning is the way in which Israel furthers its colonial ambitions, while in time of war the colonial project is pursued through the deliberate destruction of Palestinian settlements, with the use of advanced military aircraft and helicopters (Graham, 2004b). In conclusion, spatial planning and military raids are complementary aspects of urbicide as a geopolitical practice, justified in the name of self-defence and protection against terrorist threats.

Figure 4.4   Israel's security fence in the Palestinian West Bank (2010)

Source: photo © Cristiana Rubatto

BOX 4.3   URBAN FILMS

THE MULTIPLE TRUTHS OF URBAN GEOPOLITICS – *BEIRUT OPEN CITY* (LEBANON, 2008, DIRECTED BY SAMIR HABKI)

Beirut Open City is a 2008 film, set in Beirut during the Syrian occupation of Lebanon in the 1990s, which followed the end of the civil war years (1975–90). The film describes parallel stories taking place in different parts of the city and ending up being increasingly interconnected as the narrative unfolds. On the one side, the film is based on the story of Khaled, a 33-year-old Egyptian photojournalist attempting to make a film about political issues in Lebanon, for which he interviews lay people, insurgents, activists and militiamen. On the other side, the film shows a young man 'accidentally' killed by the bodyguards of an American

(Continued)

(Continued)

ambassador (and filmed by Khaled), and the subsequent act of vengeance perpetrated by members of a local clan.

The title of the film explicitly evokes Roberto Rossellini's *Roma città aperta* (*Rome Open City*), a masterpiece of Italian neo-realism. *Beirut Open City* shares with Rossellini's 1945 film a number of features, most notably the attention being paid to the relationship between the city during wartime and the acts of domination and resistance. Habki's film takes a closer look into the complexity and the contradictions of everyday life and public affairs in Beirut: secular institutions and political parties co-exist with traditional clan lineages and religious politics; the power of pro-Syrian politicians is confronted with that of American diplomats; mass media are corrupt, while city life is permeated by fear, suspicion and ungovernable violence. In other words, the city at the time of the civil war was far from being an 'empty' space; on the contrary, it was a space filled with a number of parallel and conflicting power relationships, in the absence of any kind of truth. In the film the protagonist, willing to 'represent the truth' through his camera – in line with the neo-realist imperative of political denunciation – will suffer the consequences of such an endeavour. In this context, even the identities of the characters acting in such a violent and crowded environment appear to be enigmatic: Khaled himself puzzles over the complexities of Lebanese politics, wondering whether a militiaman differs from a rebel like terrorism differs from resistance.

4.6 Conclusion: the visible and the invisible in urban geopolitics

In the previous section of this chapter, it has been argued that in permanent conflict areas the outcomes of spatial planning strategies are complementary to the destructive effects of military actions. In addition, this chapter has also shown that in geographical areas where there is no explicit conflict of military character planning regulations and surveillance devices, such as those leading to the annihilation of public space in Western cities or to the demolition of slums in cities in the South, are examples of potential 'urbicides'.

Take the latter: the violent and inhuman implications of slum-clearance campaigns are evident. This is the case of the Murambatsvina Operation that was carried out in Zimbabwe in 2005, when President Robert Mugabe launched an initiative aimed to trigger a process of large-scale redevelopment of urban slums, through the forced demolition of unauthorized settlements (homes and urban facilities). The United Nations estimates that 700,000 people were left without homes, while another 2.4 million were affected by the governmental campaign (UN, 2005).

Figure 4.5   The Porta Farm slum, Harare (Zimbabwe), before and after demolition (2002 and 2006)

Source: http://www.aaas.org (accessed May 2010) © Digital Globe

In the advanced capitalist countries, related forms of 'structural violence' arise from the implementation of urban regeneration and housing redevelopment plans, expropriating long-term residents of their livelihood, carried out by making reference to objectives of aesthetic improvement and spatial attractiveness. Even though the differences between the effects of housing redevelopment schemes in the South and in the North are notable, the North–South comparison is not inappropriate, considering that the notion of urbicide was originally proposed by Marshall Berman (1996) with reference to the demolition of derelict housing complexes in the Bronx district in New York City. Along these lines, investigating the politics of urban regeneration in Reading (South of England, UK), Mike Raco (2003) has shown how in the 'revanchist' neoliberal city governmental efforts are concentrated on the 'needs' of property developers and real estate investors, rather than on those of local communities. In this context, the design of aesthetically pleasing, comfortable and safe places brings about an ontologically violent practice: the physical removal of the so-called 'social polluters' (individuals and social groups whose presence is associated with the deterioration of the urban environment: Urry, 1995) and their relocation in other – less visible – areas of the city.

To conclude, this chapter has focused on what is probably the most neglected dimension of urban politics, particularly in mainstream scholarship and public discourse: the socio-spatial relations at the urban scale regulated by violence 'in the last instance'. In doing so, the chapter has tried to demonstrate that drawing a veil over the violence accompanying the building of a socio-spatial order at the urban level, which is only one among several others, has the effect of making this violence invisible, impersonal and naturally given, leading to the delegitimization of democratic dissent. This twofold danger – the normalization of violence and the annihilation of democracy – characterizes the public sphere not only of cities involved in military conflicts, but also of cities in which violence hides in the shadows and sometimes behind the apparent banality of urban-design techniques, neighbourhood-regeneration processes, spatial segregation phenomena and urban-security policies.

Note

1   The 'broken windows' metaphor holds that, if the broken windows (the minor signs of disorder) are not regularly fixed, major problems and disorders will spread across society. This means that those being responsible for minor crimes and acts of deviance, such as prostitutes, the homeless and the beggars, deserve the same treatment as that for those committing serious crimes (Herbert, 2001).

part three

POLITICS AS CONTESTATION

5
Urban Justice: Struggles and Movements

Key Issues and Themes

The field of critical urban studies is deeply concerned with the notion of social justice. Since the 1970s the interest in social justice has been revived by the writings of political thinkers and moral philosophers such as John Rawls, Michael Walzer, Michael Sandel, Iris Marion Young and Amartya Sen.

The spatialization and more specifically the urbanization of the notion of social justice are due to Henri Lefebvre and David Harvey respectively. The former has introduced the path-breaking concept of 'the right to the city', which has prepared the ground for subsequent elaborations on socio-spatial justice. The latter has critically applied philosophical discussions over social justice to the analysis of the contemporary city in a context of advanced capitalism and emerging postmodernism.

Contemporary struggles for social justice are centred on life-related issues such as housing and income, health and the environment. In doing so, they shed light on what can be defined the 'living politics of the city', which can be considered as opposed to the government-led urban biopolitics analysed in Chapter 4.

Struggles and mobilizations around environmental justice are particularly relevant within contemporary urban politics. A critical approach to environmental justice links environmental issues to broader socio-spatial inequalities associated with the capitalist pattern of economic development and socio-spatial organization.

5.1 Introduction: the ethical turn in democratic politics

In many respects, the notion of justice can be viewed as the other side of the coin with regard to the themes with which this book has dealt in the previous chapters: the shift to neoliberalism and its urbanization, the evolution of governmental techniques and practices in late-capitalist societies, the reliance on violence (and its exhibition) as an ordinary way of governing urban social relations in times of globalizing terrorism and allegedly intensified crime. These phenomena can be understood from an alternative point of view, one which looks at the struggles for social justice arising from the power dynamics in contemporary urban politics.

In the past two or three decades, in the context of the neoliberal transformation of capitalist economies and societies, social justice has become a 'hot' topic within public and scholarly debates. On the one hand, ultraliberal thinkers have questioned the idea itself of social justice, for being prey to vested interests of organized actors (such as the labour unions) and political lobbies (Hayek, 1978). On the other hand, the exponents of progressive political and intellectual movements, particularly those advocating liberal and post-socialist positions, such as the feminist theorists in the United States, have looked with renewed enthusiasm at the notion of social justice, after the disillusionment that followed the collapse and the discredit of 'real' socialism as well as the crisis of class consciousness that had forged political and social conflict in the twentieth century (Brown, 2001).

On the progressive side of the political–intellectual spectrum, some authors have expressed scepticism about the notion of social justice, arguing that the political and intellectual relevance acquired by ethical and moral values fostering the ideal of social justice is symptomatic of the broader 'post-political' condition characterizing advanced liberal societies. For example, political theorist Chantal Mouffe (2005) has observed that contrasting positions within public debates are no longer defined along the lines of the right/left dichotomy and of class dualism, but on the basis of what is presumed to be 'right' and 'wrong'. The political, Mouffe concludes, is increasingly incorporated into the ethical-moral realm, losing its ambition to radically transform existing socio-economic relationships. Other left-leaning writers, however, such as David Harvey, while advocating resolutely Marxist positions, have recognized the relevance of social justice as a 'practice' and as a 'discourse'. Harvey particularly emphasizes the importance of social justice as a powerful discourse capable of mobilizing political action (Harvey, 1996).

Broadly speaking, apart from the reservations of some authors, there is no doubt that there is revived interest in the notion of social justice within the progressive field. This notion is intended to challenge the hegemony acquired in the last decades by values reflecting the markedly individualistic ethics prevailing in contemporary societies, such as the utilitarian approach to inter-personal relations, the entrepreneurialization of administrative and political agency, the increased competition not only at the economic level but also in the realm of social and cultural activities. At a more practical level, as Harvey has pointed out, social justice discourse plays an important role in the mobilization of contemporary social movements and political organizations: from the new generation of liberation movements in the South (such as the *Ejército Zapatista de Liberación Nacional* in the Mexican state of Chiapas, with its slogan '*democracia, justicia y libertad*') to the transnational networks of 'anti-globalization' associations and movements, and from the opinion campaigns advocating the rights of cultural and religious minorities (the Tibetans, the Kurds, the Palestinians, etc.) to the urban struggles for social rights and services (housing, employment and wages, health care) and for a different relationship with the environment. In some countries, recent years have also witnessed – particularly in Western Europe and Latin America – the rise or the revival of leftist parties, sometimes even taking part in government coalitions, which have used social justice as a catchword in their political discourse: from *Die Linke* in Germany and the *Socialistische Partij* in The Netherlands to the neo-Bolivarian indigenist parties that have taken the lead in the national governments of Venezuela and Bolivia.

As the next section of this chapter will show, the theoretical debate dealing with the notion of justice within the liberal and progressive fields reflects the heterogeneity of positions that this ideal brings together, ranging from the foundational distributive approaches (drawing inspiration from the path-breaking work of John Rawls) to subsequent theorizations emphasizing the practical and self-reflective potential of social justice as a discursive terrain for a variety of social movements arising from the postmodern and post-Fordist transition: most notably, the contributions of Iris Marion Young and of David Harvey, which are theoretically differentiated but in many respects politically contiguous. The latter theoretical sensibility has brought an increased awareness of social justice as an inherently 'localized' and contingent value, firmly embedded in the institutions and spaces of everyday life. In this context, cities are portrayed as rich condensations of social experiences, spatio-temporal dimensions and related political arenas (Amin and Graham, 1997) and therefore as crucial sites where rights are claimed and social and environmental injustices are denounced. The urbanization of (in)justice, stressed by several authors in recent years (Merrifield and Swyngedouw, 1996; Mitchell, 2003; Nicholls and Beaumont, 2004), is not just a theoretical-conceptual construction or a political-ideological proposition, but it is a thesis supported by empirical evidence: even though rural spaces have witnessed the rise or the resurgence of important social movements, in the North but especially in the South of the world, cities and metropolitan areas – also as a consequence of their renewed centrality acquired in an era of globalization – have even expanded their historical role as spaces dedicated to democratic and egalitarian politics. The struggles over social justice, therefore, offer an exemplification of the egalitarian and democratic thrust of urban politics in times of globalization, postmodernity and neoliberalism. Moreover, in concentrating on life-related issues, such struggles are manifestation of what will be defined the 'living politics of the city', which can be considered as opposed to the government-led urban biopolitics analysed in Chapter 5.

5.2 Social justice in question: equality, recognition, domination

In the last thirty or forty years, the perceived loss of the well-being achieved during the expansive stage of post-war capitalism has sparked lively debates on the notion of social justice. Pioneering contributions to this debate have originated in the intersected domains of moral, legal and political philosophical studies, but a number of human and social sciences have also contributed to the discussion by applying ideas and concepts to specialized fields of enquiry: from heterodox economics and social theory to human geography and the cognate socio-spatial disciplines.

The starting point of this debate is the publication of *A Theory of Justice* by John Rawls in 1971. This ambitious book was intended to offer a 'theory of justice' capable of bringing together the ideal of social contract with that of individual freedom. Rawls's attempt was noteworthy, considering the fact that in orthodox liberalism the notion of freedom is at unease with a unitary conception of society. As it has been already pointed out (Chapter 3), the so-called 'classical' liberalism (from Locke and Hume to John Stuart Mill) builds on the assumption that economic and social well-being is optimized when individuals are enabled to freely pursue their own interests, provided that their actions do not limit the freedom of other individuals. A leading exponent of contemporary orthodox liberalism is the already mentioned Friedrich von Hayek, who alerted readers to the dangers associated with the commonly held notion of social justice in limiting the development of what he defined – along with other 'pure' liberal thinkers of the last century, such as the great philosopher of science Karl Popper – 'Open Society', as opposed to the 'Big Government' advocated by socialists and other proponents of state-led socio-economic regulation (Hayek, 1978).[1]

As an attempt to reconcile individual freedom and societal well-being, Rawls's work distinguishes itself from 'classical' as well as from coeval orthodox liberal positions. The idea of social contract, which he places at the centre of his theory, is drawn from the contractualist tradition tracing its origins back to the Enlightenment era (from the aforementioned Locke to Rousseau and Kant). Like Enlightened philosophers who postulated the existence of a 'state of nature', Rawls begins the illustration of his theses by presupposing the existence of an 'original position' preceding the constitution of society. Building on this abstract point of view, he contends that the recognition of basic freedoms (of association, vote, property) is preliminary to the objective of reducing inequalities of status and wealth. On the basis of this assumption, Rawls argues that advocates of social justice should be committed to reconciling individual freedom with an equality of opportunities and the reduction of status and economic disparities. This objective is to be achieved through a just distribution not only of quantifiable goods (such as the income, first of all), but also of immaterial endowments (rights, powers, opportunities). In the subsequent years, the derived notion of 'distributive justice' has come to represent a key concept within contemporary reflections on justice in political and moral philosophy.

Reinterpreting Rawls's theory from a pluralistic perspective, Michael Walzer (1983) has identified the principles of 'free exchange', 'merit' and 'need' as leading criteria (at one and the same time contradictory and complementary to each other) for the redistribution of goods and immaterial endowments in a variety of societal spheres, each one being characterized by different and to some extent alternative rationalities. For instance, the principle of 'merit' is suited to the selection of quali-fied and talented individuals, but is not suited to the evaluation of the agency of those belonging to the lowest social strata, such as the poor, for whom the principle of 'need' is the most appropriate in social justice terms. The pluralistic rereading of Rawls's theory of justice has been accompanied, within the philosophical debate, by its neo-communitarian reformulation. A leading exponent of the latter strand of thinking is Michael Sandel (1982) who has reconnected the theory of justice and the related demand for the recognition of individual rights to the values and moral imperatives of communities. However, beyond the intentions of Sandel and other progressive interpreters of communitarianism, communitarian discourse has served to legitimize not only community-based claims of citizenship and participation founded on ideals of solidarity and cooperation, but also 'inimical' social practices and public policies, pursued in the name of self-defence (see Chapter 4). Owing to this intrinsic ambivalence, communitarian arguments are frequently mobilized within the framework of conservative or even reactionary appropriations of social justice as a political catchword, justifying social practices and public policies that are in stark contrast to the conventionally democratic-egalitarian character of social-justice discourse.

In the late 1980s, the harmonious dialectic that had taken shape within the debate over social justice amongst liberal thinkers in their various articulations (contractu-alists, pluralists, communitarians) was broken by the emerging political theorizations of the so-called post-structuralist feminism. The work of Iris Marion Young (1990), particularly the book entitled *Justice and the Politics of Difference*, has been notably influential in this respect. Even though Young shares with Rawls and his pluralistic followers the emphasis on difference, in her view injustice does not arise from dis-tributive disparities, as Rawls and Walzer believe, but from relations of 'domination' preventing those socially and politically weaker from participating and spelling out their claims in the public sphere. To Young, the distributive approach to social justice is inappropriate when it comes to redistributing immaterial endowments, particu-larly those relating to the rights and the entitlements of the less powerful. From this standpoint, attention should be drawn – Young argues – to the 'institutional context' regulating societal domains (the labour market, the family, the political system), most notably to decision-making processes and the regulation of power relations. In her view, public policies should be committed to dynamically adapting institutional processes and regulations to constantly changing social conditions and relations. For this reason, Young rejects an abstract and formalistic approach to social justice (as in the mainstream liberal-pluralistic tradition inspired by Rawls). Rather, critical theory should advocate a genuinely political view of justice-related issues, one that pays attention to the everyday demands for the recognition of difference and the democratic inclusion of the disadvantaged groups within the public sphere (see also Young, 2000).

In her analysis, Young ideally refers to the experience of the 'new left' in the 1960s and the 1970s: the movements of workers and the unemployed, those for the environment, as well as those advocating the rights of African-American and Hispanic communities, of women, homosexuals, the disabled and other disadvantaged groups under conditions of oppression and marginalization. Far from demanding an identity-based legitimization of disadvantaged groups, as communitarians do, in Young's view the politics of difference transgresses pre-fixed identities by nurturing practices of dialogue and social interaction among unevenly empowered subjects. In this context, urban life appears to be a fertile ground for the development of a 'politics of difference'. Unlike rural and suburban spaces, characterized by social homogeneity and political stability, the disorderly character of urban life has the potential for achieving a social order based on the principle of 'being together of strangers' (Young, 1990, p. 237): a situation of coexistence and respect among strangers in which individuals and social groups are motivated to transgress their respective senses of belonging. However, according to Young, three obstacles are put in the way of the attaining of such a goal in contemporary capitalist societies: first, the financial power of large firms, from which municipalities derive the majority of their revenues; second, the dynamics of decision-making in local administrations favouring elite interests; finally, the residential segregation of disadvantaged minority groups (Young, 1990).

Alongside important differences, Young's analysis has affinities with David Harvey's critical appraisal of the 'liberal theses' on social justice which he published in 1973, just two years after the publication of *A Theory of Justice*. In *Social Justice and the City* David Harvey, at the time an emerging exponent of the new 'radical geography', built a theoretical framework which reflected the political tensions of the 1970s in the United States and Western Europe, but also in more peripheral countries of Latin America, Africa and Asia. Having appeared amidst a decade of political and intellectual turmoil, the book underlined the relationship between the distribution of power and the dynamics of wealth production in advanced capitalist societies, linking social-justice issues to the contradictions of capital accumulation. In doing so, Harvey offered an understanding of social justice which considered the role of the capitalist mode of production, an aspect overlooked not only within foundational theorizations of social justice but also within pluralistic reformulations and feminist critiques.

In a subsequent book entitled *Justice, Nature and the Geography of Difference*, Harvey has examined the reasons behind this lacuna (Harvey, 1996). After the publication of the highly successful *The Condition of Postmodernity*, Harvey's contribution to the understanding of the economic and cultural consequences of postmodernity was highly distinguished, being recognized as a milestone in contemporary social and human sciences. His interpretation of the postmodern condition is founded on a renewed version of historical-geographical materialism, which he subsequently uses as a basis for the appraisal of contemporary theorizations of social justice, particularly those of poststructuralist feminists. Far from misrecognizing the relevance of social justice as a philosophical horizon and public discourse within progressive politics and scholarship, Harvey's contribution to the discussion is intended to reassert class-consciousness's relative primacy over those senses of belonging (gender, ethnicity, age) that are at the centre of post-structuralist theorizations of postmodern societies. In doing so, Harvey creatively reformulates Marxian dialectic materialism, appropriating postmodern notions of 'positionality' and 'situatedness', which allow him to reconceptualize class-consciousness as a multidimensional, context-specific sense of belonging. From this standpoint, also the theme of 'environmental justice' – Harvey's main objective in his reappraisal of social justice discourse – should be understood in class and anti-capitalist terms, because those being more affected by processes of environmental degradation are low-income countries and the lower social classes. In fact, while the advanced capitalist countries have saturated their environmental carrying capacity, the poor countries are treated like 'the wasteland of the world', on the basis of a cynical principle of 'redistribution' of wastes (including toxic ones), accommodating the interests of the powerful countries and being more or less overtly advocated even by high officials of international organizations, such as the World Bank's chief economist Larry Summers in the early 1990s (id.). The other victims of environmental degradation processes are the lower classes, in the North and in the South of the world, who are more likely to reside near contaminated sites or in areas that are more vulnerable to the effects of extreme 'natural' events, such as earthquakes and floods (as has happened in New Orleans first with Hurricane Katrina in 2005 and then with the oil contamination of the marine environment in 2010: see Box 5.2, pp. 153–4).

Even though Harvey's book was strongly criticized by the feminists for hastily dismissing the importance of gender and other socio-cultural senses of belonging in reasserting the relative primacy of class consciousness (McDowell, 1998), he has had the undoubted merit of having integrated environmental issues into debates on social justice, linking the critique of ecological degradation to the contradictions of capitalism; a view of environmental issues which at the time was still marginal in the academic discussion but had been already embraced by several social movements mobilizing for environmental justice across the world. The dichotomy that has characterized the debate within the academic and political left – between those laying emphasis on the recognition of the diversity of subjective positionalities, like Young and other radical feminists, and those focusing on issues of wealth and power redistribution, like Harvey from a Marxian perspective and Rawls and the pluralists from a liberal perspective – has been critically addressed by philosopher Nancy Fraser (1997) who has tried to offer a reunified critical stance toward social justice. In doing so, she has argued that the conflicting dimensions of recognition and redistribution are to be reconciled in novel ways through the lens of transformative thinking. According to Fraser, the distributive thesis should be reframed against the background of a political strategy aiming at modifying social relations under capitalism, while those advocating a politics of recognition should be critical of the senses of belonging received from mainstream society, destabilizing established divisions between social groups and formations.

In the light of this debate, the following sections of this chapter will show how the variety of positions coexisting within the academic debate on social justice are reflected into the experiences of social-justice movements in contemporary cities.

5.3 Rights to the city

The first author to offer explicitly spatial reflections on social justice was Bleddyn Davies (in particular in his work published in 1968, in which he coined the notion of 'territorial justice') within the framework of a critical evaluation of welfare services in Great Britain. However, it is only after the publication of Harvey's work in the 1970s that the notion of socio-spatial justice has received a more systematic theorization, acquiring substantial relevance within the agenda of radical geography studies. Having abandoned the deductive and formalistic theoretical models inspiring his previous work in the 1960s, Harvey came to terms with the political and philosophical thought of that time, opting in particular for the neo-Marxist positions. As already anticipated in the previous section and more accurately illustrated in Chapter 3 of this book, in Harvey's view the dynamics of the capitalist mode of production, particularly in relation to the financial and the housing sectors, are central to the production and reproduction of socio-spatial inequalities and, therefore, to the urban politics of social justice (Harvey, 1973).

Along with *Social Justice and the City*, an essential reference within the debates on socio-spatial justice is the work of Henri Lefebvre, a pioneering contributor to the critical theory of social space and a major source of inspiration for a number of important theorizations and strands of research in this field. Whereas Harvey and other Marxists have called attention to the role of structural factors, Lefebvre's concept of the 'right to the city' (Lefebvre, 1968) has shed light on the subjective-relational dimension within the dynamics of space production at the urban scale: city dwellers (rather than citizens conventionally identified within the boundaries of the nation-state) give rise to struggles claiming the right to urban life and the primacy of the 'use value' over the 'exchange value' of urban spaces. It should be noted that by 'space' Lefebvre referred not only to the material space (i.e. the built environment), but also to its metaphorical, immaterial and programmatic dimension (Lefebvre, 1974). The production of urban space, therefore, does not imply merely the modification of the fabric of the city, but also the generation of broader, multi-dimensional socio-spatial relations. For instance, the localization of an industrial plant or of an infrastructure mobilizes a variegated set of socio-spatial relations linked to material, social and symbolic factors, altogether constituting the 'political' dimension of the urban process (Purcell, 2003; McFarlane and Rutherford, 2008). In this vein, the notion of the 'right to the city' underlies the possibility of autonomous space production within and beyond the horizon of the capitalist imperative of socio-spatial organization and economic development.

In reviving the Marxian dichotomy between use value and exchange value, Lefebvre's notion of the 'right to the city' was intended to restore the primacy of the use value as a way of envisioning an egalitarian, post-capitalist society. This means that the ownership of the means of production or of urban land does not entail the freedom to act by the capitalist class. It is not acceptable that landlords and manufacturers freely decide to demolish an obsolete building or to close an unproductive factory. In Lefebvre's view, these decisions have such an impact on the lives of city dwellers that the latter should have a voice in these matters, playing a part in the formulation of planning and policy strategies. In terms of urban social justice, rather than denying the legitimacy of private property, this implies asserting the basic principle that private interests should not undermine general well-being.

The conceptual perspective that has just been briefly outlined looks at the role of contentious movements contesting urban-restructuring plans that appear to be socially discriminatory, such as those leading to the gentrification of inner-city neighbourhoods and working class areas. Gentrification is the phenomenon occurring when long-term residents are forced or induced by market mechanisms to relocate, following the demolishing of obsolete housing complexes, the subsequent reconstruction of attractive residential lots and the related rise of house prices, both to buy and to rent, in neighbourhoods undergoing processes of urban regeneration and real-estate revitalization. The relocation of long-term residents is normally followed by the social upgrading of the neighbourhood, with the influx of new inhabitants belonging to the middle-upper classes (Lees et al., 2008). The notion of gentrification was coined in the 1960s with reference to the social ascent of neighbourhoods in central London, but this phenomenon was not new in the history of the capitalist city, being experienced already in the nineteenth century, for instance at the time of the demolition and reconstruction plans ordered by Prefect Baron Hausmann in the historic neighbourhoods of Paris, in which riots and popular insurgencies frequently originated (Harvey, 2003). Albeit historically associated with the evolutionary dynamics of the capitalist city, processes of gentrification have been intensifying in the era of globalization and urban neoliberalism, as the imperative of economic growth has replaced that of wealth redistribution prevailing in the Keynesian era (N. Smith, 1996; Cameron, 2003).

Figure 5.1   Struggles against gentrification in Dalston, London

Source: http://www.autonomousgeographies.org (accessed June 2010) © Jenny Pickerill

Another factor behind the expansion of gentrification processes is the 'cultural-ization' of the urban public sphere, starting with its more radical and transgres-sive expressions and then being subsumed within the circuits of capital accumulation (see Chapter 2). The triumph of gentrification, at the same time, has revived neighbourhood-based struggles over housing issues: the 'right to stay put' (the right to not be removed from the long-term place of residence), vig-orously claimed by social movements and community organizations resisting evictions and foreclosures in global cities such as New York and London where land rent is most profitable, can be understood as the materialization of the Lefebvrian ideal of the 'right to the city' (Newman and Wyly, 2006). In recent years, a larger number of cities across the United States and Western Europe alike have witnessed the rise of anti-eviction campaigns as a response to the effects of the residential mortgage default of 2007–08, which has led to the execution of countless foreclosures particularly affecting members of ethnic minorities and socially excluded groups (cf. Chapter 3).

5.3.1 The living politics of the city: democratic challenges and enigmas

As already said, the recognition of the 'right to the city' as a fundamental principle of social justice presupposes that urban dwellers are given a voice in the decisions concerning not just the production and transformation of urban spaces, but their actual lives, being these decisions concerned with the foundations of human life such as health, housing and also the living income, as we shall see. The notion of the 'the right to the city' thus acquires renewed relevance as an example of the 'living politics of the city' (Patel, 2010), but it also becomes more enigmatic owing to ongoing processes of deterritorialization. On the one hand, real-estate projects and broader initiatives of urban renewal are increasingly managed by economic and political agents that are autonomous from the conventional spaces of territorial government (the nation-state, the local state, etc.), such as international organizations and transnational firms. In places strongly connected to the networks and flows of the world economy, such as the global cities, the sources of legitimacy pertaining to hegemonic economic-political actors are undecipherable by definition. On the other hand, also the identity of subaltern actors claiming social justice and citizenship rights, such as international migrants and ethnic minorities, whose contribution is vital to urban economies in times of globalization, is constitutively uncertain, being nurtured by multidimensional, fluid allegiances (Sassen, 1996a; Isin, 2000; Purcell, 2003; see Chapter 6).

The deterritorialization of societal government (or the government of societies 'at a distance': Rose, 1999) takes place in an era characterized by an expansion of the power to control and regulate human bodies and lives, a phenomenon widely known as 'biopolitics'. In this context, the health and the biological profile of city dwellers are subjected to multiscalar processes of government and regulation. The governmentalization of health and the related discourses on biosecurity, however, engender a variety of responses at the grassroots level: from the demands of social justice raised by queer groups mobilizing around the rights of AIDS patients in the 1980s and the 1990s (Highleyman, 2002; see also Chapter 6 on sexual citizenship) to the community responses to pandemic alarms such as the SARS and the avian flu, dealing with institutional failures in the management of the states of emergency (Ali and Keil, 2008). In the face of such growing concern about urban biopolitics and the implications for social justice, there are a number of unresolved questions. What are the prerogatives of local and state governments as regards the management of 'global' emergencies? To what extent can 'the right to the city' be applied to these 'states of emergency'? Finally, who is entitled to address life-related issues in a context of spatially stretched decision-making processes and of increasingly globalized socio-environmental phenomena?

Whereas biopolitical issues are still enigmatic in terms of social justice, urban movements focusing on income issues are oriented towards a more conventionally egalitarian approach to social justice. An interesting example in this regard is that of the 'living wage' campaigns conducted in the United States and in Europe by coalitions of labour unions, social activists and faith-based grassroots organizations (the living wage is a monetary compensation given by the government to low-income individuals who are jobless or employed on a casual basis; see also Box 5.1). The urban dimension of living-wage campaigns is twofold: first, the actors forming a coalition taking the lead in the campaign mutually recognize on the basis of the sharing of common urban experience; second, living-wage campaigns identify local governments as key interlocutors, rather than the employers or state governments, as happens in conventional workers' struggles. In the United States, the living-wage movement took shape in the early 1990s, achieving political recognition and even concrete results in the form of municipal ordinances for the living wage that were approved in 22 medium- and large-sized municipalities (the first was Baltimore in 1993, followed by Minneapolis, San Francisco, New York and Los Angeles, amongst others). The positive responses at the municipal level, with the allocation of public funds for the living wage, have followed in the wake of the pressure exerted by the campaigners on local governments. According to some commentators, the success of these campaigns brings light on a resurging redistributive approach to urban policy (Martin, 2001), contrary to the commonly held view (see in Chapter 3 Peterson's theorization of 'city limits') that local administrations are inevitably oriented towards the promotion of economic growth, rather than of redistribution, because their fiscal base depends upon the attraction of economic investors.

Struggles for social justice, therefore, touch on crucial aspects of the process of social reproduction in capitalist cities, such as housing, the income and increasingly also issues of health and 'biosecurity', giving shape to what has been defined the 'living politics of the city'. As Mark Purcell (2008) points out, grassroots movements – rather than offering policy solutions, a task pertaining to local, regional and national governments – have the ability to revitalize urban democratic politics, bringing social justice claims back into institutional processes largely influenced by the interests of politico-economic elites.

BOX 5.1   URBAN FILMS

MIGRANT WORKERS AND UNION STRUGGLES IN THE POST-METROPOLIS – *BREAD AND ROSES* (USA/EU, 2000, DIRECTED BY KEN LOACH)

Ken Loach is a director who became widely known for his films depicting the difficult lives of working-class people in a neoliberal society, particularly in Great

Britain after the Thatcher era (*Raining Stones* and *Riff Raff* being the most famous). *Bread and Roses* (the title draws on a famous slogan originally coined for a textile strike in Massachusetts in 1913) was his first film set in the United States during the Reagan Administration. The film fictionalizes the early stages of the 'Justice for Janitors' campaign in Los Angeles in the late 1980s, a social movement fighting for the rights of cleaners and caretakers across the US and Canada, which was started in 1985 in response to the low wages and minimal health-care coverage in this highly deregulated sector (see Aguiar and Herod, 2006).

The film narrates the vicissitudes of Maya, a young illegal immigrant who risks being raped by one of the men who led her across the border (the so-called *coyotes*) at her arrival in the United States. In Los Angeles, Maya meets her sister Rosa, working as a cleaner in a huge office building. Rosa's life is difficult: her husband is no longer able to work because of diabetes, while the service firm employing her (Angel Cleaning Services) does not provide any health insurance. Maya joins her sister in the company, quickly realizing the number of injustices and harassments that immigrants have to suffer in the workplace. However, the encounter with Sam, a young union organizer, urges Maya and other janitors to fight for fair wages and dignified conditions. The film shows the difficulties in organizing the campaigns, the employer retaliation against the unionized workers, as well as the internal conflicts among the janitors.

The city of Los Angeles – widely portrayed as the archetype of contemporary post-Fordist and postmodern urbanism (see Soja, 2000) – is a perfect venue for this film. With an ever-growing community of Hispanics (44.4 per cent of the entire population in 2008: see Brookings Institute, 2010), the Los Angeles experience points to the ways in which the self-organized struggles of an increasingly multinational and casualized workforce compensate, on the one hand, for the limits of mainstream unionism and, on the other hand, for those of national regulations unable to ensure decent working conditions. *Bread and Roses* shows, however, that those taking the lead of union campaigns have to face threats and intimidation, often received in subtle ways, as happens to Sam when he is scolded by his boss, who suggests him identifying 'easier targets', arguing that the fight against Angel Cleaning Services is not a good strategy in terms of career development. Moreover, in his speeches Sam reveals a close linkage of the union with the Democratic Party, resulting in a limitation of the union's political autonomy. Despite these limits and threats, Ken Loach's message is clear: the deprived condition of marginal workers should be addressed not through irrational actions (Maya's act of stealing has a tragic end, forcing her to return to her country of origin), but through political engagement and labour-union organizing.

(Continued)

(Continued)

The urban space plays a highly symbolic role in the story. As pointed out by Fojas (2007), at the beginning of the film Maya is forced out of a plaza by security guards, but in the concluding scenes she and her colleagues have occupied the same plaza. The appropriation of urban space is key to the workers' strategy aimed at gaining public attention, but at the same time the city is also an alienating space for migrant workers, one in which subaltern 'minorities' like the Latinos (who are the largest ethnic group in Los Angeles) have to celebrate their traditions and emphasize their sense of community belonging in order to acquire visibility.

5.4 Justice movements: limits and potentialities

Historically, cities have been venues for protest and contentious movements 'from below'. In this sense, cities are institutionally 'thick' (see Amin and Thrift, 1995), in terms of associative experiences, collective memory of struggles and protests, and existing formal and informal networks in which a wide range of minorities, social groups and organizations become involved. This multifaceted repertoire of subjectivities, associational processes and collective movements constitutes an institutional 'potential' producing an experience of the urban public sphere as a 'common place' bringing together singularities of different origin (Negri, 2008) see also Section 6.5. Through their 'presence' and 'co-presence' in the public sphere (see Chapter 6 on the 'politics of presence') urban singularities give rise to a variegated set of 'publics' and 'counterpublics', the latter being the manifestation of 'constituent forces' incessantly reviving the idea and the practice of democracy – democracy being understood not just as a 'governmental form' but as a process of permanent experimentation led by subaltern groups (Negri, 1992; Fraser, 1995b).

The perspective on urban democracy that has just been outlined has commonalities with Young's conceptualization of the public sphere as a place of 'coexistence amongst strangers', but it also differentiates from the latter for the emphasis placed on cities as loci of production of subjectivities and institutions that are autonomous from the established authorities. In order to fully appreciate the institutional 'potential' of social justice movements, it is worth analysing in greater detail their profile, the dynamics of claim-making arising from their presence in the public sphere, as well as the ways in which they are commonly represented by the wider public. This analysis allows us to critically evaluate an understanding of cities as 'common places' interconnecting a multiplicity of singularities.

In the 1970s, Manuel Castells was the first social scientist to offer a systematic and theoretically informed examination of grassroots movements from an urban perspective. In his noted book on the 'urban question', at the time welcomed as a foundational Marxist theorization of the urban process under capitalist conditions, Castells related the development of social movements in late-capitalist societies to the expansion of collective consumption and to the consequent increase in government spending (Castells, 1972). In the remainder of his career, having left aside this conceptual perspective as a consequence of his own abandonment of Marxist structuralism as well as of broader historical circumstances (the crisis of the Keynesian mode of regulation), Castells first scrutinized the socio-cultural and organizational traits of urban movements in the capitalist city (Castells, 1983); then, he threw light on the qualitative shift towards identity-based dynamics of mobilization, in the context of the transition to the so-called 'informational society' (Castells, 1997; cf. Rossi, 2010a).

Even though in his more recent work Castells has correctly emphasized the importance of the cultural-informational turn in re-shaping the forms of collective action, an identity-centred explanation of social movements is only partially acceptable. The next chapter will explore the phenomenon of citizenship movements under the rubric of 'politics of presence', which is only partly driven by identity-based factors of belonging. This analysis will show that urban movements can be committed to transgressing conventional identities, even those of minority groups, struggling over a multidimensional urban citizenship that exceeds the conventional limits of the nation-state and its legitimate institutions but also those of their groups and communities of affiliation. However, there is no doubt that there are movements whose motivations arise from the discrimination of positionalities variously based on ethnicity, gender and sex, while there are other movements developing around issues that are independent from such positionalities. The previously analysed movements mobilizing around living wage campaigns and for 'the right to stay put' are examples of urban social movements that cannot be associated with any specific group and community. On the other hand, other justice movements – such as that of homosexuals struggling for the rights of AIDS patients – are intimately linked to group-based allegiances.

Moreover, it is not only the social profile of grassroots movements to be diversified, but also social justice demands to be ambivalent and rife with contradictions. Indeed, the struggles for social justice and the related claims are not necessarily associated with a progressive ethos of solidarity and equality. Owing to the intrinsic complexity and the contradictory essence of the urban public realm and to the variety of actors mobilizing around urban social issues, there are groups and movements of active citizens that are typical expressions of the so-called 'revanchist urbanism', claiming the right to live in a city where the homeless and other marginal subjects are removed from the urban space (N. Smith, 1996; see Chapter 4). As Mustafa Dikeç (2001) has observed, these demands are discursively justified by neoliberal arguments focusing on the inviolability of individual and community rights, most notably those to physical integrity and security. In this context, the conventional wisdom maintains that the rights of urban residents are threatened by socially tolerant attitudes towards groups ignoring the rules of 'civilization' and 'naturally' tending to adopt deviant behaviours. These arguments are mobilized in support of governmental and citizens' campaigns aiming at 'cleansing the city'. From the standpoint of orthodox liberalism, justice-related claims are always legitimate, both those arising from the conviction that individual rights are being threatened by deviant subjects and those linked to the will to improve the well-being of disadvantaged groups.

The contrast between mutually opposing modes of claim-making drawing on the ideal of social justice (one reflecting an egalitarian politics of emancipation, the other arising from a politics of inimicality) is not always clearly defined. In some cases, social movements happen to shift from being commonly included among the progressive forces of society to being assimilated into the grey and morally indefensible space of the 'post-political'. Mustafa Dikeç's analysis of the way in which the disorganized movements of young proletarians in the banlieues have been represented within public discourse in France is illustrative of this metamorphosis. While in their early stages (the 1980s) the protests and even the revolts of the marginalized youngsters living in the banlieues (the vast majority of them being of foreign origin, mostly from the North African ex-colonies) were treated as phenomena having at least implicit political significance, in subsequent years the renewed emphasis placed on fear, insecurity and violence within public discourse has led to the depoliticization, the stigmatization and finally the moral rejection of the young rioters. The banlieues are now viewed as a problem of governability, in terms of control of potential or actual disorder, rather than as producers of phenomena of social exclusion (youth unemployment, marginality, poverty, school dropouts, etc.). In the neoliberal context, however, whereas some movements are relegated to a post-political condition, other movements are co-opted as eccentric and creative contributors to the revitalization of urban capitalism. Take the example of the squatter movement in Amsterdam: historically formed as a way of standing up for the right to affordable housing (and to the city more generally) from an anti-capitalist perspective, over the last twenty years squatters have been splitting between those retaining a strong political commitment (anarchists and far-left activists) and those focusing more explicitly on the production of underground culture. In light of these changing (and contested) identities, the mainstream society and the political parties alike have changed their attitudes towards the squatter movement, shifting from requests for policies of control and repression to the acceptance and even the appreciation of alternative lifestyles and the reconsideration of the squatter movement as a source of creative urbanism (Uitermark, 2004).

At the beginning of this section, emphasis has been placed on the 'institutional thickness' of the urban environment as regards the development of social-justice movements and the revitalization of democratic politics. This does not mean that cities serve merely as sites stimulating the formation of social movements. Cities are also nodes and 'spaces of convergence' for networks of movements and associations mobilizing around issues of global and local relevance (Routledge, 2003). The

Figure 5.2 Homeless in an underground station, Tokyo (2008)

Source: photo © Federico Rota

formation of 'transnational' networks of movements and grassroots organizations has a practical purpose (the sharing of experiences among activist groups and the strengthening of social-justice campaigns at a global scale), but should be read also in light of the 'moral turn' (D. Smith, 1997) and the varying geographies of 'responsibility' (Massey, 2004) taking shape in contemporary societies. On the one hand, these networks build on the assumption that decisions and institutional processes originating in distant places and regions have strong implications at the local scale (for instance, the decisions taken by the World Trade Organization or by multinational companies affect food-consumption practices across the world); on the other hand, these networks are aware of the fact that in an increasingly interconnected world our everyday actions (such as the purchase of consumption goods) have repercussions at a larger scale well beyond our intentions (Barnett et al., 2008), contributing to the reproduction of phenomena of social and environmental injustice (for instance, the exploitation of workers and the contamination of ecosystems in low-income countries), as the next section of this chapter will show with reference to the latter.

5.5 Justice, globalization and the environment

Even though emphasis has been previously placed on the 'fertility' of urban spaces in the generation of social movements, it should be noted that the achievements of these movements transcend the physical and also imaginary boundaries of urban societies. Mark Purcell (2003) has argued that, despite the fact that Lefebvre associated a specific force of transformation with the 'urban revolution', his reflections have broader relevance with respect to the human condition. This means that Lefebvre's notion of the 'right to the city' should be applied to a wide-ranging set of issues relating to the everyday life of city dwellers, for instance those concerning their environmental citizenship (see also section 6 in Chapter 1). In this context, a 'right to dwell' broadly conceived can be taken as a point of departure for the building of a 'substantive' and 'absolute' urban democracy, one in which city dwellers are entitled to exert an influence (through a universal 'right to politics': Dikeç, 2001) on matters concerning their living environment. This goal is to be attained by allowing local communities (starting from the neighbourhood level) to take part in decision-making processes dealing with issues relating to the transformation of the environment and its preservation, the quality of consumption goods, the design of sustainable housing.

The approach outlined above – which could be defined 'neo-Lefebvrian' – relates the goal of social justice to the generation of a political order based on the ideal of 'substantive' democracy, which views the democratic process as a permanent legitimization 'from below' of the established institutions. For their emphasis on issues of agency and empowerment, the neo-Lefebvrian theses have commonalities with the theory of justice as a space of 'capabilities' (understood as 'the capacity to act' and privileged over principles of utility and social contract) elaborated by economist Amartya Sen (1999, 2009) and applied by sociologist Martha Nussbaum (1999, 2006) to the condition of disadvantaged groups, such as women in poor countries and the disabled. The political-philosophical tenets of neo-Lefebvrian thinking, however, are more radical than those of Sen and Nussbaum, having stronger affinities with post-Marxist theorizations of absolute democracy (such as those of Toni Negri and Jacques Rancière). Theorists of absolute democracy look at social conflict as a constituent force within the democratic process, viewing the assignment of rights and the attribution of capacities for self-government to subaltern groups as the outcome of adversarial confrontation; on the other hand, proponents of the theory of capabilities believe that the achievement of social justice is the result of a consensual agreement amongst different groups, and in their view this is the distinguishing feature of the democratic process.

Despite the diversity of political and philosophical approaches, these strands of thinking reflect the changes incurred by justice movements in recent years. Compared to those in the twentieth century, urban social movements have broadened the scope of their campaigns, the sphere of relations with other actors and geographical spaces, adopting a multidimensional stance towards social and environmental issues and the ways in which these are practically addressed. Whereas social movements in the 1960s and the 1970s focused their campaigns on the recognition of social rights for the subaltern classes and of civil rights for the ethnic minorities, over time global justice-related issues have acquired a prominent position within the public realm of contemporary cities. The globalization of social-justice movements is threefold:

1 At an institutional level: justice movements increasingly tend to transgress national boundaries in their organizational structures, developing through networks of cooperation in which a variety of actors becomes involved in the South as well as in the North of the world.
2 In spatial terms: the process of claim-making becomes multi-scalar, which means that social movements are aware of the relevance of local issues, but these issues are reconsidered in light of the policies and the recommendations of supranational organizations such as WTO, NATO and IMF.
3 In temporal terms: the temporalities of social-justice movements are multidimensional; social movements are no longer exclusively focusing on contemporary problems and issues, but are increasingly concerned with prospective issues that are likely to shape the future of the earth and mankind: environmental change, intergenerational justice, the transformation of demographic structures and the socio-cultural implications linked to the geographical expansion of international migratory flows.

The organizational and spatio-temporal reconfiguration of contemporary social movements was highlighted by critical theorists of social justice already in the late 1980s and the 1990s, most notably by the aforementioned Iris Marion Young and David Harvey, who – despite their divergences – shared an emphasis on the contingent and relational character of social justice struggles and issues. Expanding this view, the global dimension of social movements therefore should be understood through a new lens: the 'globalism' of social justice movements is not interchangeable with the traditional 'internationalism' of the workers' and socialist movement; rather, global justice movements are better represented by an ideal of 'situated cosmopolitanism' (Pollock et al., 2000), which evidences the diversity of socio-cultural and organizational practices. On the other hand, the narratives adopted by social movements, particularly in the promotion of campaigns and initiatives, are not naturally given, but are the outcome of a complex and indeterminate dialectic between reality, representation and its discursive translation (Dixon et al., 2008). To justice movements the fact of presenting social and environmental issues of local relevance as a consequence of globalization, neoliberalism or climate change is the result of a process of agenda building and consciousness-raising, but is also a

Figure 5.3   Protests against the privatization of municipal enterprises in Cali, Colombia (2004)
Source: © http://www.justiceforcolombia.org (accessed June 2010)

discursive exercise aimed at connecting existing campaigns to those conducted by other activist groups across the world.

In this context, mobilizations around environmental issues offer significant examples of the spatio-temporal and organizational repositioning of contemporary social movements. The politics of environmental change is deeply permeated by the dialectic developing between politico-geographical scales, social practices and a plurality of economic, political and administrative actors, including grassroots movements formed by activists and residents which are increasingly influential in the public sphere of contemporary cities. Just like the right to the city should be understood more widely as a right to dwelling and to politics, claims of 'environmental justice' should not be understood in merely conventional terms as a demand for landscape protection and nature preservation. Under the banner of environmental justice, contemporary social movements organize campaigns reconnecting environmental problems to broader phenomena of social injustice: for instance, campaigns and protests against the opening of landfill sites (like those conducted in suburbs of the metropolitan area of Naples, in Italy, at the time of the waste crises of 2008 and 2010) and other dangerous infrastructures located close to densely populated areas, or those denouncing the fact that ethnic minorities (such as African-Americans and Asians in the United States) are more exposed to environmental dangers associated with unhealthy living conditions as compared to the white majority (Schlosberg, 2007).

It is not only neo-Marxist authors such as David Harvey or radical social movements who present environmental campaigns against the background of a discourse of social justice. Rather, it is now commonly accepted the idea that 'the environmental' and 'the social' are intimately interconnected as regards justice-related issues. According to Bunyan Bryant, a pioneering scholar in this field, environmental justice refers to:

> those cultural norms and values, rules, regulations, behaviors, policies, and decisions to support sustainable communities, where people can interact with confidence that their environment is safe, nurturing, and productive. Environmental justice is served when people can realize their highest potential, without experiencing the 'ism'. Environmental justice is supported by decent paying and safe jobs; quality schools and recreation; decent housing and adequate health care; democratic decision-making and personal empowerment; and communities free of violence, drugs and poverty. These are communities where both cultural and biological diversity are respected and highly revered and where distributed justice prevails. (Bryant, 1995, p. 6)

The above definition explicitly draws on the philosophical strand of thinking dealing with distributive justice originally inspired by John Rawls and further developed by Michael Walzer and other liberal and post-liberal authors (such as Iris Marion Young), but at the same time it is also influenced by the theory of capabilities proposed by Sen and Nussbaum. Regardless of philosophical influences, variously Marxist or liberal, environmental justice has relentlessly gained in popularity within scholarly and public debates over the last two decades or so, being embraced by an increasing number of urban social movements. Critical socio-spatial scholars have contributed to the revived interest in environmental issues, particularly within the framework of the so-called 'urban political ecology' which is committed to bringing issues of class, ethnicity and gender back in the environmentalist policy agenda and discourse, drawing on Harvey's reflections on the relationships between capitalism and the environment (Keil, 2003; Bickerstaff et al., 2009).

Adopting the standpoint of urban political ecology, Debbané and Keil (2004) have taken into account issues of 'distributive justice' arising from water resource management in their social implications (the access discriminated on the basis of ethnicity and income) and in light of contextual differences, with comparative reference to Toronto (Canada) and Hermanus (South Africa). The political, societal, economic and institutional features associated with each national context are of decisive importance: in Canada, the struggle over the access to water is related to broader campaigns against neoliberalism and the privatization of public services; in South Africa, the disparities of access to water between the black and the white communities is viewed as a legacy of the apartheid regime (see also Bond and McInnes, 2006). Issues relating to the uneven access to a 'common good' such as water can be observed and analysed from the standpoint of the disadvantaged groups or from that of politico-economic elites exploiting this resource in order to consolidate their hegemonic position. In this context, Giglioli and Swyngedouw (2008) have shown that the problem of water scarcity in Sicily, which recently culminated in the crisis of 2002, has been opportunistically used as a form of rent-seeking by local elites so as to attract funding from the state (financing maintenance of existing water-supply systems rather than projects of environmental management attempting to solve the problem in a socially just manner).

Conflicts over water management are just one manifestation of the ways in which issues of environmental injustice are revelatory of broader socio-spatial inequalities. The effects of 'natural' disasters in urban areas (earthquakes, floods, etc.) are notoriously socially uneven: living in a white, upper-class neighbourhood or in a deprived and ethnically segregated area makes the difference when cities are affected by 'extreme' physical phenomena. Pre-existing inequalities have been tragically brought to light by Hurricane Katrina which devastated vast portions of the city of New Orleans in 2005 (see Box 5.2). While 'black' neighbourhoods were strongly affected by the devastation, the white communities of residents were largely untouched by the most serious consequences of the flood, benefitting also from quicker and more efficient programmes of housing rehabilitation (Rydin, 2006). The ultra-liberal approach dominating at that time within the Bush Jr. Administration prevented the US Federal Government from taking the lead in an efficient strategy for recovery in favour of disadvantaged groups and dilapidated areas (Peck, 2006). The inertia of Federal Government thereby induced communities of city dwellers in New Orleans to organize neighbourhood committees demanding the redevelopment of the most damaged residential spaces (Irazábal and Neville, 2007). As the grassroots response to the effects of Hurricane Katrina demonstrates, neighbourhood-based urban social movements mobilizing for environmental justice offer possible alternatives to conventional approaches to environmental issues, based on the neoliberal ideal of the ecologically 'active' and 'responsible' citizen (Marinetto, 2003). As Erik Swyngedouw has pointed out, drawing on the insights of a radical critic of neoliberalism like Slavoj Žižek (2006), the mainstream view on sustainability reflects the post-political degeneration of contemporary societies, refusing conflict and the opposition between alternative socio-political options as a basis of the broader democratic process dealing with environmental issues, while limiting itself to the identification of technical solutions which do not question the existing political, societal and economic order (as in the case of anti-emissions policies, 'green' incentives, etc.: see Chapter 1).

Figure 5.4 Unauthorized settlements hiding behind open-field disposal sites in St. Louis, Senegal (2006)

Source: photo © Matteo Puttilli

BOX 5.2   URBAN FILMS

GOVERNING THE DISASTER – *WHEN THE LEVEES BROKE: A REQUIEM IN FOUR ACTS* (USA, 2006, DIRECTED BY SPIKE LEE)

Hurricane Katrina hit the city of New Orleans – one of the poorest metropolitan areas in the United States, with a high percentage of black population – in August 2005, killing more than 1,500 people, causing unprecedented human suffering and the destruction of vast spaces of built environment (about 80 per cent of

(Continued)

(Continued)

New Orleans was flooded). The four-hour documentary film by Spike Lee gives voice to local residents, activists, celebrities and politicians commenting on the disaster. The documentary illuminates the ways in which an event that has been conventionally presented as a 'natural' disaster has reinforced pre-existing socio-spatial inequalities. Moreover, Spike Lee's work helps reconstruct the dynamics of pre- and post-hurricane emergency politics. In doing so, it shows that local residents often know the hidden truth behind 'natural' catastrophes. Residents of New Orleans reported, most notably, that water was leaking from the canals months before Hurricane Katrina caused the levee system to collapse: this means that the timely detection of the leak by the authorities could have prevented the catastrophic breach. After having done nothing to prevent the disaster, the state and the Federal authorities mismanaged the process of evacuation, making no provisions to help people without a car (namely, the poor, the elderly and the sick), who had been in fact those hit most by the disaster (according to the 2000 Census almost one third of the entire population of New Orleans were without private mobility). Not only the process of evacuation but the whole set of post-disaster emergency and recovery plans have proven inadequate: from the Katrina survivors crammed into the New Orleans Superdome and Convention Centre, which caused considerable emotional distress, to the unregulated process of resettlement in severely damaged areas.

Hurricane Katrina and its aftermath have inspired a wide range of interpretive endeavours in literature and the figurative arts. David Simon, known for being the creator of the successful TV series *The Wire* describing the deprived urban environment of Baltimore, has scripted *Treme* (2010), a new TV series centred on the lives of musicians residing in the Tremé neighbourhood of New Orleans in the years following the hurricane. Dave Eggers has published *Zeitoun* (2009), a non-fiction account of a Syrian-American immigrant and his turbulent experience during Hurricane Katrina, showing how the neoliberal politics of environmental emergency has also fomented the rising prejudice against the Arabs and the Muslims. Finally, Spike Lee has produced a follow up to *When the Levees Broke*, entitled *If God Is Willing and Da Creek Don't Rise*, a film documenting both the ongoing process of urban redevelopment five years after Katrina and the reactions to the new environmental disaster caused by the British Petroleum oil spill in the Gulf of Mexico, which flowed for three months from April 2010, reaching the Louisiana coastline with serious consequences on the marine environment and the local economy of New Orleans and the surrounding region.

5.6 Conclusion: the encounter between institutionalist and Marxist perspectives

As the last section of this chapter has shown, the importance of urban social movements for environmental justice rests on the fact that their struggles point to the ways in which ecological issues should be understood and practically addressed within the context of existing socio-spatial and economic relationships. In capitalist cities, such relationships are characterized by socio-spatial inequalities and uneven access to decision-making processes: the former are usually underlined within the framework of Marxian critiques of the capitalist mode of production and the related model of urban and regional development, such as those provided by David Harvey and the proponents of 'urban political ecology'; the latter are customarily stressed within the framework of liberal and post-liberal critiques (from the contractualist and pluralist positions to the radical-feminist critique by Iris Marion Young and the more moderate version proposed by Martha Nussbaum) of the institutional dynamics producing conditions of exclusion and oppression of socio-cultural minorities.

In the struggles for socio-spatial justice the conventional dichotomy between Marxist and liberal positions, which has divided the progressive academic field over the last three decades, is de facto overcome by the attention simultaneously drawn both to structural inequalities and socio-institutional exclusions. Social movements are aware of the fact that the combination and the overlapping of these forms of inequalities and exclusions give rise to common situations of urban injustice. At the political and scholarly levels, however, an effort to productively confront and possibly integrate on novel bases two approaches – Marxist and liberal – to social justice that in many respects are complementary is still far from materializing. This would entail bringing together the liberal emphasis on institutional issues with the Marxist privileged focus on the capitalist mode of production, challenging the conventional dichotomy between the 'economic' and the 'institutional' as determinants of social injustice. In fact, on the one hand, conditions of oppression and social injustice do not arise only from existing institutional dynamics, as radical (post-)liberal theorists contend; on the other hand, the structure and the form of social movements is not just a product of the urban capitalist process, as neo-Marxist theorists maintain.

Rather, a radical version of institutionalism, hybridized and mediated with the Marxist attention towards the configuration and the contradictions of capitalism, would drive us to analyse the ways in which subaltern groups and urban social movements autonomously develop institutional potentials: namely, the capacity to reinvent institutions and to revitalize democratic practice (as shown, for instance, by local communities' response to Hurricane Katrina in New Orleans). In the final instance, the evolution and even the survival of the capitalist city and of its government structures are closely dependent on subaltern actors' ability to revivify the existing political-institutional process through autonomous struggles and mobilizations.

Note

1   This is worth noting that the Conservative leader David Cameron, the newly
    appointed Prime Minister of Great Britain after the uncertain 2010 general election,
    has put forward the thesis of 'big society' as the flagship project of government's
    mandate. It would seem a departure from orthodox liberal ideas of 'open society' and
    the like, which had been unconditionally supported by previous leaders of the Tories
    in Britain, after Margaret Thatcher's neoliberal (counter)revolution in the 1980s (see
    Chapter 3 in particular). Cameron's notion of 'big society' draws on communitarian
    ideas and discourses about the responsible citizen and political community, which
    had been already brought to the fore by the New Labour Party at the time of Blair's
    mandates (see Chapter 4 and below in this chapter). In doing so, Cameron offers a
    communitarian solution to the crisis of neoliberalism after the decline in popularity
    of free market ideas caused by the financial crash of 2008–09.

6
Urban Citizenship: Insurgencies and Recognition

Key Issues and Themes

The spaces of 'national citizenship', understood as a simultaneously legal, cultural and societal sense of belonging, have been eroded by the forces of globalization and neoliberalism.

While the advent of globalization has undermined the primacy of state-centred citizenship, the resurgence of the local scale of governance and economic development has led to the re-emergence of cities and metropolitan areas as crucial spaces of contention over the recognition of minority identities and a variety of shifting positionalities.

The city is the space in which a denationalized dimension of collective and individual belonging appears to be founded on truly cross-national relationships and socio-spatial practices. Urban citizenship, therefore, intersects with post-national senses of belonging and the everyday cosmopolitanism of international migrants.

Along with the recognition of ethnicity and cultural difference, sexuality represents a contentious terrain for minority politics in contemporary cities. The negotiation of sexual citizenship typically reproduces the contradictions of the politics of recognition in a context of neoliberal urban governance.

6.1 Introduction: the crisis of national citizenship

The transformations of citizenship are central to contemporary reflections dealing with the changes associated with the shift towards societal configurations that appear to be more fluid and open, getting rid of the senses of belonging dominating in the twentieth century and in the broader course of modernity. In an era of advanced globalization and postmodernity, the terrain of citizenship becomes at one and the same time more dynamic and rich but also uncertain and ungraspable, being exposed – as this chapter will show – to the influence exerted by a wide range of political, social and cultural forces and related spatial entities, which are not always easily identifiable.

Since the time in which the modern nation-state formed in Europe (approximately between the fifteenth and the seventeenth centuries), the idea and the experience of citizenship have been forged primarily by two closely interrelated allegiances: one based on belonging to the national community; another one relating to the jurisdictional order formalized in a state-led constitutional design. The modern and contemporary notion of citizenship thus powerfully evokes the sense of national belonging and the corresponding political, institutional and administrative layer of the nation-state, drawing on two sources of legitimization: the first is cultural, fostered by the inclusion in a national collectivity (linguistic, symbolic, imaginary); the second is political-juridical, built upon the assignment of rights and duties, which are distinctive of liberal democracies.

The contemporary experience of citizenship in Western countries is not limited to the cultural and political-legal dimensions, tracing their origins back to the rise of the modern state and of a bourgeois civil society respectively. In addition to those previously existing, a third dimension has taken shape during the twentieth century: that of 'substantive' citizenship, which has laid the social foundations (material and no longer exclusively formal and spiritual) underpinning the linkage between citizenship and the national state. Indeed, in the last century the experience of citizenship has been intimately linked to societal well-being, pursued through the state-led provision of public services in the form of the so-called 'welfare state' (Marshall, 1950). The actually achieved prosperity has neither been socially homogeneous, nor has it been uniform and constant in time and space, not only at the world scale, but also within the smaller circle of the advanced capitalist countries. The variety of national models of capitalism and the related patterns of political-economic regulation have produced a strong diversification of the ways in which substantive citizenship has been pursued and has finally materialized. Spatio-temporal variegation aside, in the course of the twentieth century contemporary citizenship, understood as a sense of formalized belonging to a collectivity exceeding the boundaries of the proximate community, has been built on the contribution, on the one hand, and the benefit, on the other hand, that the citizen has offered or has reaped within the process of wealth redistribution: the assignment of rights and duties has been accomplished through access to public services provided by the state (the rights) and through the payment of taxes and other obligations like the military service (the duties).

The three-dimensional characterization of citizenship (cultural, legal and substantive), identified within the boundaries of the national state, has prevailed until the last quarter of the twentieth century. Since then, the primacy of national citizenship has been undermined, on the one hand, by the gradual shrinkage of the nation-state's public sphere; on the other hand, by the increased relevance of extra-state decision-making processes, relating to politico-geographical scales that have acquired a renewed role in the globalized world (Sassen, 1996b). The formation of a 'trans-scalar' system of societal government is, therefore, the most visible effect, widely debated at the political and scientific levels in recent years, of the process that has led to the 'creative destruction' of the former political-territorial order (commonly defined 'modern' or 'Westphalian') and to the rise of a multi-level political-jurisdictional form (Falk, 2000). The fiscal crisis of the state in the 1970s, the consequent decline of Keynesian regulation and, finally, the neoliberal counter-revolution in the 1980s opened the way for the shaping of an increasingly post-national citizenship regime, one in which the nation-state, however, still retains a pivotal role in distributing and rendering accountable powers of governance, upwards towards international organizations and downwards towards sub-national governing bodies (Hirst and Thompson, 1995).

The coming sections of this chapter will analyse the constructive effects linked to the crisis of national citizenship, namely the 'geographies of belonging' that have arisen in this context and the related consequences for urban democratic politics. As this chapter will show, the rise of differentiated spaces of belonging should be seen as the result of the mobilization of unevenly empowered actors and subjectivities. In this context, cities and municipalities, which were major venues for the institutionalization of political agency until the formation of the modern nation-state, have become central to the reconfiguration of contemporary citizenship.

6.2 The promises of urban citizenship

While the advent of globalization has undermined the primacy of state-centred citizenship, the resurgence of the local scale of governance and economic development has led to the re-emergence of cities and larger metropolitan areas as crucial spaces of contention over the recognition of minority identities and a variety of shifting positionalities. The renewed centrality of cities is the consequence of economic, demographic and cultural processes: first, cities' increased role as directional centres in the advanced capitalist countries of the West as well as in rising economic super-powers such as China, Brazil and India; second, the rising rates of urbanization (understood as a demographic phenomenon) in the low-income as well as the emerging countries of the Global South, particularly in sub-Saharan Africa and East Asia; third, the global expansion of urban lifestyles, especially those of Western origin, favoured by the diffusion of powerful information technologies such as the Internet in the first instance.

These processes have led social scientists to emphasize the relevance of 'urban citizenship' in a context of declining nation-state. As anticipated, the rise of urban citizenship is related to that of 'cosmopolitan', or 'post-national', citizenship within public and scholarly debates. The contours of the latter, however, are still uncertain, and its experience is judged to be elitist and class-biased (Calhoun, 2002), despite international organizations' endeavours to instil in their members a de-nationalized moral conduct, as the case of the European Union emblematically shows (Walters and Haahr, 2005). Conversely, the sense of affiliation with the urban community appears to be grounded in the everyday practices and acts of citizenship, otherwise exposed to the risks of displacement and anomy associated with globalization (Isin, 2000). In many respects, however, the idea of urban citizenship does not contradict that of 'cosmopolitanism'. In fact, the city is the space in which a denationalized dimension of collective and individual belonging is founded on truly cross-national relationships and socio-spatial practices – for the concentration of international migrants and ethnic minorities in urban areas (Rogers, 2000; Söderström, 2006) – rather than on merely ideological statements or programmatic politics, such as those stemming from the liberal ideal of the cosmopolitan political community (see Archibugi et al., 1998).

The celebration of the virtues of urban citizenship in an era of globalization has taken the form also of a neo-utopian thinking looking at the city as a space of co-presence and dialogue (Sennett, 1999) and as a terrain of democratic imagination going beyond the limits of representative institutions (Amin et al., 2000). An influential precursor of this optimistic attitude towards the progressive political qualities of the urban experience is Henri Lefebvre, whose writings on the city have been enthusiastically rediscovered over the last two decades within Anglophone urban studies (see Lefebvre, 1996). Lefebvre believed that the urban environment is most suited to the pursuit of an egalitarian and just society: as a spatial horizon in socialist-revolutionary terms, and as a site of contestation and struggle for the emancipation of subaltern classes within existing capitalist societies (Lefebvre, 1970).

The decline of the national dimension of citizenship and the rise of post-national and urban forms of institutionalized or insurgent citizenship intermesh with the proliferation of senses of belonging to minority groups. An increasingly influential view in the social sciences holds that these changes should be ascribed to the broader decline of universalistic modes of thought, triggered by the neo-communitarian turn by which group-based claims and identities acquire renewed influence with respect to citizenship and the related set of rights and responsibilities as well as of behaviours and lifestyles (Maffesoli, 1988; Taylor, 1992; Etzioni, 1993). In spite of conservative and even reactionary degenerations, the neo-communitarian turn has been interpreted also in progressive terms by political theorists looking at the mutations in citizenship and social belonging as an opportunity for the rethinking of emancipatory politics. In this context, Nancy Fraser has argued for the reconciliation of the politics of redistribution, received as a legacy of the twentieth century's welfare state and the related form of substantive and universalistic citizenship, with the politics of recognition, customarily associated with the 'post-socialist' era, which focuses on identity-based claims and related demands for social inclusion posed by minority groups (Fraser, 1995a; see Chapter 5).

Along with that of 'community', the key word of the contemporary political lexicon, as regards the changing meaning and experience of citizenship, is therefore 'minorities'. The last three decades have witnessed the rise of a wide range of minorities struggling for the recognition of ethno-national identities, religious beliefs and sexual orientations. These groups are motivated to express their presence in the public sphere (and the related 'rights to the city') as a response to perceived discrimination and disadvantage, which frustrates the individual and collective aspirations of their members. Cities are not only the places where such claims are spelled out, but are also sites where allegedly fixed ('essentialized', as critical social scientists put it) group-based senses of belonging are destabilized. The distinguishing feature of what is commonly understood as 'urban citizenship' – the sense of affiliation with the urban community deriving

Figure 6.1　Use of urban space for play in Santiago de Cuba (2004)

Source: photo © Federico Rota

from the realm of everyday life – is the fact of bringing together, in either complementary or contradictory forms, the assertion and the hybridization of group-based
identities and practices.

From this perspective, the discussed notion of the 'right to the city', originally
proposed by Henri Lefebvre and recently applied to contemporary debates on
urban social justice (see Chapter 5), is re-conceptualized by urban scholars against
the backdrop of group-based processes of mobilization, representation and subjectification. Some authors have thus suggested to pluralize the Lefebvrian notion of
the 'rights to the city', understood as the spatialization of the 'right to difference'
(Holston, 1998; McCann, 1999). The 'rights to the city' are not necessarily associated with demands for public services (housing, transportation, health care) or with
the envisioning of an inclusive and just socio-spatial order, advocated by contemporary justice movements (see Chapter 5). Rather, their formulation is intended to
assert the presence of 'other' subjectivities and their right to the appropriation of
urban spaces and the negotiation of urban citizenship (Purcell, 2003). To put it
differently, conflicts and mobilizations taking shape around the everyday meaning
and practice of urban citizenship shed light on the importance of the 'politics of

Figure 6.2   A public space in Brussels, Belgium (2008)
Source: photo © Alberto Vanolo

presence' in contemporary societies (Phillips, 1998). In such a politics the recognition of the 'right to be different' is a crucial objective in the pursuit of urban democracy.

The 'politics of presence' coexists and in some respects is closely interrelated with social-justice struggles, the former being more specifically focused on group-based claims of recognition while the latter is concerned with social issues of potentially universal relevance. What urban justice and citizenship movements share is the search for an 'absolute' form of democracy, one in which life-related issues (the living politics of the city discussed in Chapter 5), claims of recognition, the contestation of the injustices of capitalism, the critical scrutiny of the contradictions of the neoliberal regime of societal governance and finally the autonomous institutional processes triggered by urban social movements constitute the essence of urban democracy.

6.3 The globalization of migration and the multiple geographies of belonging

In the contemporary city viewed as a 'difference machine' (Isin, 2002), the sense of belonging that more coherently reflects the 'spirit' of the age of globalization and the socio-cultural changes associated with it is in many respects that of ethnicity (and religious affiliation). Historically, urban conglomerations have been favourite destinations for international migrants aspiring to settle on a temporary or permanent basis in the host country. The link between an ancient phenomenon such as that of human migration and urbanization (understood both as a demographic and socio-cultural process) took form in the second half of the nineteenth century, in the wake of the process of industrialization in Western countries and particularly in the United States. Since then, migrations have made a decisive contribution to demographic growth in cities and metropolitan areas of the industrialized countries: from the transoceanic migrations that brought hundreds of thousands of people from Europe to North America (a neo-industrial city like Chicago shifted from having 10,000 inhabitants in 1860 to almost two million in 1910) to the contemporary migratory movements expanding across the globe through international but also local and interregional flows. Illustrative of the more recent stages of migration processes is the case of Shenzen, which is in many respects comparable to that of Chicago and the other neo-industrial towns in the nineteenth century: located in the densely industrialized Pearl River Delta (currently one of the world's leading manufacturing regions), in the South of China, the city has expanded from having 300,000 inhabitants at the end of the 1970s to about three million in the mid-1990s, with a vertiginous increase in the rate of 'temporary' residents, particularly of rural migrants moving to the city, which are reported to be approximately double the number of 'permanent' residents. In contemporary

China, internal migration has implications not only in demographic and economic terms, but also at the political-juridical level, as migrants coming from other regional contexts are discriminated, particularly as regards access to public services and civil rights: a form of denied citizenship based on ethno-cultural origin which has historically affected immigrants of foreign origin also in advanced capitalist countries such as Germany and Japan (Solinger, 1999).

In the contemporary era of globalization, which has been influentially portrayed as the 'age of migration' (Castles and Miller, 2003), an increasing number of cities and regions which used to be almost exclusively places of departure have become magnets for domestic and international migrants: those in neo-industrialized China of course, but also a countless number of cities and regional spaces scattered all over the world, from Southern Europe to the Middle East and North Africa, from the emerging economies of East Asia to those in South Africa. In Southern Europe, Italy is illustrative of the changing patterns of international migration and the issues arising from these processes: while until the post-war decades Italy was mainly a place of departure towards the Americas and other countries of Western Europe, today this country is at the crossroads of the expanding migratory flows crossing the Mediterranean sea. The influx of migrants and their permanent settlement raises important questions regarding the assignment of political and social rights to the new comers and the 'second generations' and their process of social integration. Social problems such as housing precariousness and labour exploitation are most serious in those areas inhabited by immigrants that are affected by civil-rights discrimination, notably in the interstices of urban and metropolitan areas (in peripheral and inner-city neighbourhoods) as well as in the agricultural countryside of the 'Mezzogiorno' (see Cristaldi, 2002; Krasna and Nodari, 2004).

Another major distinctive feature of contemporary processes of migration is the diminishing importance of colonial legacies and long-term routes of commercial exchange, which were still predominant in the post-war decades (as testified by the concentration of North and West African immigrants in France, of Indonesians and Surinamese in The Netherlands, of Indians and Pakistanis in the United Kingdom, of Turks and Kurds in Germany, and so on). Over the last thirty years, emerging routes and migration relations have taken shape: from the settlement of new ethno-national groups in the high-income countries (such as the Arabs in the United States, the Eastern Europeans in the Euro-Mediterranean region, and the South East Asians in Japan) to the expansion of diasporic communities (the best-known being the Chinese and the Philippines) and the formation of socio-economic and cultural networks associated with migration (especially in religious affairs and in the trade sector). The emerging dynamics and forms of international migration processes give rise to a complex 'politics of belonging', throwing light on the limits of citizenship exclusively identified within the boundaries of the nation-state (Castles and Davidson, 2000).

Ongoing mutations in citizenship are the consequence not only of the importance acquired by extra-national sources of belonging (gender, race, place of living,
religion), but also of the fact that the migration experience is more fragmented and
geographically mobile, compared to the past, when migrants were accustomed to
associate their lives and those of the subsequent generations with the country where
they first settled. Rather, contemporary migrations tend to have a temporary and
circulatory character, being characterized by frequent back-and-forth movements
and intensified exchanges between the host country and the home country, thanks
also to the new information and transportation technologies (Vertovec and Cohen,
1999). In recent times, empirical evidence of such qualitative changes has been
provided by the economic downturn of 2008–09, when a growing number of
international migrants residing in previously booming national economies (for
instance, the Eastern Europeans in Ireland and the United Kingdom, the North
Africans in Spain) have decided to go back to their countries of origin. At the time
of writing (November 2010), it is not clear whether these return flows are permanent or temporary. In any case, this decision has been imposed by the shrinking
opportunities in the job market, particularly in the construction sector in which
migrants were employed in previous years, which within a short space of time has
shifted from being the engine of national economies to being responsible for the
big credit crunch which has brought a halt to the process of globalization of the
world economy.

Return migrations should be understood not only in terms of defence responses
to the effects of economic recession hitting the most vulnerable groups of the
migrant population. In their policy documents, international organizations under-
line the shift from a dualistic migration process, based on the opposition between
'here' (the host country) and 'there' (the home country), to a more fluid and
dynamic configuration forged by permanent exchange of information and experiences deriving from the circulation of the most qualified migrants in terms of
human capital (Wickramasekara, 2009; cf. Vertovec, 2002). Migrant elites returning
to their countries of origin, for instance in sub-Saharan African countries such as
Ivory Coast and Ghana, after migrating in Europe or the United States, increasingly
embark on projects of innovative entrepreneurship, while in the past being employed
in the public sector (now saturated) was the common objective for return migrants
(Ammassari, 2004). Acting as entrepreneurs within innovative sectors (such as
information and communication technologies) demands being constantly 'on the
move', using the country of origin (and return) as an interface node in transnational
business networks, rather than as the permanent place of residence and work like it
used to be in the past. Phenomena of incessant movement and circulation, along
with those taking the form of diasporic networks and communities, are at the
origin of the formation of material and immaterial spaces of 'dual' and 'flexible'
citizenship, drawing on multiple senses of belonging and a variety of socio-cultural
values (Ong, 1999).

Figure 6.3   Migrants at the border between Thailand and Myanmar (2009)

Source: photo © Germana Chiusano

BOX 6.1   URBAN FILMS

ETHNIC BUSINESS AND COMMUNITY NETWORKS AS A POLITICS OF RECOGNITION – *LA GRAINE ET LE MULET (THE SECRET OF THE GRAIN)* (FRANCE, 2007, DIRECTED BY ABDEL KECHICHE)

Finding it hard to integrate into the mainstream of the host society, immigrants rely on solidarity networks tying the members of ethnic groups. This is the key idea behind this film by the Franco–Algerian director Abdel Kechiche. The story is centred on food, and particularly on couscous, in an unnamed French Mediterranean seaport city (probably Marseille). Slimane Beiji, a 61-year-old man, father of two sons and one daughter, is suddenly fired because of 'flexibility' policies, after three years of shipyard work under hazardous conditions. Finding himself in an unwaged status, he has to deal with a difficult family situation (he is divorced from his wife, living by himself in a room of his lover's hotel). He is thus eager to improve his economic situation, by becoming an entrepreneur. His project is to renovate an old rusty ship turning it into a restaurant serving fish with couscous. In doing so, he has to negotiate a number of conditions with local institutions and private actors, such as the municipality, the banks (to get a loan), the port authority (for planning permission). Being a low-income, immigrant worker, the negotiation process proves intricate (despite the help of Latifa, his lover, who holds French citizenship). This leads him to mobilize his inner circle of close friends and immediate family members in support of his project, including his former wife (Souad), his children and above all his lover's daughter (Ryn).

The story revolves around characters showing dignity and humanity, but also behaving in contradictory ways under difficult circumstances. The film offers a realistic description of a close-knit community of expatriate Maghrebis in France, whose positionality within the host society transgresses long-established community boundaries essentially thanks to the symbolic power of ethnic food culture and of couscous most particularly.

6.3.1 The local spaces of citizenship: from *ius soli* to *ius domicilii*

The multifarious configuration assumed by migration flows has contradictory effects on the conventional link between citizenship and nationality, but also on the ways in which this link becomes an object of contestation and contention. The nation-state remains the political-juridical entity entitled to exert control over international borders, to grant immigration visas and political asylum, to authorize temporary visits for business or tourism and finally to 'concede' legal citizenship. Nowadays, the nation-state, therefore, mostly retains its sovereignty concerning migration affairs, as the state's jurisdiction over this field can be subjected only to international agreements which are reached on a voluntary basis.

The situation of undocumented aliens (or 'illegal', as they are often labelled in public discourse) is illustrative of how national states remain the authorities entitled to establish the legal boundaries of citizenship. The phenomenon of undocumented migrants has expanded over the last twenty or thirty years, when countries attracting the largest shares of international migrants have toughened border controls and have enacted severe legislation against illegal aliens. In the United States, the historically positive attitude towards international migrants, which led to the approval of the generous Immigration and Nationality Act in 1965, has been eroded by subsequent legislations: a bill approved in 1996 introduced the category of individuals being 'illegally present' in the national territory; in 2001, the Congress passed the Patriot Act in response to the 9/11 terrorist attacks, allowing amongst other surveillance procedures the pre-emptive detention of 'suspected' aliens, including those regularly residing in the US territory. In Europe, the adoption of the Schengen Agreement in 1985 and its implementation since 1990, on the one hand, has allowed the free travel of European citizens within the boundaries of the signing countries, giving rise to the so-called 'borderless Europe' (now consisting of 25 countries); on the other hand, it has strengthened the cooperation amongst national agencies involved in border controls, creating what has been defined 'fortress Europe' (Kofman, 1995), where the freedom to move for some (the citizens) coexists with the increasingly stricter restrictions being imposed on the 'other' (the international migrants aspiring to settle in Europe). In doing so, the 'liberal paradox' of economic openness and national political closure characterizing immigration policy in European countries over the post-war decades has been reproduced in the context of 'unified Europe' as an opposition between the 'outside' and the 'inside' (see Hollifield, 1992).

In the global North, therefore, the last two or three decades have witnessed the expansion of the phenomenon of unauthorized (or 'illegal') immigrants (around 11 million in the United States and up to 8 million in the European Union, according to official estimates[1]), staying in the host country even for several years and frequently bringing in immediate family members. Apart from those born in countries recognizing birthright citizenship (such as the United States – see also below), the younger members of illegal migrant families experience the strongest sense of injustice, as they are denied access to social and civil rights in countries in which they have grown and have received their education. As Monica Varsanyi (2006) has shown with reference to Los Angeles in California, the problems created by the denial of formal citizenship can be alleviated by the local state's provision of civil rights as well as of documents proving the identity of unauthorized migrants, through local non-citizen voting (in school-boards elections, for instance), in-state tuition for undocumented students and driver licences. Surveillance procedures that have been recently adopted at the federal level, however, are weakening the local-administrative pathway to citizenship. Driver licences, for instance, were used as a universally accepted form of identification until the approval of the Real ID Act in 2005, which established stricter standards for state-issued driver licences and other identification cards. In Western European countries, where regional governments and other localities have an established role as service-providers, the local-administrative pathway to substantive citizenship is even more clearly delineated than in the United States. In these contexts, urban citizenship is built upon local policies that represent a de facto consent for the formal membership of individuals who are already regular participants in the life of their immediate communities (see Rogers and Tillie, 2001).

The described phenomena shed light on the important link – conventionally unrecognized by national jurisdictions and international law – between place of residence and citizenship for undocumented migrants. While the national and federal levels of government witness the rise of exclusionary dynamics of formal membership, the opportunities offered by local states adopting progressive legislations towards residing migrants call attention to the emancipatory potential of *ius domicilii* (residents are entitled to social and political rights denied at the national and federal levels), as opposed not only to the conventional *jus sanguinis* (or right of blood, by which access to citizenship is conditioned upon the ethno-national affiliation of ancestors), which is historically prevailing in Europe, but also to *jus soli* (or birthright citizenship, important examples being the United States and France, but also Germany since 2000), which is more inclusive than the former but it persistently links the recognition of nationality and citizenship to the nation-state as a place of birth.

6.3.2 The practices of urban citizenship

There is not only the local structure of institutional opportunities that grants access to citizenship rights for those being excluded from formal membership. Extra-state access to substantive citizenship can be also the consequence of the 'politics of presence' taking shape at the grassroots level, on the basis of ethnicity, gender and class, in the multiethnic spaces of contemporary cities and metropolitan areas. Minority politics can take the form either of organized urban social movements or of silent and invisible social practices, namely individual and collective behaviours reproduced in time and space fostering a sense of affiliation with the urban community. The environment of cities, and most notably that of globalized urban and metropolitan areas, is particularly favourable to the politics of presence. The so-called global cities, a term originally used with reference to the directional centres of the world economy (London, Tokyo and New York, according to Saskia Sassen's 1991 pioneering work) and in more recent years applied to a larger number of cities across the world (see Chapter 1), are indeed crucial spaces in which informal social practices and explicit political claims coalesce under the banner of 'post-national citizenship' (Isin, 2000).

The organized movements of ethnic minorities and the practices of citizenship do not take place in a vacuum, having to deal with a complex and contested politics of multiculturalism, which has become a pillar of contemporary political life within liberal democracies but also in numerous newly democratized countries. In Western countries, in particular, the recognition and the social and political integration of ethnic minorities are commonly held policy objectives for national governments and also local administrations (as shown in the previous section), even though these processes increasingly take place under conditions of ethnic and political tension. Inter-ethnic contrasts and conflicts have indeed arisen in numerous countries across Europe, including those that are not new to the immigration experience.

This situation has led scholars and policy analysts to signal the crisis of multicultural citizenship in Europe (Triandafyllidou et al., 2006). Examples of these tensions are scattered all over Europe. Cities in Northern England, in Britain, in 2001 and in minor subsequent events, witnessed violent incidents between British Asians and white youths, the latter being provoked by ultra-nationalist political groups such as the British National Party (Amin, 2003; Phillips, 2006), while the terrorist attacks on London's public transportation system in July 2005 carried out by four unsuspected Muslim men living in the United Kingdom have exacerbated prejudice towards ethno-religious minorities. Similar feelings have emerged in the tolerant and cosmopolitan city of Amsterdam, in the Netherlands, following the assassination of filmmaker Theo Van Gogh and other minor episodes of Islamic radicalism (Uitermark et al., 2005), which have prepared the ground for the rise of the anti-Islamic PVV (the Party for Freedom led by the charismatic Geert Wilders) as the third largest political party in the newly elected Parliament in 2010. Islamophobic sentiments are also behind recurring discussions over the use of the 'veil' (the hijab) by Muslim women in France, albeit justified by reference to Republican values of *parité* (sex equality) and *laïcité* (secularism) (Body-Gendrot, 2002). In the last decade, in France these discussions have taken place in a context characterized by continuous tension materializing in violent clashes between young proletarians of foreign origin (particularly of North African origin) and the police that erupted in the *banlieues* of the metropolitan areas of Paris and Lyon (see Chapter 5).

Although they take less explicit and institutionalized forms compared to those in the West, minority practices and claims of urban citizenship are also present in emerging countries of the global South where politico-economic elites and the wider public alike are reluctant to recognize the distinctive identity of ethnic minorities, particularly of minorities allegedly threatening the state and the moral integrity of the nation. The latter is the case for cities in which ethnic divisions are linked to broader geopolitical conflicts. From this point of view, the Middle East, an area which is central to the understanding of contemporary international relations at the world scale, offers evidence of the complex politics of urban citizenship taking shape in ethnically fractured cities, particularly those in which there is one dominant national or ethnic group.

With reference to this context, geographer Anna Secor (2004) has analysed the condition of Kurdish women of rural origin living in the Turkish city of Istanbul. In the absence of a government policy of recognition and social inclusion, Kurdish women mobilize a wide array of strategies and tactics taking place within the realm of everyday life, in the attempt to renegotiate their second-class citizenship. In Turkey, the national government does not recognize the regional and national identity of Kurds and the related linguistic, cultural and religious background (such as the Kurdish dialects forming a distinct macro-language). As Anna Secor points out, notwithstanding the discriminatory attitude towards this ethnic group, living in Istanbul – a large city of 12 million inhabitants in which about 250,000 immigrants settle every year on a permanent or temporary basis – offers Kurdish women the opportunity to participate in a learning process of citizenship formation. Such a goal is pursued by developing socio-spatial strategies combining explicit claims of minority belonging (in the context of community life and participation in women's associations) with uses of anonymity, especially within disciplined and institutionalized settings such as the school and the workplace. The combination of strategies claiming the right to be recognized as a nation with those aimed at exhibiting an apparent sense of affiliation with the mainstream national identity testifies to the complex and contradictory politics of citizenship formation in a country like contemporary Turkey deeply marked by the struggles of an 'insurgent' ethnic minority. An urban environment like that of Istanbul, therefore, proves to be fertile ground for the rise of 'spaces of insurgent citizenship' (Holston, 1998), owing not only to the conditions of anonymity characterizing metropolitan areas, but also to the opportunities for social emancipation offered to women of rural origin. Even though they have access to formal membership, the sense of affiliation with the urban community allows these women to escape a twofold destiny of marginality, deriving from the fact of being Kurdish and women respectively, while engaging in a process of 'substantive' citizenship claiming.

Another example of minority politics taking shape in the Middle Eastern region is the Arab-Israelis (or Palestinian-Israelis, according to an unusual but in principle more correct definition) living in the seven ethnically 'mixed' cities in Israel, with a vast majority of inhabitants of Jewish origin (around 80 per cent): Haifa, Tel Aviv, Lydda, Ramla, Acre, Nazareth, Jerusalem. With reference to this context, Leibovitz (2007) has analysed the processes of political mobilization and the struggles for substantive citizenship in the cities of Haifa and Tel Aviv-Jaffa, where the presence of the population of Palestinian origin is recognized by municipal authorities, even though the process of recognition takes place − for instance, in the 'red' Haifa (the stronghold of the political left in Israel) − mainly at the symbolical level, while the effective representation of Palestinian interests and claims within the local institutions is limited. Being excluded from the institutionalized sites of local politics is only one aspect of the process of marginalization. In a densely populated and economically dynamic city like Tel Aviv, the Arabs − the vast majority residing in the Jaffa district − experience the highest levels of social exclusion, housing hardship and school drop-out. This condition of political and social marginalization, and of discriminated citizenship, has been denounced for many years by Palestinian civil-society organizations, both of Christian and Muslim descent, such as Harabitta, an association based in Tel Aviv, which has taken the lead in several political and opinion-making campaigns advocating the rights of the Palestinian-Israelis since the late 1970s. Local authorities have responded to these mobilizations by relegating the radical organizations to the margins of the local institutional arena (and the related system of subsidies), while privileging dialogue with allegedly moderate and collaborative associations, in many cases of religious orientation rather than of political-nationalist (and secularist) background as in the case of Harabitta and others. In Israel, a formally liberal democracy, though deeply marked by the colonial domination over the Palestinians (see Chapter 5), the politics of citizenship is therefore shaped by a contradictory dialectic between the local structure of opportunities and the selective incorporation of minority claims and interests, on the one hand, and the national scale of government, characterized by persisting geopolitical impasse with strong implications for international relations, on the other hand.

The relatively advanced institutionalization of minority politics and particularly of the relationships between civil-society organizations and local governments thus differentiates the Israeli-Palestinian political arena from the Turkish-Kurdish one. Even though the Palestinians living in formally democratic Israeli cities such as Tel Aviv and Haifa are enabled to draw on political opportunity structures, while the Kurds and particularly the Kurdish women in Turkey are denied political participation, these minorities have in common a stance towards the city as the spatiality devoted to the struggles for substantive citizenship. The latter take place in the presence of state-level political systems leaving no room not only for their recognition as a nation, but even for their capacity to exert influence on broad political-economic processes and for pursuing their aspirations to individual or collective emancipation. While for ethnic minorities struggling for recognition the risk of 'normalization' (through the cooptation within the dominant governmental rationality) lies in the institutionalization of their claims and discourses, for social movements forming around another major source of diversity such as sexuality the same risk lies in the commodification of their role and identity, which undermines the foundations of radical and dissident action.

6.4 Dissidence or normalization: the quandaries of sexual citizenship

The previous chapter of this book has underlined the importance of I.M. Young's theory of 'the politics of difference' for contemporary debates on social justice. In referring to the city as a venue for the politics of difference, Young (1990) argues that the encounter with the stranger characterizing everyday life in urban environments is an erotic experience, owing to our instinctual attraction towards the Other. There is no doubt that the urban experience of difference has been always associated with the intersected realms of the erotic and the sexual: in fact, prior to the arrival and the settlement in large cities of the contemporary 'others' par excellence like the migrants (even though migration is an ancient phenomenon, its urbanization and internationalization trace their origins back to the age of industrialization and to that of globalization, respectively, as previously said in this chapter) are sexual minorities that almost by definition embody the senses of 'alterity' and otherness attached to the urban experience, to be either stigmatized or celebrated by the established authorities and public opinion alike.

Today, the ambivalent attitude towards sexual alterity takes the form of a contradictory politics, combining a proud assertion of the sense of belonging to the homosexual community with the assimilation and cooptation within the spaces of institutional governance and the circuits of the capitalist urban economy. In order to appreciate the contemporary significance of the assertion of homosexual identity it is worth referring to a foundational moment in gay activism, namely the so-called 'Stonewall riots' (from the name of the nightclub where it all began), which erupted in 1969 as a protest over police raids on gay bars in the 'alternative' (and subsequently gentrified) Greenwich Village of Manhattan, in New York City. An act of insubordination and civil disobedience is thus at the origin of the gay movement, like other discriminated urban minorities (such as the African-Americans in the United States). In the following years, movements advocating the rights of homosexuals formed across the United States and in Western Europe alike, symbolically referring to the Stonewall riots. Since then, the gay movement has embarked on a complex evolutionary pathway leading to the recognition of its constitutive claims, but also to their institutionalization, with the formation of professional organizations representing the gay community and also with the proliferation of pro-gay initiatives promoted by local governments in collaboration with civil-society organizations (Cooper, 2006). The process of institutionalization has a number of positive aspects, as it brings to light needs and social issues relating to the situation of homosexuals, who are for instance still victims of acts of discrimination and harassment. However, the other side of the coin of the phenomenon of recognition is the normalization of homosexual subjectivity and its incorporation into the politico-administrative machine. Being aware of this danger, radical 'queer' movements have constantly renewed the 'tradition' of claiming the right to sexuality as an exercise of dissident citizenship and resistance against assimilation.[2] Recent years, generally characterized by the rise of a worldwide movement contesting global capitalism and neoliberalism, have seen the production of non-institutionalized, autonomous queer spaces – in the form of improvised events and street performances as well as physical spaces (like squatted buildings) challenging conventional forms of sociality – in which the rituals of mainstream gay politics and culture are ironically deconstructed (Brown, 2007).

The stubborn dissidence of large sectors of the homosexual movement does not stem only from sentiments of pride, but is also an active response to a growingly pervasive tendency to domesticate insurgent sexual subjectivities, for instance by making them instrumental in the revitalization of urban capitalist economies. Today, this tendency is fostered by the culturalization of an increasing number of realms of city life (see Chapter 2); a process encouraging the legitimization and celebration of gay identities within the public sphere and their subsumption within the urban capitalist process. A crucial sector in which the 'integration' of gay communities into the mechanisms of the urban capitalist economy becomes explicit is the housing market: as previously said (Chapter 4), this sector is central to the structuring and regeneration of urban capitalism, particularly in the context of the neoliberal deregulation of mortgage markets and the associated 'financialization of home' (Aalbers, 2008; see Chapter 4). The leitmotif of early debates on homosexuality within urban scholarship concerned the role of homosexuals (along with artists and other creatives) as gentrifiers of culturally attractive neighbourhoods. Despite the stereotypes and even the 'urban legends' constructed around the gay–gentrification nexus (Lees, 1996), there is no doubt that in some contexts homosexuals have made a decisive contribution to broad processes of urban regeneration and more specifically to real-estate revitalization, particularly in neighbourhoods and areas of special significance for gay and lesbian communities: the already mentioned Greenwich Village in Manhattan and Park Slope in Brooklyn, both in New York City; the Marais, the old Jewish quarter in central Paris, and a host of culturally vibrant and tolerant urban areas located in the largest cities of the United States, Europe and even Eastern Asia (cf. Lauria and Knopp, 1986).

In a book on sexual citizenship, British scholars David Bell and Joe Binnie (2000) have reflected on the ambivalence of the urban politics taking shape around the recognition of sexual minorities. Writing from the geographical standpoint, they reconstruct the multiscalar spatialities of sexual minorities' senses of affiliation: from transnational sexual citizenship, produced by the globalization of culture and lifestyles, to urban citizenship, associated with the transformation of the contemporary city into a leisure and entertainment machine, one capable of increasing the value of sexual minority identities through the construction of Gay Villages, the organization of Gay Pride parades, and the invention of a number of spaces and events dedicated to the celebration of homosexual difference, enjoyed by tourists and other city users and consumers. Ironically, as a result, these celebrations lead not just to the recognition of sexual minorities, but to the desexualization of the ways in which sexual alterity is commonly represented, being reduced to a quickly consumable icon of the 'creative city'.

In a subsequent article dealing with issues relating to the urban governance of sexual citizenship, Bell and Binnie (2004) have engaged with the work of Iris Marion Young, questioning the romanticism of her thesis about the intrinsic eroticism of city life, while highlighting the difficult and dilemmatic process of sexual citizenship formation. On the one hand, sexual minorities struggle for the recognition of their community identity and for obtaining adequate civil rights; on the other hand, they deal with the temptation of becoming involved in the seductive and economically rewarding mechanisms of the entrepreneurial city, epitomized by the representation of the gay as a 'good citizen' in a neoliberal context of urban renaissance, like in Richard Florida's theorization of the creative city. In their view, the dialectic between the recognition and the commodification of homosexual identities and subjectivities follows in the wake of the compromise that is at the origin of the constitution of a legitimate citizenship space for the queer movement: the assignment of rights and duties, on which the process of citizenship negotiation is founded, takes the form of an exchange between the act of recognition by mainstream society and the commitment by those being recognized ('the minorities') not only to behaving in a decent way, but also to actively contributing to the achievement of general prosperity and to accepting the 'rules of the game' as residents, consumers and economic agents. On the basis of the implicit compromise that is behind the negotiation of citizenship, there is a dynamic of selective legitimization of minority spaces, practices and codes of conduct by mainstream society and the established authorities. The homosexual is portrayed as an active and responsible citizen, when he or she dresses the part of homebuyer, real-estate investor, wealthy consumer or creative professional. On the other hand, homosexual communities are seen as an intrusive presence, when they express a desire to display their bodies as a way of asserting their sexuality: in this case, local-government managers resort to segregated spaces (the 'red light districts'), rigidly disciplined and regulated for sanitary purposes (Bell and Binnie, 2000).

From the vantage point of sexual minorities' ambivalent space of citizenship one can observe, therefore, the contradictions and the dilemmas of urban governance at the time of neoliberalism. The neoliberal practice of governance and citizenship is founded on the recognition that freedoms (of verbal and physical expression) and capabilities ('capacities to act') are key to the pursuit of the 'right to be different' (cf. Tully, 1999). The process of recognition produces selective dynamics of inclusion and institutionalization through an array of norms of behaviour, formalized rules and routinized conventions, underlying a complex politics of 'distinction'. This observation brings us to some concluding reflections on citizenship and the practice of absolute democracy in the contemporary city.

Figure 6.4   Italian government's campaign against homophobia (November 2009)

Source: http://www.pariopportunita.gov.it (Italian Ministry for Equal Opportunities; accessed November 2009)

Note: The text on the left translates as follows: 'Certain differences never matter in life. Refuse homophobia.' The denser text on the right (on the back of the leaflet) reads: 'Refuse homophobia, don't be the different one.' Note the ambiguity in the phrase 'don't be different', which implicitly reaffirms the social stigma towards 'diversity'.

BOX 6.2   URBAN FILMS

BEING HOMOSEXUAL IN ISRAEL/PALESTINE – *HA BUAH* (*THE BUBBLE*) (ISRAEL, 2006, DIRECTED BY EYTAN FOX)

The changing forms and dynamics of the politics of sexual citizenship across the world are closely related to the local politico-institutional context and to socio-cultural specificities. Whereas Western cities generally witness an ambivalent process of recognition of sexual minorities and incorporation into local governance structures, sexual-minority groups living in cities in the South experience persistent dynamics of exclusion and stigmatization. From this perspective, Israel is a peculiar case of tolerant attitude towards the 'insiders' (the Israeli citizens) combined with the social and cultural marginalization of the 'absolute outsiders' (the Palestinians) as well as the 'internal outsiders' (the Arab citizens of Israel: cf. section 6.3.2).

Ha Buah (*The Bubble*) is a film describing the impossible love relationship between two young men, the Israeli Noam and the Palestinian Ashraf. The urban setting is central to the narrative: on the one side, the progressive and cosmopolitan Tel Aviv appears as a bohemian space of freedom and fun, where the two young men are free to express their feelings in public. However, the actual situation of Tel Aviv is that of 'a bubble', an oasis of happiness and tolerance in an ethnically divided country where religious tensions and fundamentalisms are strong and where Palestinians live under conditions of apartheid. One of the two protagonists, Ashraf, is a Palestinian without a permit to stay in Israel and this forces him to keep his identity secret, using a fake name (Shimi). At the same time, being homosexual is hardly accepted by Palestinian society, even in the relatively large city of Nablus where he lives. When Ashraf's future brother-in-law, a Hamas activist, discovers that Ashraf is gay, he starts threatening him about revealing his secret unless he marries his cousin. Even Ashraf's sister, who is particularly close to him, hesitates to accept her brother's sexual orientation.

In addition to cultural prejudice, the political conflict between Israelis and Palestinians nullifies the very possibility of regular relationship. A bomb attack in Tel Aviv triggers a chain of violence leading first to the death of Ashraf's sister and subsequently to Ashraf's decision to commit a suicide attack in Tel Aviv – an extreme act of desperation that will lead to the death of the two lovers. Tel Aviv's representation in the film challenges the stereotypical image of a Middle Eastern city, with an example of a cosmopolitan, 24-hour city, only occasionally hit by terrorist attacks (unlike Jerusalem which is under permanent terror threat).

> Rather, Tel Aviv appears as a normalized space of exception, where the freedom to act and the possibility of presence (of being irresponsibly young, homosexual, anti-militarist) coexists with a state of permanent fear and constantly imminent suspension of the law.

6.5 Conclusion: the 'common place' of citizenship

The illustrative part of this chapter has focused on the experiences of two social groups, the international migrants and the sexual minorities – leaving aside those of other disadvantaged minorities such as the disabled, children and the elderly – which are revelatory of the potential but also the ambivalent implications of the struggles over urban citizenship. While being at odds with the national state and the conventional spaces of representative democracy, these groups look at the urban realm as a venue for the process of claim-making, even though the issues they raise are not necessarily 'urban' in the strict sense, such as those relating to the access to social and political rights for migrants and the recognition of alterity for sexual minorities. Migrants and sexual minorities view the city as a space of belonging challenging the constraints of group-based identities as well as a shelter space, which arises from the assemblage of experiences, social practices and claims. This role of the city as a source of 'relationality' (cf. Massey, 2005) and 'protection' for the excluded and marginalized minorities is not played by other political spatialities: neither by the legitimate space par excellence such as the nation-state, which is responsible for the vast majority of injustices and absences for which disadvantaged groups mobilize, nor by the space of the 'international community', which is still evanescent in political-juridical terms, being either powerless or under the yoke of national interests.

In an era of advanced neoliberalism, the urban realm is fertile ground for democratic politics, but is also a space being governed in systematic and sophisticated ways, through the selective recognition of freedoms and the redistribution of capacities to act. Processes of incorporation are enacted not only by local and national governments, but also by the forces of post-Fordist capitalism, those capable of mobilizing powerful mechanisms of seduction and cooptation of alternative subjectivities and the related affective qualities and institutional potential. This implies that the contemporary city, with its public sphere attracting subjectivities located in a fluid space at the crossroads between contestation and participation within processes of urban government and wealth accumulation, should not be seen as a space of innocence, where the lost ideal of democratic citizenship, betrayed by the decline of the nation-state and by the fading cosmopolitanism of the elites, lastly resurrects.

Rather, the city is a 'common place' (see the notion of the common in Hardt and Negri, 2009), at one and the same time ordinary and unpredictable, which contributes to the pursuit of egalitarian and democratic politics by collecting a multifaceted repertoire of citizenship practices, hanging between the search for autonomy and the temptation of political, economic and cultural normalization.

Notes

1   Data for USA from http://www.census.gov ; data for EU from Eurostat (2010), p. 192.
2   Literally, *queer* means strange, unusual, but nowadays this term is commonly associated with homosexual people, relating in particular to activist movements challenging monistic understandings of gay culture and identity. A related term, which takes into account the pluralism of homosexual culture, is LGBT (*Lesbian Gay Bisexual Transgender*). Activists and radical intellectuals – such as Michael Warner (1999) – lay emphasis on this term as opposed to those positions accepting the normalization of homosexuality, for instance through the recognition of gay marriage, a widely debated issue in the United States and other liberal democracies. In theoretical terms, a major source of inspiration for the queer movement is the work of Judith Butler and her critique of gender essentialism and dualism (especially Butler, 1990).

Conclusion: Beyond Post-neoliberal Melancholia

This book has explored the different, interrelated and conflicting at the same time, dimensions of urban politics in an era of globalization, postmodernity and neoliberalism. In doing so, it has tried to convey a multifaceted view of the ways in which cities have become places that are central to the understanding of the contemporary globalized, and still globalizing, world. Historically, cities have offered to politico-economic elites a wide range of opportunities for economic growth, but the last three decades have witnessed the rise of cities as relatively autonomous agents of economic development and competitiveness in a context of deeply restructured socio-spatial relations involving a variety of politico-geographical scales and related actors. The politics of urban growth, the capital accumulation strategies being devised at the urban level, the cultural-economic processes leading to the generation of geographical imaginaries and public discourses are crucial to the present age of globalization, one in which economic development endeavours have to combine with the ability to generate iconic consciousness through strategies of representation.

These processes have taken place in a world which is growingly interconnected, as the globalization rhetoric has put it for many years, but it appears also to be increasingly variegated in terms of hybridization of governance cultures and development pathways. The powerful 'ideas from America' dictating the politics of becoming in contemporary cities – from the global city to the creative city and to the resilient city – have travelled around the world, but in doing so they have also fused with local cultures of governance, entrepreneurship and the existing socio-spatial relationships of power, as contemporary politico-economic elites become reluctant to passively adopt policy recipes imported from elsewhere. Even though the success of neoliberalism lies in the fact of being a highly mobile and flexible governmental technology, its normative effects on the strategies of economic development are recurrent: the financialization of the housing sector, urban boosterism and the organization of hallmark events and mega-projects as a way of attracting public and private investments, the discursive emphasis on green and knowledge-based economies and on 'creative' industries as promised lands for economic growth and urban renaissance.

Today, while the world economy is dealing with a global economic recession originally triggered by the subprime mortgage crisis, China – the new frontier of urban entrepreneurialism in the year of the ambitious Shanghai Expo 2010 – is experiencing an unprecedented housing boom, which is leading real estate to become the engine of the national economy along with export-led manufacturing sectors. However, in April 2010 the national government had to introduce a series of measures aimed at reducing speculative demand for housing, by imposing restrictions on the supply of mortgages (Naughton, 2010); then, in October 2010, in the context of what international mass media have depicted as 'currency wars' between the world's economic superpowers (China and the United States above all), China's central bank announced an increase in the official rate of interest, a decision taken for the first time in the last three years, in order to avoid a property bubble like the one that hit capitalist economies in 2008–09, leading to the first worldwide recession of the globalization era. While China tries to moderate the potentially pernicious exuberance of the housing market, 'ghost towns', abandoned construction sites, unsold houses and shop closures have already proliferated in cities across the advanced capitalist world in times of global recession, after years of prosperity and apparently unlimited growth.

Cities are, therefore, at one and the same time active agents and victims of current economic turbulences. They are active agents, because the financial and fiscal crisis was originally caused by the residential mortgage default in the United States (see Chapter 3). On the other hand, they are major victims of the recession, not just because of the already mentioned spatial effects but also because of the generation of new urban outcasts: residents facing home foreclosure, migrants losing their jobs, public-sector employees being made redundant, casualized workers losing social-security benefits. In responding to this situation, national governments are looking for innovative politico-economic visions and strategies, capable of boosting a persistently anaemic growth. The two countries that had been in the forefront in the 'neoliberal (counter)revolution' in previous decades, the United States and Great Britain, are those where an exit strategy appears to be particularly urgent and impelling. The former is tempted by a return to Keynesianism, through an expansionary fiscal policy led by government spending, even though the Federal Administration led by President Obama has to face a neo-conservative backlash all across the country demanding lower property taxes and reduced market regulation. The latter, having witnessed in 2010 the Conservatives returning to power after 13 years of New Labour governments, is inclined to reproduce Thatcherite policies of fiscal austerity and public-sector downsizing, despite the reference to the pursuit of an alleged 'Big Society', which in principle advocates active citizenship and community involvement as a way to alleviate the effects of socio-economic restructuring, but in practice is likely to lead to the rise of a neo-charitable welfare system and a neo-paternalistic state.

In a context in which national politico-economic elites are finding it hard to find effective ways of getting out of the economic recession, advanced capitalist societies are being sunk into a deep melancholia, comparable to the sense of post-imperial melancholia analysed by Paul Gilroy (2004) in his reflections on the rise of assimilationist impulses towards the ethnic minorities in Britain. While nation-states respond to uncertainty and fear by resorting to economic nationalism combined with austerity plans on a domestic level, it is in the interstices of societies that one can still see a light of hope: namely, in what this book has identified, drawing on the insights of French philosopher Jacques Rancière, as the third dimension of urban politics, the politics as contestation led by poor residents struggling for their right to stay put, by marginalized ethnic and sexual minorities demanding recognition, and by a variety of campaigners for citizenship and social justice. This 'politics of the common' (Hardt and Negri, 2009) adds to the previously described scenario a dynamic of contestation which is to be understood not just as the capacity to resist the consequences of socio-economic and state restructuring processes, but is to be viewed as a source of institutional formation and also of economic experimentation. In their struggles and campaigns touching on life-related issues such as housing and food, social services and a living income, substantive citizenship and sexuality, grass-roots social movements and civil-society groups bring to light a 'living politics of the city' (Patel, 2010), which complements and at the same time stands in contrast to the hegemonic bio-politics, merely concerned with disciplinary issues of safety and protection from the infecting and the deviant 'Other'.

If cities and the wider capitalist societies want to get rid of the sense of post-neoliberal melancholia into which they are currently sunk, the living politics highlighted by contemporary urban social movements may show the way forward. 'You must change your life', as philosopher Peter Sloterdijk (2009) has put it in his recent book, is an 'absolute imperative' that can be applied not only to individuals but also to the larger society. That means, building on Sloterdijk's notion of 'anthro-potechnique', that societies should be concerned with the search for discipline and method understood as a democratic practice and training. Urban neoliberalism prospered in an era characterized by unconditional belief in self-regulating markets, including housing markets. The illusion of ownership society, which symbolically traces its origins back to the adoption of Proposition 13 in California in 1978 and which was brought again to the fore of public debate by President George W. Bush in the mid-2000s, with the emphasis he placed on the neoliberal ideal of home-ownership (see Chapter 3), drew on a sense of optimism and euphoria, which has been replaced by dictates of realism and rigour as soon as the recession has taken shape. Looking back at the last decade, the 2000s, one cannot fail to notice the way in which unbridled optimism and grey realism have followed one another in a neurotic fashion within the space of few months. Changing city life means, therefore, training the citizen and the larger urban community to cope with the limits of urban economic development and to contribute to the search for an alternative model of wealth generation and redistribution by restoring a sense of connection to the helpless Other and the struggling minorities.

Glossary

accumulation   The process of value creation resulting in the formation of economic, social, cultural or political capital.

actors   The subjective entities performing actions, discourses, representations and acts of resistance on the basis of their identities, interests and needs within the urban public realm.

belonging   The socio-political process leading to the development of a sense of attachment to a place or a social group (a prerequisite for the rise of a space of citizenship).

biopolitics   The hegemonic politics of life itself within advanced liberal societies.

capabilities   The capacity to act and achieve a recognized presence on the public sphere.

citizenship   The codification of contested and fluid identities.

city branding/marketing   The commodification of the image of the city.

commodification   The primacy of exchange-value over use-value in the management of social relations.

community   The visible outcome of a politics of belonging at the level of neighbourhood, ethnicity and other relatively bounded socio-spatial units.

competitiveness   The conventional justification for actions and projects carried out in the name of the well-being of an urban community.

cosmopolitanism   The post-national politics of belonging in which cities act as crucial arenas.

creativity   The distinctive feature of thriving urban economies in a context of post-Fordism and immaterial capitalism.

crisis   The disruption of the established socio-spatial and economic order.

democracy   The ultimate goal of progressive politics either in formal or absolute/substantive terms.

development   The pursuit of an allegedly more prosperous society.

difference   A long-standing attribute of urban societies currently associated with the variety of socio-cultural positionalities coexisting in postmodern times.

elites Groups and classes that have attained a hegemonic position within urban societies.

gated communities A residential space of exception regulated in the last instance by violence.

globalization The politico-economic era characterized by the heightened circulation of commodities, bodies and discourses at a world scale.

governance A pluralistic practice of governing based on the negotiation and the coordination of the decision-making process.

governmentality The wide array of techniques, procedures and regulations giving rise to a governmental rationality.

homeownership The social goal of making the commodification and individualization of housing more acceptable in capitalist neoliberal societies.

institutions The variegated set of formal and informal rules, conventions, organizations and shared behaviours regulating socio-spatial relations.

justice The acknowledgement of the right and wrong in urban politics.

minorities Subaltern groups in urban societies identified along ethnic, religious, gender/sexual lines.

multiculturalism The ambivalent politics of presence, recognition and assimilation/integration taking shape around minority claims of diversity.

narratives The discursive strategy linked to a politics of representation.

negotiation The institutionalized way in which decisions are made in a context of urban governance.

neoliberalism The renewed belief in self-regulating markets.

police The preservation of a pre-fixed socio-spatial order by means of coercion, allowed by the state monopoly on the legitimate use of force.

positionality The contingent role performed by individuals and social groups in relation to others.

presence The very fact of being there and the associated claim to be granted recognition by the mainstream society.

recognition The government's response to a grassroots politics of presence.

redistribution The allocation of rights, duties and responsibilities between individuals, social groups and territories.

regeneration/renewal The expected outcome of a strategy aimed at tackling urban decline.

regime   The capacity to govern through the mobilization of a broad range of actors, coalitions, rationalities and governance structures.

regulation   The set of legal and informal norms shaping the agency of individuals, groups and collectivities.

resilience   The routinized capacity to recover from disasters and other unpleasant events in today's crisis-laden world.

responsibility   The feature that makes socio-spatial subjects (actors and spaces) accountable in liberal societies, thus allowing competition.

strategies   The social construction of rationalities and actions aimed at achieving purposes that are conducive to the well-being of a community or a private entity.

References

Aalbers, M. (2008) 'The financialization of home and the mortgage market crisis', *Competition and Change*, vol. 12, no. 2, pp. 148–166.

Aalbers. M.B. (ed.) (2009) 'Symposium on the sociology and geography of mortgage markets', *International Journal of Urban and Regional Research*, vol. 33, no. 2, pp. 281–442.

Adorno, T.W. and Horkheimer, M. (1947) *Dialektik der Aufklärung.* Amsterdam: Querido (Eng. transl.: *Dialectic of Enlightenment.* London: Verso, 1997).

Agamben, G. (1995) *Homo sacer. Il potere sovrano e la nuda vita.* Turin: Einaudi (Eng. transl. *Homo Sacer: Sovereign Power and Bare Life.* Stanford, CA: Stanford University Press, 1998).

Agamben, G. (2002) 'Security and terror', *Theory and Event*, vol. 5, no. 4, pp. 1–2.

Agamben, G. (2003) *Lo stato di eccezione.* Turin: Bollati Boringhieri (Eng. transl. *State of Exception.* Chicago, IL: University of Chicago Press, 2005).

Agnew, J. (2002) *Making Political Geography.* New York: Oxford University Press.

Aguiar, L.L.M. and Herod, A. (eds) (2006) *The Dirty Work of Neoliberalism: Cleaners in the Global Economy.* Malden, MA: Blackwell.

Ali, S.H. and Keil, R. (eds) (2008) *Networked Disease: Emerging Infections in the Global City.* Oxford: Blackwell.

Allen, J. (2003) *Lost Geographies of Power.* Oxford: Blackwell.

Amin, A. (1994) 'Post–Fordism: models, fantasies and phantoms of transition', in A. Amin (ed.), *Post–Fordism: A Reader.* Oxford: Blackwell, pp. 1–39.

Amin, A. (2002) 'Ethnicity and the multicultural city: living with diversity', *Environment and Planning A*, vol. 34, no. 6, pp. 959–980.

Amin, A. (2003) 'Unruly strangers? The 2001 urban riots in Britain', *International Journal of Urban and Regional Research*, vol. 27, no. 2, pp. 460–463.

Amin, A. (2005) 'Local community on trial', *Economy and Society*, vol. 34, no. 4, pp. 612–633.

Amin, A. (2006) 'The good city', *Urban Studies*, vol. 43, no. 5–6, pp. 1009–1023.

Amin, A. and Graham, S. (1997) 'The ordinary city', *Transactions of the Institute of British Geographers*, vol. 22, no. 4, pp. 411–429.

Amin, A. and Thrift, N.J. (1995) 'Institutional issues for the European regions: from markets and plans to socioeconomics and powers of association', *Economy and Society*, vol. 24, no. 1, pp. 41–66.

Amin, A. and Thrift, N.J. (2002) *Cities: Reimagining the Urban.* Cambridge: Polity Press.

Amin, A., Massey, D. and Thrift, N. (2000) *Cities for the Many Not the Few.* Bristol: Policy Press.

Amin, S. (2006) 'The millenium development goals. a critique from the south', *Monthly Review*, vol. 57, no. 10, pp. 1–15.

Ammassari, S. (2004) 'From nation–building to entrepreneurship: the impact of élite return migrants in Côte d'Ivoire and Ghana', *Population, Space and Place*, vol. 10, no. 2, pp. 133–154.

Archibugi, D., Held, D. and Köhler, M. (eds) (1998) *Re–imagining Political Community: Studies in Cosmopolitan Democracy*. Cambridge: Polity Press.

Arif, Y. (2008) 'Religion and rehabilitation: humanitarian biopolitics, city spaces and acts of religion', *International Journal of Urban and Regional Research*, vol. 32, no. 3, pp. 671–689.

Atkinson, R. and Easthope, H. (2009) 'The consequences of the creative class: the pursuit of creativity strategies in Australia's cities', *International Journal of Urban and Regional Research*, vol. 33, no. 1, pp. 64–79.

Bae, Y. and Sellers, J. (2007) 'Globalization, the developmental state and the politics of urban growth in Korea: A multi-level analysis', *International Journal of Urban and Regional Research*, vol. 31, no. 3, pp. 543–560.

Baghwati, J. (2004) *In Defense of Globalization*. New York: Oxford University Press.

Bagnasco, A. and Le Galès, P. (1997) 'Les villes européennes comme société et comme acteur', in A. Bagnasco and P. Le Galès (eds), *Villes en Europe*. Paris: La Découverte, pp. 7–43 (Eng. transl. *Cities in Contemporary Europe*. Cambridge: Cambridge University Press, 2000).

Barnett, C. (2001) 'Culture, policy, and subsidiarity in the European Union: from symbolic identity to the governmentalisation of culture', *Political Geography*, vol. 20, no. 4, pp. 405–426.

Barnett, C., Cloke, P., Clarke, N. and Malpass, A. (2008) 'Consuming ethics: articulating the subjects and spaces of ethical consumption', *Antipode*, vol. 37, no. 1, pp. 23–45.

Bauman, Z. (1997) *Postmodernity and its Discontents*. Cambridge: Polity Press.

Bauman, Z. (1999) *In Search of Politics*. Cambridge: Polity Press.

Beaumont, J. (2008) 'Faith action on urban social issues', *Urban Studies*, vol. 45, no. 10, pp. 2019–2034.

Bell, D. and Binnie, J. (2000) *The Sexual Citizen*. Cambridge: Polity Press.

Bell, D. and Binnie, J. (2004) 'Authenticating queer space: citizenship, urbanism and governance', *Urban Studies*, vol. 41, no. 9, pp. 1807–1820.

Bello, W. (2004) *Deglobalization: Ideas for a New World Economy*. New York: Zed Books.

Bennett, J. (2010) *Vibrant Matter: A Political Ecology of Things*. Durham, NC: Duke University Press.

Berman, M. (1996) 'Falling towers: city life after urbicide', in D. Crow (ed.), *Geography and Identity*, Washington, DC: Maisonneuvre Press, pp. 172–192.

Bickerstaff, K., Bulkeley, H. and Painter, J. (2009) 'Justice, nature and the city', *International Journal of Urban and Regional Research*, vol. 33, no. 3, pp. 591–600.

Bishop, R. and Clancey, G. (2004) 'The city-as-target, or perpetuation and death', in S. Graham (ed.), *Cities, War, and Terrorism*. Oxford: Blackwell, pp. 54–74.

Blanchard, O.J. (1987) 'Reaganomics', *Economic Policy*, vol. 2, no. 5, pp. 15–56.

Blakely, E.J. and Snyder, M.G. (1997) *Fortress America: Gated Communities in the United States*. Washington, DC: Brooking Institution Press.

Blinnikov, M., Shanin, A., Sobolev, N. and Volkova, L. (2006) 'Gated communities of the Moscow green belt: newly segregated landscapes and the suburban Russian environment', *GeoJournal*, vol. 66, no. 1–2, pp. 65–81.

Blomley, N. (2004) *Unsettling the City: Urban Land and the Politics of Property*. London: Routledge.

Body-Gendrot, S. (2002) 'Living apart or together with our differences?', *Ethnicities*, vol. 2, no. 3, pp. 367–385.

Boltanski, L. (2009) *De la critique. Précis de sociologie de l'émancipation*. Paris: Gallimard.

Bond, P. and McInnes, P. (2006) 'Decommodifying electricity in postapartheid Johannesburg', in H. Leitner, J. Peck and E.S. Sheppard (eds), *Contesting Neoliberalism*. New York: Guilford, pp. 157–178.

Bourdieu, P. (2000) *Les structures sociales de l'économie*. Paris: Seuil (Eng. transl. *The Social Structures of the Economy*. Cambridge: Polity, 2005).

Boyle, M. (1999) 'Growth machines and propaganda projects: a review of readings of the role of civic boosterism in the politics of local economic development', in A.E.G. Jonas and D. Wilson (eds), *The Urban Growth Machine: Critical Perspectives Two Decades Later*. Albany, NY: State University of New York Press, pp. 55–70.

Brenner, N. (1999) 'Globalisation as reterritorialisation: the rescaling of urban governance in the European Union', *Urban Studies*, vol. 36, no. 3, pp. 431–451.

Brenner, N. (2000) 'The urban question: Reflections on Henri Lefebvre, urban theory and the politics of scale', *International Journal of Urban and Regional Research*, vol. 24, no. 2, pp. 361–378.

Brenner, N. (2004) *New State Spaces: Urban Governance and the Rescaling of Statehood*. Oxford: Blackwell.

Brenner, N. and Theodore, N. (2002) 'Cities and the geographies of "actually existing neoliberalism"', *Antipode*, vol. 34, no. 3, pp. 341–347.

Brookings Institute (2010) *State of Metropolitan America*. Published report; http://www.brookings.edu/reports/2010/0509_metro_america.aspx.

Brown, G. (2007) 'Mutinous eruptions: autonomous spaces of radical queer activism', *Environment and Planning A*, vol. 39, no. 11, pp. 2685–2698.

Brown, M. (2009) 'Public health as urban politics, urban geography: venereal power in Seattle, 1943–1983', *Urban Geography*, vol. 30, no. 1, pp. 1–29.

Brown, M. and Staeheli, L.A. (2003) '"Are we there yet?" Feminist political geographies', *Gender, Place and Culture*, vol. 10, no. 3, pp. 247–255.

Brown, W. (2001) *Politics Out of History*. Princeton, NJ: Princeton University Press.

Bruggmann, J. (2009) *Welcome to the Urban Revolution: How Cities are Changing the World*. New York: Bloomsbury Press.

Bryant, B. (ed.) (1995) *Environmental Justice: Issues, Policies, and Solutions*. Washington DC: Island Press.

Bulkeley, H. and Betsill, M. (eds) (2005) *Cities and Climate Change: Urban Sustainability and Global Environmental Change*. London: Routledge.

Bunnell, T. (2008) 'Multiculturalism's regeneration: celebrating Merdeka (Malaysian independence) in a European Capital of Culture', *Transactions of the Institute of British Geographers*, vol. 33, no. 2, pp. 251–267.

Buruma, I. (2008) 'Abu Dhabi, stad als modern themapark', *NRC Handelsblad*, 1 November.

Butler, J. (1990) *Gender Trouble: Feminism and the Subversion of Identity*. New York: Routledge.

Caldeira, T. (2001) *City of Walls. Crime, Segregation, and Citizenship in São Paulo*. Berkeley, CA: University of California Press.

Calhoun, C. (2002) 'The class consciousness of frequent travelers: towards a critique of actually existing cosmopolitanism', in S. Vertovec and R. Cohen (eds), *Conceiving Cosmopolitanism. Theory, Context and Practice*. New York: Oxford University Press, pp. 86–109.

Cameron, S. (2003) 'Gentrification, housing redifferentiation and urban regeneration: "Going for Growth" in Newcastle upon Tyne', *Urban Studies*, vol. 40, no. 12, pp. 2367–2382.

Cartier, C. (2001) *Globalizing South China*. Oxford: Blackwell.

Castells, M. (1972) *La Question urbaine*. Paris: Maspero (Eng. transl. *The Urban Question. A Marxist Approach*. London: Arnold, 1977).

Castells, M. (1983) *The City and the Grassroots: A Cross-Cultural Theory of Urban Social Movements*. London: Arnold.

Castells, M. (1989) *The Informational City*. Malden, MA: Blackwell.

Castells M. (1997) *The Power of Identity*. Malden, MA: Blackwell.

Castells, M. and Hall, P. (1994) *Technopoles of the World*. London: Routledge.

Castells, M. and Mollenkopf, J. (eds) (1991) *Dual City: Restructuring New York*. New York: Russell Sage Foundation.

Castles, S. and Davidson, A. (2000) *Citizenship and Migration: Globalization and the Politics of Belonging*. London: Routledge.

Castles, M. and Miller, M.J. (2003) *The Age of Migration: International Population Movements in the Modern World*. New York: Guilford Press (third edition; first edition 1998).

Chen, X. (ed.) (2009) *Rising Shanghai: State Power and Local Transformations in a Global Megacity*. Minneapolis, MN: Minnesota University Press.

Cochrane, A. (2004) 'Modernisation, managerialism and the culture wars: the reshaping of the local welfare state in England', *Local Government Studies*, vol. 30, no. 4, pp. 481–496.

Cochrane, A. (2007) *Understanding Urban Policy: A Critical Approach*. Oxford: Blackwell.

Cochrane, A. and Jonas, A. (1996) 'Re-imagining Berlin: world city, national capital or ordinary place?', *European Urban and Regional Studies*, vol. 6, no. 2, pp. 145–164.

Cochrane, A., Peck, J. and Tickell, A. (1996) 'Manchester plays games: exploring the local politics of globalization', *Urban Studies*, vol. 33, no. 8, pp. 1319–1336.

Compagna, F. (1967) *La politica delle città*. Bari: Laterza.

Cook, I. (2006) 'Beijing as an "internationalized metropolis"', in F. Wu (ed.), *Globalization and the Chinese City*. London: Routledge, pp. 63–84.

Cooper, D. (2006) 'Active citizenship and the governmentality of local lesbian and gay politics', *Political Geography*, vol. 25, no. 8, pp. 921–943.

Coward, M. (2009) *Urbicide. The Politics of Urban Destruction*. London: Routledge.

Cox, K.R. (1993) 'The local and the global in the new urban politics: a critical view', *Environment and Planning D: Society and Space*, vol. 11, no. 4, pp. 433–448.

Cox, K.R. and Mair, A.J. (1988) 'Locality and community in the politics of local economic development', *Annals of the Association of American Geographers*, vol. 78, no. 2, pp. 307–25.

Cox, K.R. and Mair, A.J. (1991) 'From localised social structures to localities as agents', *Environment and Planning A*, vol. 23, no. 2, pp. 197–213.

Cristaldi, F. (2002) 'Multiethnic Rome: towards residential segregation?', *GeoJournal*, vol. 58, no. 2–3, pp. 81–90.

Cussett, F. (2003) *French theory: Foucault, Derrida, Deleuze & Cie et les mutations de la vie intellectuelle aux États-Units*. Paris: La Decouverte.

Dahl, R. (1961) *Who Governs? Democracy and Power in an American City*. New Haven, CT: Yale University Press.

Davies, B. (1968) *Social Needs and Resources in Local Services*. London: Joseph.

Davis, M. (1990) *City of Quartz: Excavating the Future of Los Angeles*. London: Verso.

Davis, M. (1999) *Ecology of Fear: Los Angeles and the Imagination of Disaster*. New York: Vintage Books.

Davis, M. (2006a) 'Fear and money in Dubai', *New Left Review*, no. 41, pp. 47–68.

Davis, M. (2006b), *Planet of Slums*. London: Verso.

Davis, M. (2010) 'Who will build the ark?', *New Left Review*, no. 61, pp. 29–46.

Debbané, A.–M. and Keil, R. (2004) 'Multiple disconnections: environmental justice and urban water in Canada and South Africa', *Space and Polity*, vol. 8, no. 2, pp. 209–225.

DeLeon, R.E. (1992) *Left Coast City: Progressive Politics in San Francisco, 1975–1991*. Lawrence, KS: University of Kansas Press.

Dicken, P. (2007) *Global Shift: Mapping the Changing Contours of the World Economy*. London: SAGE.

Dikeç, M. (2001) 'Justice and the spatial imagination', *Environment and Planning A*, vol. 33, no. 10, pp. 1787–1805.

Dikeç, M. (2005) 'Space, politics, and the political', *Environment and Planning D: Society and Space*, vol. 23, no. 2, pp. 171–188.

Dikeç, M. (2006) 'Two decades of French urban policy: from social development of neighbourhoods to the republican penal state', *Antipode*, vol. 38, no. 1, pp. 59–81.

Dixon, D.P., Woodward, K. and Jones III, J.P. (2008) 'Guest editorial: on the other hand ... dialectics', *Environment and Planning A*, vol. 40, no. 11, pp. 2549–2561.

Dobers, P. (2003) 'Image of Stockholm as an IT city: emerging urban entrepreneurship', in C. Steyaert and D. Hjorth (eds), *New Movements in Entrepreneurship*. Aldershot: Edward Elgar, pp. 200–217.

Doron, G. (2000) 'The dead zone and the architecture of transgression', *City*, vol. 4, no. 2, pp. 247–263.

Economist, The (2010) 'Living the dream: the Shanghai World Expo', 1 May, pp. 49–50.

Elliott, A. and Urry, J. (2010) *Mobile Lives*. London: Routledge.

Escobar, A. (1995) *Encountering Development: The Making and Unmaking of the Third World*. Princeton, NJ: Princeton University Press.

Etzioni, J. (1993) *The Spirit of Community: Rights, Responsibilities and the Communitarian Agenda*. New York: Crown.

European Commission (1999) *Sustainable Urban Development in the European Union: A Framework for Action*, Communication from the Commission to the Council, the European Parliament, the Economic and Social Committee and the Committee of the Regions; http://ec.europa.eu/regional_policy/sources/docoffic/official/communic/pdf/caud/caud_en.pdf

European Union (2007) *Territorial Agenda of the European Union: Towards a More Competitive and Sustainable Europe of Diverse Regions*, Informal Ministerial Meeting on Urban Development and Territorial Cohesion, 24–25 May; http://www.bmvbs.de (accessed December 2009).

Eurostat (2010) *Europe in Figures: Eurostat yearbook 2010*. Luxembourg: Publications Office of the European Union.

Falk, R. (2000) 'The decline of citizenship in an era of globalization', *Citizenship Studies*, vol. 4, no. 1, pp. 5–17.

Farinelli, F., Olsson, G. and Reichert, D. (eds) (1994) *Limits of Representation*. Munich: Accedo.

Farish, M. (2004) 'Another anxious urbanism: simulating defense and disaster in cold war America', in S. Graham (ed.), *Cities, War, and Terrorism*. Oxford: Blackwell, pp. 93–109.

Faulconbridge J. (2006), 'Stretching tacit knowledge beyond a local fix? Global spaces of learning in advertising service firms', *Journal of Economic Geography*, vol. 6, no. 4, pp. 517–540.

Ferguson, J. (2006) *Global Shadows: Africa in the Neoliberal World Order*. Durham, NC: Duke University Press.

Fernandes, L. (2004) 'The politics of forgetting: class politics, state power and the restructuring of urban space in India', *Urban Studies*, vol. 41, no. 12, pp. 2415–2430.

Fitzgerald, J. (2010) *Emerald Cities: Urban Sustainability and Economic Development*. New York: Oxford University Press.

Florida, R. (2002) *The Rise of the Creative Class: And How It's Transforming Work, Leisure, Community and Everyday Life*. New York: Basic Books.

Florida, R. (2005) *Cities and Creative Class*. New York: Routledge.

Flusty, S. (1997) 'Building paranoia', in N. Ellin and E.J. Blakely (eds), *Architecture of Fear*. New York: Princeton Architectural Press, pp. 13–26.

Fojas, C. (2007) 'Borderlined in the global city (of angels)', in A. Çinar and T. Bender (eds), *Urban Imaginaries. Locating the Modern City*. Minneapolis, MN: University of Minnesota Press, pp. 37–54.

Foucault, M. (1975) *Surveiller et punir: naissance de la prison*. Paris: Gallimard (Eng. transl: *Discipline and Punish: The Birth of the Prison*. New York: Random House, 1977).

Foucault, M. (1976) *Histoire de la sexualité I. La volonté de savoir*. Paris: Gallimard (Eng. transl: *The History of Sexuality Vol. 1: The Will to Knowledge*. New York: Random House, 1978).

Foucault, M. (1979) 'On governmentality', *Ideology and Consciousness*, no. 6, pp. 5–21.

Foucault, M. (2004) *Naissance de la biopolitique: Cours au Collège de France (1978–79)*. Paris: Seuil.

Fraser, N. (1995a) 'From redistribution to recognition: dilemmas of justice in a "post–socialist" age', *New Left Review*, no. 212, pp. 67–93.

Fraser, N. (1995b) 'Rethinking the public sphere: a contribution to the critique of actually existing democracy', *Social Text*, no. 25–26, pp. 56–80.

Fraser, N. (1997) *Justice Interruptus: Critical Reflections on the 'Postsocialist' Condition*. New York: Routledge.

Freud, S. (1929) *Das Ungluck in der Kultur* (Eng. transl: *Civilization and Its Discontents*. London: Penguin, 2002).

Friedmann, J. (1986) 'The world city hypothesis', *Development and Change*, vol. 17, no. 1, pp. 309–344.

Fukuyama, F. (1989) 'The end of history?', *The National Interest*, no. 16, pp. 3–18.

Galluccio, F. (2007) 'L'impero e le sue scale: "metafisica" del potere, tracce per una geografia minore', *Rivista Geografica Italiana*, vol. 113, no. 1, pp. 27–45.

Giddens, A. (1998) *Third Way: The Renewal of Social Democracy*. Cambridge: Polity Press.

Giglioli, I. and Swyngedouw, E. (2008) 'Let's drink to the great thirst! Water and the politics of fractured techno-natures in Sicily', *International Journal of Urban and Regional Research*, vol. 32, no. 2, pp. 392–414.

Gilroy, P. (2004) *After Empire: Melancholia or Convivial Culture?* London: Routledge.

Glasze, G. (2006) 'Segregation and seclusion: the case of compounds for western expatriates in Saudi Arabia', *GeoJournal*, vol. 66, no. 1–2, pp. 83–88.

Goffman, E. (1974) *Frame Analysis: An Essay on the Organization of Experience*. Boston, MA: Northeastern University Press.

Gonzalez, S. (2006) 'Scalar narratives in Bilbao: a cultural politics of scales approach to the study of urban policy', *International Journal of Urban and Regional Research*, vol. 30, no. 4, pp. 836–857.

Gordon, I. and Buck, N. (2005) 'Introduction: cities in the new conventional wisdom', in N. Nuck, I. Gordon, A. Harding and I. Turok (eds), *Changing Cities: Rethinking Urban Competitiveness, Cohesion and Governance*. Basingstoke: Palgrave, pp. 78–93.

Gottmann, J. (1961) *Megalopolis*. Cambridge, MA: MIT Press.

Graham, S. (2004a) 'Introduction: cities, warfare, and states of emergency', in S. Graham (ed.), *Cities, War, and Terrorism*. Oxford: Blackwell, pp. 1–25.

Graham, S. (2004b) 'Cities as strategic sites: place annihilation and urban geopolitics', in S. Graham (ed.), *Cities, War, and Terrorism*. Oxford: Blackwell, pp. 31–53.

Graham, S. (2006) 'Cities and the "war on terror"', *International Journal of Urban and Regional Research*, vol. 30, no. 2, pp. 255–276.

Gramsci, A. (1948–51) *Quaderni dal carcere*. Turin: Einaudi. (Eng. transl. *Prison Notebooks*. New York: Columbia University Press, 2010).

Gregory, D. (2006a) 'Vanishing points. Law, violence, and exception in the global war prison', in D. Gregory and A. Pred (eds), *Violent Geographies. Fear, Terror, and Political Violence*. London: Routledge, pp. 205–236.

Gregory, D. (2006b) '"In another time–zone, the bombs fall unsafely …": targets, civilians and late modern war', *The Arab World Geographer*, vol. 9, no. 2, pp. 88–111.

Habermas, J. (1962), *Strukturwandel der Öffentlichkeit. Untersuchungen zu einer Kategorie der bürgerlichen Gesellschaft*. Neuwied: Luchterhand (Eng. transl. *The Structural Transformation of the Public Sphere*. Cambridge, MA: MIT Press, 1989).

Hall, P. (1966) *The World Cities*. London: Weidenfeld & Nicolson.

Hall, P. (2000) 'Creative cities and economic development', *Urban Studies*, vol. 37, no. 4, pp. 639–649.

Hall, S. (1997) *Representation: Cultural Representations and Signifying Practices*. London: SAGE.

Hall, T. and Hubbard, P. (eds) (1998) *The Entrepreneurial City: Geographies of Politics, Regime and Representation*. Chichester: Wiley.

Hamnett, C. (1994) 'Social polarisation in global cities: theory and evidence', *Urban Studies*, vol. 31, no. 3, pp. 401–424.

Hancock, M. and Srinivas, S. (2008) 'Spaces of modernity: religion and the urban in Asia and Africa', *International Journal of Urban and Regional Research*, vol. 32, no. 3, pp. 617–630.

Harding, A. (1997) 'Urban regimes in a Europe of the cities?', *European Urban and Regional Studies*, vol. 4, no. 4, pp. 291–314.

Harding, M. (1994) 'Elite theory and growth machine', in D. Judge, G. Stoker and H. Wolman (eds), *Theories of Urban Politics*. London: SAGE, pp. 35–53.

Hardt, M. and Negri, A. (2000) *Empire*. Cambridge, MA: Harvard University Press.

Hardt, M. and Negri, A. (2009) *Commonwealth*. Cambridge, MA: Harvard University Press.

Harloe, M. (ed.) (1977) *Captive Cities: Studies in the Political Economy of Cities and Regions*. London: Wiley & Sons.

Harloe, M. (2001) 'Social justice and the city: the new "liberal formulation"', *International Journal of Urban and Regional Research*, vol. 25, no. 4, pp. 889–897.

Harvey, D. (1973) *Social Justice and the City*. London: Arnold.

Harvey, D. (1989a) *The Condition of Postmodernity*. Oxford: Blackwell.

Harvey, D. (1989b) *The Urban Experience*. Baltimore, MD: Johns Hopkins University Press.

Harvey, D. (1989c) 'From managerialism to entrepreneurialism: the transformation in urban governance in late capitalism', *Geografiska Annaler B: Human Geography*, vol. 71, no. 1, pp. 3–17.

Harvey, D. (1996) *Justice, Nature and the Geography of Difference*. Oxford: Blackwell.

Harvey, D. (2003) *Paris, Capital of Modernity*. London: Routledge.

Hayek, F.A. von (1978) *Law, Legislation and Liberty: The Mirage of Social Justice*. London: Routledge & Kegan Paul.

He, S. and Wu, F. (2009) 'China's emerging neo-liberal urbanism: perspectives from urban redevelopment', *Antipode*, vol. 41, no. 2, pp. 282–304.

Healey, P. (2004) 'The treatment of space and place in the new strategic spatial planning in Europe', *International Journal of Urban and Regional Research*, vol. 28, no. 1, pp. 45–67.

Herbert, S. (2001) 'Policing the contemporary city: fixing broken windows or shoring up neo–liberalism?', *Theoretical Criminology*, vol. 5, no. 4, pp. 445–466.

Herbert, S. (2006) *Citizens, Cops, and Power: Recognizing the Limits of Community*. Chicago, IL: University of Chicago Press.

Highleyman, L. (2002) 'Radical queers or queer radicals? Queer activism and the global justice movement', in B. Shepard and R. Hayduk (eds), *From ACT UP to the WTO: Urban Protest and Community Building in the Era of Globalization*. London: Verso, pp. 106–120.

Hinchliffe, S., Kearnes, M.B., Degen, M. and Whatmore, S. (2005) 'Urban wild things: a cosmopolitical experiment', *Environment and Planning D: Society and Space*, vol. 23, no. 5, pp. 643–58.

Hirst, P. and Thompson, G. (1995) 'Globalization and the future of the nation-state', *Economy and Society*, vol. 24, no. 3, pp. 408–442.

Hoffmann, L.M., Fainstein, S.S. and Judd. D.R. (eds) (2003) *Cities and Visitors: Regulating People, Markets and City Space*. Oxford: Blackwell.

Hollifield, J. (1992) *Immigrants, Markets and States: The Political Economy of Post-War Europe*. Cambridge, MA: Harvard University Press.

Holston, J. (1998) 'Spaces of insurgent citizenship', in L. Sandercock (ed.), *Making the Invisible Visible: A Multicultural Planning History*. Berkeley, CA: University of California Press, pp. 37–56.

Hudson, R. (2005) *Economic Geographies: Circuits, Flows and Spaces*. London: SAGE.

Imrie, R. and Raco, M. (2000) 'Governmentality and rights and responsibilities in urban policy', *Environment and Planning A*, vol. 32, pp. 2187–2204.

Irazábal, C. and Neville, J. (2007) 'Neighbourhoods in the lead: grassroots planning for social transformation in post-Katrina New Orleans?', *Planning Practice and Research*, vol. 22, no. 2, pp. 131–153.

Irazábal, C. and Punja, A. (2009) 'Cultivating just planning and legal institutions: a critical assessment of the South Central Farm struggle in Los Angeles', *Journal of Urban Affairs*, vol. 31, no. 1, pp. 1–23.

Isin, E.F. (2000) 'Introduction: democracy, citizenship and the city', in E.F. Isin (ed.), *Democracy, Citizenship and the Global City*. New York: Routledge, pp. 1–21.

Isin, E.F. (2002) *Becoming Political*. Minneapolis, MN: Minnesota University Press.

Jacobs, J. (1969) *The Economy of Cities*. New York: Random House.

Jameson, F. (1981) *The Political Unconscious: Narrative as a Socially Symbolic Act*. Ithaca, NY: Cornell University Press.

Jenks, M., Burton, E. and Williams, K. (eds) (1996) *The Compact City: A Sustainable Urban Form?* London: Spon Press.

Jessop, B. (1997) 'The entrepreneurial city: re-imaging localities, redesigning economic governance, or restructuring capital?', in N. Jewson and S. MacGregor (eds), *Transforming Cities: Contested Governance and New Spatial Divisions*. London: Routledge, pp. 28–41.

Jessop, B. (2001) 'Institutional re(turns) and the strategic–relational approach', *Environment and Planning A*, vol. 33, no. 7. pp. 1213–1235.

Jessop, B. (2002) 'Liberalism, neoliberalism, and urban governance: a state-theoretical perspective', *Antipode*, vol. 34, no. 3, pp. 452–472.

Jessop, B. (2004a) 'Critical semiotic analysis and cultural political economy', *Critical Discourse Studies*, vol. 1, no. 2, pp. 159–174.

Jessop, B. (2004b) 'Hollowing out the nation-state and multilevel governance', in P. Kennett (ed.) *A Handbook Of Comparative Social Policy*. Cheltenham: Edward Elgar, pp. 11–25.

Jessop, B., Sum, N.-L. (2000) 'An entrepreneurial city in action: Hong Kong's emerging strategies in and for (inter)urban competition', *Urban Studies*, vol. 37, no. 12, pp. 2287–2313.

Jonas, A. and While, A. (2007) 'Greening the entrepreneurial city? Looking for spaces of sustainability politics in the competitive city', in R. Krueger and D. Gibbs (eds), *The Sustainable Development Paradox: Urban Political Economy in the United States and Europe*. New York: Gilford Press, pp. 123–159.

Jonas, A. and Wilson, D. (eds) (1999) *The Urban Growth Machine: Critical Perspectives Two Decades Later*. Albany, NY: State University of New York Press.

Jones, M. (2009) 'Phase space: geography, relational thinking, and beyond', *Progress in Human Geography*, vol. 33, no. 4, pp. 487–506.

Judd, D.R. and Parkinson, M. (eds) (1990) *Leadership and Urban Regeneration: Cities in North America and Europe*. Newbury Park, CA: SAGE.

Judd, D.R. and Swanstrom, T. (1998) *City Politics: Private Power and Public Policy*. New York: Longman.

Kaika, M. (2005) *City of Flows: Modernity, Nature, and the City*. London: Routledge.

Kaika, M. and Swyngedouw, E. (2000) 'Fetishizing the modern city: the phantasmagoria of urban technological networks', *International Journal of Urban and Regional Research*, vol. 24, no. 1, pp. 120–138.

Kaldor, M. (1999) *New and Old Wars: Organized Violence in a Global Era*. Cambridge: Cambridge University Press.

Kanai, M. and Ortega-Alcázar, I. (2009) 'The prospects for culture-led urban regeneration in Latin America: cases from Mexico and Buenos Aires', *International Journal of Urban and Regional Research*, vol. 33, no. 2, pp. 483–501.

Katz, C. (1996) 'Towards minor theory', *Environment and Planning D: Society and Space*, vol. 14, no. 4, pp. 487–99.

Kavaratzis, M. and Ashworth, G.J. (2005) 'City branding: an effective assertion of identity or a transitory marketing trick?', *Tijdschrift voor Economische en Sociale Geografie*, vol. 96, no. 5, pp. 506–514.

Keil, R. (2003) 'Urban political ecology', *Urban Geography*, vol. 24, no. 8, pp. 723–738.

Keil, R. (2009) 'The urban politics of roll-with-it neo-liberalization', *City*, vol. 13, no. 2–3, pp. 231–245.

King, A.D. (2000) 'Postcolonialism, representation, and the city', in G. Bridge and S. Watson (eds), *A Companion to the City*. Oxford: Blackwell, pp. 261–269.

Kofman, E. (1995) 'Citizenship for some but not for the others: spaces of citizenship in contemporary Europe', *Political Geography*, vol. 14, no. 2, pp. 121–137.

Kong, L. (2007) 'Cultural icons and urban development in Asia: economic imperative, national identity, and global city status', *Political Geography*, vol. 26, no. 4, pp. 383–404.

Krasna, F. and Nodari, P. (eds) (2004) 'L'immigrazione straniera in Italia. Casi, metodi e modelli', *Geotema*, special issue, no. 23.

Krätke, S. (2004), 'City of talents? Berlin's regional economy, socio-spatial fabric and "worst practice" urban governance', *International Journal of Urban and Regional Research*, vol. 28, no. 3, pp. 511–529.

Kulcsar, L. and Domokos, T. (2005) 'The post-Socialist growth machine: the case of Hungary', *International Journal of Urban and Regional Research*, vol. 29, no. 3, pp. 550–563.

Landry, C. (2000) *The Creative City: A Toolkit for Urban Innovators*. London: Earthscan.

Landry, C. (2006) *The Art of City Making*. London: Earthscan.

Lauria, M. and Knopp, L. (1986) 'Towards an analysis of the role of gay communities in urban renaissance', *Urban Geography*, vol. 6, no. 1, pp. 152–169.

Lees, L. (1996) 'In the pursuit of difference: representations of gentrification', *Environment and Planning A*, vol. 28, no. 3, pp. 453–470.

Lees, L., Slater, T. and Wyly, E.K. (2008) *Gentrification*. London: Routledge.

Lefebvre, H. (1968) *Le droit à la ville*. Paris: Anthropos.

Lefebvre, H. (1970) *La Révolution urbaine*. Paris: Gallimard (Eng. transl. *The Urban Revolution*. Minneapolis, MN: University of Minnesota Press, 2003).

Lefebvre, H. (1974) *La Production de l'espace*. Paris: Anthropos (Engl. transl. *The Production of Space*. Oxford: Blackwell, 1991).

Lefebvre, H. (1996) *Writings on Cities*. Oxford: Blackwell.

Le Galès, P. (1998) 'Regulations and governance in European cities', *International Journal of Urban and Regional Research*, vol. 22, no. 3, pp. 482–506.

Legg, S. (2007) *Spaces of Colonialism: Delhi's Urban Governmentalities*. Oxford: Blackwell.

Leibovitz, J. (2007) 'Faultline citizenship: ethnonational politics, minority mobilisation, and governance in the Israeli "mixed cities" of Haifa and Tel Aviv–Jaffa', *Ethnopolitics*, vol. 6, no. 2, pp. 235–263.

Leisch, H. (2002) 'Gated communities in Indonesia', *Cities*, vol. 19, no. 5, pp. 341–350.

Leitner, H. and Sheppard, E. (2002) '"The city is dead, long live the net": harnessing european interurban networks for a neoliberal agenda', *Antipode*, vol. 34, no. 3, pp. 495–518.

Lever, W.F. and Turok, I. (1999) 'Competitive cities: introduction to the review', *Urban Studies*, vol. 36, no. 5–6, pp. 791–793.

Levine, M. (1987) 'Downtown redevelopment as an urban growth strategy: a critical appraisal of Baltimore renaissance', *Journal of Urban Affairs*, vol. 9, no. 2, pp. 103–123.

Levy, D.C. and Bruhn, K. (2006) *Mexico. The Struggle for Democratic Development*. Berkeley, CA: University of California Press.

Lévy, J. (1994) *L'Espace légitime: sur la dimension géographique de la fonction politique*. Paris: Press de la Fondation Nationale des Sciences Politiques.

Lévy J. (1997) *Europe, une géographie*, Paris: Hachette (Italian edition: *Europa: Una geografia*, Edizioni di Comunità, Turin 1999).

Lévy, J. and Lussault, M. (eds) (2003) *Dictionnaire de la géographie et de l'espace des sociétés*. Paris: Belin.

Ley, D. (2003) 'Artists, aestheticisation and the field of gentrification', *Urban Studies*, vol. 40, no. 12, pp. 2527–2544.

Logan, J.R. (2002) 'Three challenges for the Chinese city: globalization, migration, and market reform', in J.R. Logan (ed.), *The New Chinese City: Globalization and Market Reform*. Oxford: Blackwell, pp. 3–21.

Logan, J.R. and Molotch, H. (1987) *Urban Fortunes: The Political Economy of Place*. Berkeley, CA: University of California Press.

Lucas, R. (1988) 'On the mechanics of economic development', *Journal of Monetary Economics*, vol. 22, no. 1, pp. 3–42.

Luke, T.W. (2004) 'Everyday technics as extraordinary threats: urban technostructures and non-places in terrorist action', in S. Graham (ed.), *Cities, War, and Terrorism*. Oxford: Blackwell, pp. 120–136.

MacLeod, G. (2002) 'From urban entrepreneurialism to a "revanchist city"? On the spatial injustices of Glasgow's renaissance', *Antipode*, vol. 34, no. 3, pp. 602–624.

Maffesoli, M. (1988) *Le Temps des tribus*. Paris: Méridiens Klincksieck (Eng. transl. *The Time of the Tribes: The Decline of Individualism in Mass Society*. London: SAGE, 1996).

Marcuse, P. (2000) 'Cities in quarters', in G. Bridge and S. Watson (eds), *A Companion to the City*. London: Blackwell, pp. 270–281.

Marcuse, P. (2006) 'Security or safety in cities? The threat of terrorism after 9/11', *International Journal of Urban and Regional Research*, vol. 30, no. 4, pp. 919–929.

Marglin, S. and Schor, J.B. (eds) (1991), *The Golden Age of Capitalism: Reinterpreting the Postwar Experience*. New York: Oxford University Press.

Marinetto, M. (2003) 'Who wants to be an active citizen? The politics and practice of community involvement', *Sociology*, vol. 37, no. 1, pp. 103–120.

Markusen, A. (2006) 'Urban development and the politics of a creative class: evidence from the study of artists', *Environment and Planning A*, vol. 38, no. 10, pp. 1921–1940.

Marshall, T.H. (1950) *Citizenship and Social Class and Other Essays*. Cambridge: Cambridge University Press.

Marston, S. (2000) 'The social construction of scale', *Progress in Human Geography*, vol. 24, no. 2, pp. 219–242.

Martin, I. (2001) 'Dawn of the living wage: the diffusion of a redistributive municipal policy', *Urban Affairs Review*, vol. 36, no. 4, pp. 470–496.

Massey, D. (2004) 'Geographies of responsibility', *Geografiska Annaler B: Human Geography*, vol. 86, no. 1, pp. 5–18.

Massey, D. (2005) *For Space*. London: SAGE.

Massey, D., Quintas, P. and Wield, D. (1992) *High Tech Fantasies: Science Parks in Society, Science and Space*. London: Routledge.

McCann, E. (1999) 'Race, protest, and public space: contextualising Lefebvre in the U.S. city', *Antipode*, vol. 31, no. 2, pp. 163–184.

McCann, E. (2007) 'Inequality and politics in the creative city-region: questions of livability and state strategy', *International Journal of Urban and Regional Research*, vol. 31, no. 1, pp. 188–196.

McCann, E. (2010) 'Urban policy mobilities and global circuits of knowledge: toward a research agenda', *Annals of the Association of American Geographers*, vol. 101, no. 1, pp. 107–130.

McDowell, L. (1998) 'Some academic and political implications of *Justice, Nature and the Geography of Difference*', *Antipode*, vol. 30, no. 1, pp. 3–5.

McFarlane, C. and Rutherford, J. (2008) 'Political infrastructures: governing and experiencing the fabric of the city', *International Journal of Urban and Regional Research*, vol. 32, no. 2, pp. 363–374.

McNeill, D. (2003) 'Rome, global city? Church, state and the Jubilee 2000', *Political Geography*, vol. 22, no. 5, pp. 535–556.

Memoli, M. (2005) *La città immaginata: Spazi sociali, luoghi, rappresentazioni a Salvador de Bahia*. Milan: Angeli.

Merrifield, A. and Swyngedouw, E. (eds) (1996) *The Urbanization of Injustice*. New York: New York University Press.

Minca, C. (2005) 'The return of the camp', *Progress in Human Geography*, vol. 29, no. 4, pp. 405–412.

Mingione, E. (ed.) (1996) *Urban Poverty and the Underclass: A Reader*. Oxford: Blackwell.

Mitchell, D. (1997) 'The annihilation of space by law: the roots and implications of anti-homeless laws in the United States', *Antipode*, vol. 29, no. 3, pp. 65–89.

Mitchell, D. (2003) *The Right to the City: Social Justice and the Fight for Public Space*. New York: Guilford Press.

Molnar, V. (2010) 'The cultural production of locality: reclaiming the "European City" in post-Wall Berlin', *International Journal of Urban and Regional Research*, vol. 34, no. 2, pp. 281–309.

Mondada, L. (2000) *Décrire la ville: La construction des savoirs urbains dans l'interaction et dans le texte*. Paris: Anthropos.

Mouffe, C. (2005) *On the Political*. London: Routledge.

Moulaert, F., Rodriguez, A. and Swyngedouw, E. (eds) (2005) *The Globalized City: Economic Restructuring and Social Polarization in European Cities*. Oxford: Oxford University Press.

Mukhija, V. (2003) *Squatters as Developers? Slum Demolition and Redevelopment in Mumbai, India*. Aldershot: Ashgate.

Mumford, L. (1961) *The City in History*. New York: Harcourt Brace.

Naughton B. (2010) 'The turning point in housing', *China Leadership Monitor*, no. 33 (http://www.hoover.org/publications/china-leadership-monitor).

Negri, A. (1992) *Il potere costituente: Saggio sulle alternative del moderno*. Varese: Sugarco (Eng. transl. *Insurgencies. Constituent Power and the Modern State*, Minneapolis, MN: Minnesota University Press, 1999).

Negri, A. (2008) *Fabbrica di porcellana: Per una nuova grammatica politica*. Milan: Feltrinelli (Eng. transl. *The Porcelain Workshop: For a New Grammar of Politics*. Cambridge, MA: MIT Press, 2008).

Newman, K. and Wyly, E.K. (2006) 'The right to stay put, revisited: gentrification and resistance to displacement in New York City', *Urban Studies*, vol. 43, no. 1, pp. 23–57.

Newman, P., Beatley, T. and Boyer, H. (2009) *Resilient Cities: Responding to Peak Oil and Climate Change*. Washington, DC: Island Press.

Newsweek (2010), "How Africa is becoming the New Asia", February 19.

Nicholls, W.J. and Beaumont, J.R. (2004) 'The urbanization of justice movements? Possibilities and constraints for the city as a space of contentious struggle', *Space and Polity*, vol. 8, no. 2, pp. 107–117.

Nussbaum, M.C. (1999) *Sex and Social Justice*. Oxford: Oxford University Press.

Nussbaum, M.C. (2006) *Frontiers of Justice: Disability, Nationality, Species Membership*. Cambridge, MA: Belknap Press.

Ó Tuathail, G. (1996) *Critical Geopolitics: The Politics of Writing Global Space*. London: Routledge.

OECD (2002) *Urban Renaissance: Glasgow: Lessons for Innovation and Implementation*. Paris: OECD Publishing.

OECD (2005) *Culture and Local Development*. Paris: OECD Publishing.

Ohmae, K. (1990) *Borderless World: Power and Strategy in the Interlinked Economy*. New York: Harper.

Olds, K. (1995) 'Globalization and the production of new urban spaces: Pacific Rim megaprojects in the late 20th century', *Environment and Planning A*, vol. 27, no. 11, pp. 1713–1743.

Olds, K. and Yeung, H.W.-C. (2004) 'Pathways to global city formation: a view from the developmental city-state of Singapore', *Review of International Political Economy*, vol. 11, no. 3, pp. 489–521.

Ong, A. (1999) *Flexible Citizenship: The Cultural Logics of Transnationality*. Durham, NC: Duke University Press.

Ong, A. (2007) 'Neoliberalism as a mobile technology', *Transactions of the Institute of British Geographers*, vol. 32, no. 1, pp. 3–8.

Orueta, F.D. and Fainstein, S. (2008) 'The new mega-projects: Genesis and impacts', *International Journal of Urban and Regional Research*, vol. 32, no. 4, pp. 759–767.

Osborne, T. and Rose, N. (1999) 'Governing cities: notes on the spatialisation of virtue', *Environment and Planning D: Society and Space*, vol. 17, no. 6, pp. 737–760.

Paccino, D. (1972) *L'imbroglio ecologico: L'ideologia della natura*. Turin: Einaudi.

Paddison, R. (1993) 'City marketing, image reconstruction and urban regeneration', *Urban Studies*, vol. 30, no. 2, pp. 339–350.

Painter, J. (1995) *Politics, Geography and Political Geography: A Critical Perspective*. London: Arnold.

Patel, R. (2010) *The Value of Nothing: How to Reshape Market Society and Redefine Democracy*. New York: Picador.

Paul, D.E. (2005) 'The local politics of "going global": making and unmaking Minneapolis–St Paul as a world city', *Urban Studies*, vol. 42, no. 12, pp. 2103–2122.

Peck, J. (2005) 'Struggling with the creative class', *International Journal of Urban and Regional Research*, vol. 29, no. 4, pp. 740–770.

Peck, J. (2006) 'Liberating the city: between New York and New Orleans', *Urban Geography*, vol. 27, no. 8, pp. 681–713.

Peck, J. (2011) 'Creative moments: working culture through municipal socialism and neoliberal urbanism', in E. McCann and K. Ward (eds), *Mobile Urbanism: Cities and Policymaking in the Global Age*. Minneapolis, MN: University of Minnesota, pp. 41–70.

Peck, J. and Tickell, A. (2002) 'Neoliberalizing space', *Antipode*, vol. 34, no. 3, pp. 380–404.

Peet, R. (2003) *Unholy Trinity: The IMF, World Bank and WTO*. London: Zed Books.

Peterson, P. (1981) *City Limits*. Chicago, IL: Chicago University Press.

Phillips, A. (1998) *The Politics of Presence*. New York: Oxford University Press.

Phillips, D. (2006) 'Parallel lives? Challenging discourses of British Muslim self-segregation', *Environment and Planning D: Society and Space*, vol. 24, no. 1, pp. 25–40.

Pierre, J. (1999) 'Models of urban governance: the institutional dimension of urban politics', *Urban Affairs Review*, vol. 34, no. 3, pp. 372–396.

Pieterse, J.N. (2002) 'Globalization, kitsch and conflict: technologies of work, war and politics', *Review of International Political Economy*, vol. 9, no. 1, pp. 1–36.

Pinson, G. (2009) *Gouverner la ville par projet: Urbanisme et gouvernance des villes européennes*. Paris: Sciences Po.

Pitcher M. A. and Graham A. (2006) 'Cars are killing Luanda: cronyism, consumerism, and other assaults on Angola's postwar, capital city', in M. J. Murray and G. A. Myers (eds) *Cities in Contemporary Africa*. New York: Palgrave Macmillan, pp. 173–194.

Pollock, S., Bhabha, H.K., Breckenridge C.A. and Chakrabarty, D. (2000) 'Cosmopolitanisms', *Public Culture*, vol. 12, pp. 577–589.

Ponzini, D. and Rossi, U. (2010) 'Becoming a creative city: the entrepreneurial mayor, network politics, and the promise of an urban renaissance', *Urban Studies*, vol. 47, no. 10, pp. 1037–57.

Pred, A. (1977) *City-systems in Advanced Economies: Past Growth, Present Processes, and Future Development Options*. New York: John Wiley & Sons.

Purcell, M. (2001) 'Metropolitan political reorganization as a politics of urban growth: the case of San Fernando Valley Secession', *Political Geography*, vol. 20, pp. 613–633.

Purcell, M. (2003) 'Citizenship and the right to the global city: reimagining the capitalist world order', *International Journal of Urban and Regional Research*, vol. 27, no. 3, pp. 564–590.

Purcell, M. (2008) *Recapturing Democracy: Neoliberalization and the Struggle for Alternative Urban Futures*. London: Routledge.

Raco, M. (2003) 'Remaking place and securitising space: urban regeneration and the strategies, tactics and practices of policing in the UK', *Urban Studies*, vol. 40, no. 9, pp. 1869–1887.

Raco, M. (2007) 'Securing sustainable communities: security, safety and sustainability in New Urban Planning', *European Urban and Regional Studies*, vol. 14, no. 4, pp. 305–320.

Raffestin, C. (1980) *Pour une géographie du pouvoir*. Paris: Libraires Techniques.

Rancière, J. (1995) *La mésentente: politique et philosophie*. Paris: Galilée (Eng. transl. *Disagreement: Politics and Philosophy*. Minneapolis, MN: University of Minnesota Press).

Rancière, J. (1998) *Aux bords du politique*. Paris: Gallimard (Eng. transl. *On the Shore of Politics*. London: Verso).

Rancière, J. (2001) 'Ten theses on politics', *Theory and Event*, vol. 5, no. 3, pp. 1–16.

Rawls, J. (1971) *A Theory of Justice*. Cambridge, MA: Harvard University Press.

Ribera-Fumaz, R. (2009) 'From urban political economy to cultural political economy: rethinking culture and economy in and beyond the urban', *Progress in Human Geography*, vol. 33, no. 4, pp. 447–465.

Rice, X. (2008) 'The President, his church and the crocodiles', *New Statesman*, 23 October.

Riddell, B. (1997) 'Structural adjustment programmes and the city in tropical Africa', *Urban Studies*, vol. 34, no. 8, pp. 1297–1307.

Rifkin, J. (2003) *The Hydrogen Economy: The Creation of the Worldwide Energy Web and the Redistribution of Power on Earth*. New York: Tatcher and Penguin.

Rizvi, F. (2007) 'Lifelong learning: beyond neo-liberal imaginary', in D.N. Aspin (ed.), *Philosophical Perspectives of Lifelong Learning*. Berlin: Springer, pp. 114–130.

Robinson, J. (2002), 'Global and world cities: a view off the map', *International Journal of Urban and Regional Research*, vol. 26, no. 3, pp. 531–554.

Rogers, A. (2000) 'Citizenship, multiculturalism, and the European city', in G. Bridge and S. Watson (eds), *A Companion to the City*. Oxford: Blackwell, pp. 282–291.

Rogers, A. and Tillie, J. (eds) (2001) *Multicultural Policies and Modes of Citizenship in European Cities.* Aldershot: Ashgate.

Rogerson, C.M. (2005) 'Globalization, economic restructuring and local response in Johannesburg – the most isolated "world city"', in K. Segbers, S. Raiser and K. Volkmann (eds), *Public Problems – Private Solutions? Globalizing Cities in the South.* Aldershot: Ashgate, pp. 17–34.

Rose, N. (1999) *Powers of Freedom: Reframing Political Thought.* Cambridge: Cambridge University Press.

Rossi, U. (2008) 'La politica dello spazio pubblico nella città molteplice', *Rivista Geografica Italiana*, vol. 115, no. 4, pp. 27–58.

Rossi, U. (2010a) 'Castells, Manuel', in R. Hutchison (ed.), *Encyclopedia of Urban Studies*, Thousand Oaks, CA: SAGE, pp. 114–119.

Rossi, U. (2010b) 'The capitalist city', in R. Hutchison (ed.), *Encyclopedia of Urban Studies*, Thousand Oaks, CA: SAGE, pp. 109–112.

Routledge, P. (2003) 'Convergence space: process geographies of grassroots globalization networks', *Transactions of the Institute of British Geographers*, vol. 28, no. 3, pp. 333–349.

Rusch, R. (2003), "Joburg: discover"; http://www.brandchannel.com

Rydin, Y. (2006) 'Justice and the geography of Hurricane Katrina', *Geoforum*, vol. 37, no. 1, pp. 4–6.

Said, E. (1978) *Orientalism: Western Conceptions of the Orient.* New York: Vintage.

Salet, W. (2008) 'Rethinking urban projects: experiences in Europe', *Urban Studies*, vol. 45, no. 11, pp. 2343–2363.

Sandel, M. (1982) *Liberalism and the Limits of Justice.* Cambridge: Cambridge University Press.

Sandercock, L. (2003) *Cosmopolis II: Mongrel Cities for the 21st Century.* London: Continuum.

Sassen, S. (1991) *The Global City: New York, London, Tokyo.* Princeton, NJ: Princeton University Press.

Sassen, S. (1995) 'On concentration and centrality in the global city', in P. Knox and P. Taylor (eds), *World Cities in a World-system.* Cambridge: Cambridge University Press, pp. 63–75.

Sassen, S. (1996a) 'Whose city is it? Globalization and the formation of new claims', *Public Culture*, vol. 8, no. 2, pp. 205–223.

Sassen, S. (1996b) *Losing Control?: Sovereignty in an Age of Globalization.* New York: Columbia University Press.

Sassen, S. (2007) *A Sociology of Globalization.* New York: W. W. Norton & Co.

Saxenian, A. (1994) *Regional Advantage: Culture and Competition in Silicon Valley and Route 128.* Cambridge, MA: Harvard University Press.

Schlosberg, D. (2007) *Defining Environmental Justice: Theories, Movements, and Nature.* Oxford: Oxford University Press.

Scott, A.J. (1988) *New Industrial Spaces. Flexible Production Organization and Regional Development in North America and Western Europe.* London: Pion.

Scott, A.J. (1998) *Regions and the World Economy: The Coming Shape of Global Production, Competition, and Political Order.* Oxford: Oxford University Press.

Scott, A.J. (2000) *The Cultural Economy of Cities.* London: SAGE.

Scott, A.J. (ed.) (2001) *Global City-Regions: Trends, Theory, Policy.* Oxford: Oxford University Press.

Scott, A.J. (2006) 'Creative cities: conceptual issues and policy questions', *Journal of Urban Affairs*, vol. 28, no. 1, pp. 1–17.

Secor, A. (2004) 'There is an Istanbul that belongs to me: citizenship, space, and identity in the city', *Annals of the Association of American Geographers*, vol. 94, no. 2, pp. 352–368.

Sen, A.K. (1999) *Development as Freedom*. New York: Anchor.

Sen, A.K. (2009) *The Idea of Justice*. London: Penguin.

Sengupta, K. (2006) 'Migrants and the Middle East: welcome to the other side of Dubai', *Independent*, Tuesday 28 March.

Sennett, R. (1999) 'The spaces of democracy', in R. Beauregard and S. Body-Gendrot (eds), *The Urban Moment. Cosmopolitan Essays on the Late 20th Century City*. London: SAGE, pp. 273–285.

Shaw, M. (2004) 'New wars of the city: relationships of "urbicide" and "genocide"', in S. Graham (ed.), *Cities, War, and Terrorism*. Oxford: Blackwell, pp. 141–153.

Shi, F. and Cai, Y. (2006) 'Disaggregating the State: networks and collective resistance in Shanghai', *China Quarterly*, no. 186, pp. 114–132.

Short, J.R. and Kim, Y.-H. (1998) 'Urban crisis/urban representations: selling the city in difficult times', in T. Hall and P. Hubbard (eds), *The Entrepreneurial City: Geographies of Politics, Regime and Representation*. Chichester: John Wiley & Sons, pp. 55–75.

Short, J.R. and Kim, Y.-H. (1999) *Globalization and the City*. Harlow: Pearson.

Sidaway, J.D. (2008) 'Subprime crisis: American crisis or human crisis?', *Environment and Planning D: Society and Space*, vol. 26, no. 2, pp. 195–198.

Simmie, J. and Martin, R. (2010) 'The economic resilience of regions: towards an evolutionary approach', *Cambridge Journal of Regions, Economy and Society*, vol. 3, no. 1, pp. 27–43.

Simone, A. (2004) *For the City Yet to Come: Changing African Life in Four Cities*. Durham, NC: Duke University Press.

Sklair, L. (2002) *Globalization: Capitalism and Its Alternatives*. Oxford: Oxford University Press.

Sklair, L. (2005) 'The transnational capitalist class and contemporary architecture in globalizing cities', *International Journal of Urban and Regional Research*, vol. 29, no. 3, pp. 485–500.

Sloterdijk, P. (2009) *Du mußt dein Leben ändern*, Frankfurt am Main as Suhrkamp (Italian translation: *Devi cambiare la tua vita*, Raffaello Cortina, Milan, 2010).

Smith, D. (1997) 'Geography and ethics: a moral turn?', *Progress in Human Geography*, vol. 21, no. 4, pp. 583–590.

Smith, N. (1984) *Uneven Development: Nature, Capital and the Production of Space*. Oxford: Blackwell.

Smith, N. (1996) *The New Urban Frontier: Gentrification and the Revanchist City*. New York: Routledge.

Smith, N. (1998) 'Giuliani time: the revanchist 1990s', *Social Text*, vol. 16, no. 4, pp. 1–20.

Söderström, O. (2006) 'Studying cosmopolitan landscapes', *Progress in Human Geography*, vol. 30, no. 5, pp. 553–558.

Soja, E.W. (1989) *Postmodern Geographies: The Reassertion of Space in Critical Social Theory*. London: Verso.

Soja, E.W. (2000) *Postmetropolis: Critical Studies of Cities and Regions*. Oxford: Blackwell.

Solinger, D.J. (1999) 'Citizenship issues in China's internal migration: comparisons with Germany and Japan', *Political Science Quarterly*, vol. 114, no. 3, pp. 455–478.

Spivak, G.C. (1999) *A Critique of Postcolonial Reason*. Cambridge, MA: Harvard University Press.

Stiglitz, J.E. (2002) *Globalization and Its Discontents*. New York: Norton.

Stone, C. (1989) *Regime Politics*. Lawrence, KS: University of Kansas Press.

Storper, M. and Scott, A.J. (2009) 'Rethinking human capital, creativity and urban growth', *Journal of Economic Geography*, vol. 9, no. 2, pp. 147–167.

Stoyanov, P. and Frantz, K. (2006) 'Gated communities in Bulgaria: interpreting a new trend in post-communist urban development', *GeoJournal*, vol. 66, no. 1–2, pp. 57–63.

Strange, S. (1997) *Casino Capitalism*. Manchester: Manchester University Press.

Swyngedouw, E. (1992) 'The Mammon quest, "Glocalization", interspatial competition and the monetary order: the construction of new scales', in M. Dunford and J. Kafkalas (eds), *Cities and Regions in the New Europe*. London: Belhaven Press, pp. 255–274.

Swyngedouw, E. (2007) 'Impossible "sustainability" and the postpolitical condition', in R. Krueger and D. Gibbs (eds), *The Sustainable Development Paradox: Urban Political Economy in the United States and Europe*. New York: Guilford Press, pp. 13–40.

Taylor, C. (1992) *Multiculturalism and the 'Politics of Recognition'*. Princeton, NJ: Princeton University Press.

Taylor, P. (1982) 'A materialist framework for political geography', *Transactions of the Institute of British Geographers*, vol. 7, no. 1, pp. 15–34.

Taylor, P. (2000) 'World cities and territorial states under conditions of contemporary globalization', *Political Geography*, vol. 19, no. 1, pp. 5–32.

Thrift, N. (2005) *Knowing Capitalism*. London: SAGE.

Tretter, E. (2009) 'The cultures of capitalism: Glasgow and the monopoly of culture', *Antipode*, vol. 41, no. 1, pp. 111–132.

Triandafyllidou, A., Modood, T. and Zapata-Barrero, R. (2006) 'European challenges to multicultural citizenship: Muslims, secularism and beyond', in T. Modood, A. Triandafyllidou and R. Zapata-Barrero (eds), *Multiculturalism, Muslims and Citizenship*. London: Routledge, pp. 1–22.

Tully, J. (1999) 'The agonic freedom of citizens', *Economy and Society*, vol. 28, no. 1, pp. 161–182.

Uitermark, J. (2004) 'Framing urban injustices: the case of the Amsterdam squatter movement', *Space and Polity*, vol. 8, no. 2, pp. 227–244.

Uitermark, J., Rossi, U. and van Houtum, H. (2005) 'Reinventing multiculturalism: urban citizenship and the negotiation of ethnic diversity in Amsterdam', *International Journal of Urban and Regional Research*, vol. 29, no. 3, pp. 622–640.

UN (2005) *Report of the Fact-Finding Mission to Zimbabwe to Assess the Scope and Impact of Operation Murambatsvina*; http://www.un.org (accessed December 2009).

UNESCO (1998) *Report of the World Commission on Culture and Development "Our creative diversity"* (2nd edition 2009). Paris: UNESCO.

Urry, J. (1995) *Consuming Places*. London: Routledge.

van der Merwe, I. (2004) 'The global cities of Sub–Saharan Africa: fact or fiction?', *Urban Forum*, vol. 15, no. 1, pp. 36–47.

van Kempen, E.T. (1994) 'The dual city and the poor: social polarization, social segregation and life chances', *Urban Studies*, vol. 31, no. 7, pp. 995–1015.

Vanolo, A. (2008) 'The image of the creative city: Some reflections on urban branding in Turin', *Cities*, vol. 25, no. 6, pp. 370–382.

Vanolo, A. (2010) 'European spatial planning between competitiveness and territorial cohesion: shadows of neoliberalism', *European Planning Studies*, vol. 18, no. 8, pp. 1301–1315.

Varsanyi, M.W. (2006) 'Interrogating "urban citizenship" *vis-à-vis* undocumented migration', *Citizenship Studies*, vol. 10, no. 2, pp. 229–249.

Vertovec, S. (2002) *Transnational Networks and Skilled Labour Migration*. Oxford: Economic and Social Research Council/University of Oxford.

Vertovec, S. and Cohen, R. (eds) (1999) *Migration, Diasporas and Transnationalism*. Cheltenham: Elgar.

Virno, P. (1996) 'Virtuosity and revolution: the political theory of exodus', in P. Virno and M. Hardt (eds) *Radical Thought in Italy. A Potential Politics*. Minneapolis: Minnesota University Press, pp. 189–209.

Virno, P. (2004) *A Grammar of the Multitude: For an Analysis of Contemporary Forms of life*. New York: Semiotext(e).

Wacquant, L. (1999) *Les prisons de la misère*. Paris: Raisons d'agir.

Wacquant, L. (2007) *Urban Outcasts: A Comparative Sociology of Advanced Marginality*. Cambridge: Polity Press.

Wacquant, L. (2008) 'The militarization of urban marginality: lessons from the Brazilian metropolis', *International Political Sociology*, vol. 2, no. 1, pp. 56–74.

Walters, W. and Haahr, J.H. (2005) *Governing Europe: Discourse, Governmentality and European Integration*. London: Routledge.

Walzer, M. (1983) *Spheres of Justice: A Defense of Pluralism and Equality*. New York: Basic Books.

Ward, K. (1997) 'Coalitions in urban regeneration: a regime approach', *Environment and Planning A*, vol. 29, no. 8, pp. 1493–1506.

Ward, K. (2006) '"Policies in motion", urban management and state restructuring: the trans-local expansion of business improvement districts', *International Journal of Urban and Regional Research*, vol. 30, no. 1, pp. 54–75.

Warner, M. (1999) *The Trouble with Normal: Sex, Politics, and the Ethics of Queer Life*. Cambridge, MA: Harvard University Press.

Warren, R. (2004) 'City streets – the war zones of globalization: democracy and military operations on urban terrain in the early twenty-first century', in S. Graham (ed.), *Cities, War, and Terrorism*. Oxford: Blackwell, pp. 214–230.

Watts, M. (2004) 'Resource curse? Governmentality, oil and power in the Niger Delta, Nigeria', *Geopolitics*, vol. 9, no. 1, pp. 50–80.

Weizman, E. (2007) *Hollow Land: Israeli's Architecture of Occupation*. London: Verso.

Wickramasekara, P. (2009) *Policy Responses to Skilled Migration: Retention, Return and Circulation*. Geneva: International Labour Office.

Williams, R. (1958) *Culture and Society*. London: Chatto & Windus.

Wilson, D. (2004) 'Toward a contingent urban neo-liberalism', *Urban Geography*, vol. 25, no. 8, pp. 771–783.

Wilson, D. and Keil, R. (2007) 'The real creative class', *Social and Cultural Geography*, vol. 9, no. 8, pp. 841–847.

Wood, A.M. (2004) 'Domesticating urban theory? US concepts, British cities and the limits of cross-national applications', *Urban Studies*, vol. 41, no. 11, pp. 2103–2118.

World Bank (1991) *Urban Policy and Economic Development: An Agenda for the 1990s*. Washington, DC: World Bank.

World Bank (2000) *Cities in Transition: World Bank Urban and Local Government Strategy*. Washington, DC: World Bank.

Wu, F. (2003) 'Transitional cities', *Environment and Planning A*, vol. 35, no. 8, pp. 1331–1338

Wu, W. (2004) 'Cultural strategies in Shanghai: regenerating cosmopolitanism in an era of globalization', *Progress in Planning*, vol. 61, pp. 159–180.

Wyly, E.K., Atia, M., Lee, E. and Mendez, P. (2007) 'Race, gender, and statistical representation: predatory mortgage lending and the US community reinvestment movement', *Environment and Planning A*, vol. 39, no. 9, pp. 2139–2166.

Yeoh, B.S.A. (1999) 'Global/globalising cities', *Progress in Human Geography*, vol. 23, no. 4, pp. 607–616.

Young, I.M. (1990) *Justice and the Politics of Difference*. Princeton, NJ: Princeton University Press.

Young, I.M. (2000) *Inclusion and Democracy*. Oxford: Oxford University Press.

Zhao, S.X.B. (2003) 'Spatial restructuring of financial centers in mainland China and Hong Kong: a geography of finance perspective', *Urban Affairs Review*, vol. 38, no. 4, pp. 535–571.

Žižek, S. (2006) *The Parallax View*. Cambridge, MA: MIT Press.

Žižek, S. (2008) 'Censorship today: violence, or ecology as a new opium for the masses'; http://www.lacan.com/zizecology1.htm (accessed May 2010).

Zukin, S. (1980) 'A decade of the new urban sociology', *Theory & Society*, vol. 9, no. 4, pp. 575–601.

Zukin, S. (1991) *Landscapes of Power: From Detroit to Disneyworld*. Berkeley, CA: University of California Press.

Zukin, S. (1995) *The Cultures of Cities*. Oxford: Blackwell.

Acknowledgements

The book is a revised and expanded version of the Italian-language *Geografia Politica Urbana*, which was published in October 2010. We'd like to thank Jamie Peck, AbdouMaliq Simone and Ola Söderström, who accepted our invitation to write a foreword to this book. We also wish to express our gratitude to Robert Rojek and Katherine Haw at SAGE. Robert enthusiastically supported our project from the very beginning; Katherine had the patience to read and edit the manuscript of two authors whose native language is not English. It goes without saying, the authors alone are responsible for any remaining errors or obscurities.

Index

Page numbers in *italics* refer to boxes and figures, *g* refers to the glossary.

consumerism 34
contestation
　globalization 8–12
　image of the city 28–30
　politics as 16–17
　representation, government and x–xii
cosmopolitanism 160, 182g
Cox, K.R. 8, 62–3, 95
　and Mair, A.J. 28, 79
creative city
　economies of diversity and discursive
　　strategies 53–9
　governmentalization 59–67
　knowledge-based capitalism 51–3
　neoliberalism and 67–8, 97
creative-class theory 52–5
　critique 55–8
crime policy and marginalized groups 91, 110–13
crisis 182g
　of national citizenship 158–9
　see also financial crisis (2008–9)
'cultural capital' 56–7
culture-led regeneration
　Europe 62–6
　see also creative city

Dakar, Senegal 90
Davis, M. 36, 46, 47–8, 93, 110, 115
Debbané, A.-M. and Keil, R. 151–2
Delhi, India 86
democracy 182g
　absolute 148, 161–2, 175
　challenges and enigmas 141–4
　ethical turn in 132–4
demolition and redevelopment 126–8
deterritorialization of urban politics 84–5
Detroit, US 58–9
development 182g
　cultural entrepreneuralism, Asia 59–62
　financialization of 76–7
　Millennium Development Goals 88
　slum clearance/demolition and redevelopment
　　126–8
　technology–creativity–urban development
　　nexus 54–5
difference 182g
　'politics of difference' 136
Dikeç, M. 17, 110–11, 145–6
discursive strategies/practices 53–9
　globalization as 10–11
Dubai, United Arab Emirates 36–7

East Asia see Asia; China
economies of diversity 53–9

Economist Intelligence Unit 57
economy
　diversity, and discursive strategies 53–9
　growth and anti-poverty policies 93–4
　political economy of representation 26
　transition 30–3
　see also capitalism/capitalist city; creative city;
　　neoliberalism
8 Mile (film) 58–9
elites 183g
　politico-economic 95–6, 179, 180–1
emotional politics of sustainability 46–9
entrepreneurial cities 82
entrepreneurship
　Asia 59–62
　return migrations 165
environmental issues 45–8
　carbon emissions 62
　globalization and social movements 148–54
　social classes 137
equality
　recognition and domination 134–8
　see also inequalities; justice
ethical turn in democratic politics 132–4
ethnicity
　and citizenship 161, 169–72
　ethnic-religious divisions 116–18
　see also migration
Eurocentrism of urban scholarship 49–50
Europe/European Union (EU) 82–3, 84, 91, 92,
　　94, 160
　ethnicity 170
　housing market 100
　migration and Schengen Agreement 168
　multi-level governance of culture-led regeneration
　　62–6
　post-Cold War urban regeneration 40–2
European City of Culture programme 62–6

fear
　communitarian self-defence 115–18
　politics of 107–15
　see also security; terrorism
Fernandes, L. 29
films
　8 Mile 58–9
　Beirut Open City 125–6
　Bread and Roses 142–4
　The Garden 88
　Gomorrah 114–15
　Ha Buah (The Bubble) 176–7
　La Graine et le Mulet (The Secret of the Grain) 166–7
　No One Knows About Persian Cats 66–7
　The Simpsons 44–5